Breaking the Illusion

Other Titles From New Falcon Publications

Breaking the Illusion

Tools For Self-Awakening

Ric Weinman

NEW FALCON PUBLICATIONS
TEMPE, ARIZONA, U.S.A.

International Standard Book Number: 1-56184-093-9

First Edition 1991
First Falcon Edition 1996

Cover art by Denise Cuttitta
Back Cover Photograph by Susanne Weinman

Note to the Reader: This book contains material that is emotionally evocative. Neither publisher nor the author is responsible for any effects which may arise as a result of following suggestions given in this book. If a reader has any questions about material in this book, he/she should consult a professional therapist.

The paper used in this publication meets the minimum requirements of the American National Standard for Permanence of Paper for Printed Library Materials Z39.48-1984

Address all inquiries to:
NEW FALCON PUBLICATIONS
1739 East Broadway Road Suite 1-277
Tempe, AZ 85282 U.S.A.
(or)
1209 South Casino Center
Las Vegas, NV 89104 U.S.A.

*For those beings
whose open hearts
help us to remember.*

Acknowledgments

I want to acknowledge my friends Kailash, Michael, and Connie for making me aware of what I could contribute; Marcy, Kate, Christine, and Kelcy, for helping me to explore myself and grow; Jerry, for not letting me take my attitudes seriously; those who made up my healing and counseling practice, for forcing me to deepen my awareness and for providing me with invaluable learning opportunities; don Juan, Seth, Ram Dass, Neem Karoli Baba, Emmanuel, and Mary Burmeister for what they taught me about myself and my reality; and my parents, all three, in appreciation.

Contents

Part III — Awakening Through The Mirror

Part IV — Reincarnation & the Incarnational Personality

Part V — Going Home

Author's Note On
The New Edition

Because this book was to be reprinted with a new title, I decided to take the time to reread it, to see if there was anything I wanted to change. I was pleased to find that, although five years of intense inner work have passed since its original publication, I was still quite satisfied with most of what I had written. Most of the changes to the original manuscript, therefore, have been quite minor, with certain exceptions: I completely changed Awareness Exercise 6, "Rooting out Limiting Beliefs"; I removed the exercise called "A Story Retold" as it really didn't contribute much; I rewrote much of Chapter 23, "Reflections of Desire," shifting its focus somewhat; in Chapter 22, "Character-Trances," I changed my description of how we hold emotional characters in the body—my earlier description was incomplete and greatly oversimplified; and I completely rewrote Chapter 29, "The Role of Previous Entrancements," shifting my focus from the original, due to new experiences I have had in this area while doing inner work on myself and with others over the last five years.

Preface

The path to inner freedom is a long one. Most of us have had our moments—we suddenly awakened out of our familiar experience of life and remembered the incredible love and laughter that is who we truly are. Yet we also discovered that expanding these moments into an enduring, ongoing experience is a very difficult task. We encountered the resistance of all our old habits, life-patterns, fears, beliefs, and attitudes that we think keep us safe. We were forced to recognize that, although people do have single, turning-point experiences that qualitatively change their entire life, personal transformation must be regarded as a process that requires commitment, awareness tools, and a willingness to open to life and new experiences. This book is designed to provide you with awareness tools that you can grow with for the rest of your life.

The foundational idea of this book is that reality is quite different from what we usually experience. There are many illusions we have accepted as truth, and this has deeply limited our experience of life. We are rather similar to a leaf which has somehow forgotten that it is part of a tree. As this leaf reaches out with its awareness, it senses other leaves, but these are now strangers. Without a conscious connection to the tree, the leaf experiences a reality in which it is fundamentally alone and is being kept alive by some unknown power outside of itself, over which it has no control. This creates in the leaf a deep sense of loss and insecurity, and a fear of annihilation. The leaf may try to control this fear, or it may get angry (and take the anger out on other leaves), or feel sorry for itself, or even form a group with other leaves that are having similar experiences. Yet there is only one way for the leaf to become cured of its fear and return to emotional harmony: it must *break free of its illusion* of separateness and remember that it is one with the tree, that it *is* the tree. In our human experience, we must remember that we are each a leaf of the Tree of Life.

The awareness tools that will be developed in this book are, in essence, designed to facilitate this kind of remembering; and they will do this in very different ways, increasing the probability that, in any particular situation, readers will have an awareness tool that will help them to transform their experience.

These awareness tools will grow out of both the concepts presented in the text and the experiences of expanded consciousness you will have when you do the awareness exercises provided, which I will guide you through, step by step. Doing the exercises is very important, for learning to create transformation is never a passive process; it must be learned experientially. By doing the exercises, the awareness tools will become real resources for you, grounded in real experience; they will become part of your living reality.

This book evolved through many years of personal meditation and inner work, and through my healing and counseling practice. The core material encapsulates what I myself had to learn to free myself from an emotional black hole that I plunged into for a number of years, that I thought I would never be free of. I wrote this book to share what I had learned and because of my desire to contribute to the extraordinary evolution of consciousness that is happening today. The first draft was written in six weeks, yet I didn't call it finished for another eight years. So this book has been filtered through a large piece of my life and growth, and I'm glad to say that although many new ideas and awarenesses have been added to the original draft, the core material presented has remained intact and my experience has simply reinforced my appreciation of the process of personal reality creation it describes.

Growing numbers of people are realizing, in one way or another, that a more profound, more fulfilling experience of life is possible. And so they have made an ongoing process of personal transformation a key to their way of life; they have become willing to continuously push against the boundaries of their self-limitations, so they can create the openness required to receive life's incredible abundance of love and joy.

My great surprise in writing this book was the degree to which it contributed to my own growth. I hope it can do as much for you.

A Note On Using This Book

Many of the awareness exercises have several parts, so you may want to break up the longer ones into more than one sitting. You may find that in the middle of an exercise you are suddenly getting tired. If you think your fatigue is being caused by emotional resistance, continue; otherwise stop and continue it at another time. If you push yourself you will not receive the benefit intended from the exercise, and you may develop a resistance to doing other exercises. A few awareness exercises suggest specific lengths of time for working with them. Feel free to take more time; yet if you take less time you will probably not get what is intended from the exercise.

If an awareness exercise works very well for you, consider using it as a daily meditation. On the other hand, please recognize that some exercises will work for you and some won't. If you are having trouble with an exercise or not getting anything from it, relax and go on; yet consider coming back to it later, for it may work for you at another time.

I strongly suggest keeping a journal while you are reading and working with this book. The journal would provide a place to record new thoughts and realizations, so you can refer back to them and keep them fresh in your mind. In addition, some of the exercises will direct you to write certain things down on paper, and these could be written directly in the journal.

Although this book has been designed for individual use, two or more people can go through the book together, sharing experiences. For one person working alone, a good method is to record the exercises and play them back, pausing when required. With two or more people, the exercises can be read to each other. Members of a group may also agree to go through a section of the book alone and then share their experiences at weekly meetings.

There are many local consciousness-raising groups that have sprung up all over the country. If you are not a member of such a group and think you would enjoy exploring this book in a group context, consider forming one yourself. Even a very small group will create an opportunity for sharing.

One last note on using this book: it has the power to help you alter your consciousness and experience reality in new ways. In the process, though, it will likely stir up old, unresolved emotional issues. It may even bring up memories of traumatic events that you suppressed completely from your conscious awareness. So before starting, ask yourself if you are truly ready and willing to open yourself to these kinds of experiences.

If you are, let's begin!

The deepest trance of all is personality: who you ... think you are as separate from everyone else. There are times when having a personality seems to me like a vastly elaborate defense erected against the mystery of living. It's as though the cultural, the familial, and individual trances we are all in contribute to one large personal dream—a world view. It's as though we were all amnesiacs, having forgotten our truer identities; seeing, like the underside of a weaving, only a fraction of what's before us, unconscious to the ground of our own being, the unregarded river of life.

— Thomas R. Condon
"Trance Personally: Language
and Hypnosis in Everyday Life,"
presented at the 1982 Southwestern
Anthropological Association convention

PART I

A Perceptual Construct

I

The Role of the Body in Creating Physical Reality (Part I)

Up to the twentieth century, "reality" was everything humans could touch, smell, see, and hear. Since the initial publication of the chart of the electromagnetic spectrum ... humans have learned that what they can touch, smell, see, and hear is less than one millionth of reality. — R. Buckminster Fuller

Because our awareness of the world is filtered through our five senses, our experience of the world is, necessarily, very limited. Although we assume that what we see is what the world really looks like, if we could see at the microscopic level, an empty house would look like a zoo—fungi climbing all over the walls, viruses floating through the air in water molecules, colonies of mites thriving in errant pieces of dust, and strange looking bacteria fighting each other, using chemical warfare. If we could see only the infrared parts of the light spectrum (essentially heat), we wouldn't see any color, things would simply glow according to how much heat they gave off, and boundaries would be less clearly defined, especially on hot days when everything would glow more intensely. On very cold days, walking outside would be somewhat like walking at night with no moon. And, if we could see at the atomic level, the world would look like bits of random chaos in mostly empty space (atoms are 99.999999999999 percent empty space). *Physical reality looks solid only because we **perceive** it to be solid.*

We take what our eyes perceive for granted and assume that what they see is Reality[1], but what they see is simply what they are designed to see. They could as easily have been constructed differently.

In a similar way, we also take our other four senses for granted. If plants could talk, we would hear them only if they spoke within a range that our ears could hear. We could have had three or six or eight senses instead of five. If we didn't have ears, think of how differently we would experience our world. On the other hand, many of us have had the experience of unconsciously picking up on someone else's thought; imagine how our experience of life would change if this ability were amplified and we heard other people's thoughts as easily as we hear our own. There are many other possibilities: we could also have been created with the ability to manifest objects, or to change at will the physical shape of our face and body. There is no logical reason why we shouldn't have the ability to do these things. It just so happens we don't.

Experiments with psychedelic drugs have shown that the world becomes very different when our biochemistry is slightly altered. We could have had trillions of different biochemistries, each of which would have created a different physical world from the one we know. It just so happens that we have our own particular biochemistry. And having it and experiencing it, we never consider that there are other possibilities; we simply take our own experience as Reality.

Although Reality is infinite, *the physical reality we experience is actually **a perceptual construct** that is created by—and therefore mirrors the unique perceptual point of view of our human "body."*[2] What we experience, therefore, is not Reality but simply our own particular human experience, constructed by our own particular kind of human "body." (Since what is perceived through the senses must always be limited and a perceptual construct, Reality Itself can be experienced only through some other means of awareness. We will explore this more in later chapters.)

---

[1]When I capitalize a word such as Reality (or Life) I am referring to that one Reality which transcends, encompasses, and gives birth to all individual realities. With the word Self, I will mean our deepest, most transcendent state of consciousness, as opposed to our everyday self.

[2]In this chapter, I often use the word "body" in quotes to counteract our familiar sense of it as a particular kind of "solid" object. The "body" only seems solid because, whatever it really is, it perceives itself as solid.

Our problem is that we have become hypnotized by our perception; we believe our perceptual construct is Reality, and so we have trapped ourselves within an experiential illusion. This is similar to what happens when we watch television. All that we really see is little glowing lights, called pixels, spaced a distance apart. But the nature of our human perception organizes the variations of light into a picture. The picture is just a perceptual construct. Yet as we stare at it, we hypnotize ourselves with the drama it represents and project onto it our own inner sense of Realness. Then we forget that we are watching visual constructions created by glowing pixels and respond emotionally to these pictures, just as if they were Real. A telephone ringing will easily jolt us out of our trance. However, it usually takes an event as drastic as an out-of-body experience to jolt us out of our entrancement with what we normally experience as reality.

The question may arise as to how we experience other people within a perceptual construct. First of all, our "bodies" are so constructed that they can see, hear, feel, smell, and even taste other "bodies." This in itself creates an interactive situation. Secondly, because we have such similar "bodies" we have similar points of view, which create perceptual constructs that are enough alike for us to have common experiences. This creates a *consensus reality*. Unfortunately, because we agree about the physical objects in this consensus reality (the earth is solid, the sky is blue, and so on) we are fooled into thinking that it exists independently of our perception, that it is Objective Reality. Yet what makes the sky blue for both of us is the nature and similarity of our perception, not some objective "blueness." If a person's viewpoint creates a sufficiently different perception (he agrees the sky exists but insists that it always turns orange the day after the full moon), we say that he is "hallucinating" and take him out of the group reality and put him in a mental hospital.

AWARENESS EXERCISE 1:
A "SOLID" OBJECT

The purpose of this exercise is to alter your sense of the "solidness" of physical reality.

PART 1

Sit comfortably, several feet away from a plant—any kind of plant—facing toward it. (Or, instead of a plant, have another person sit quietly and read, with his or her back to you, so you won't be distracted by the other person's awareness of you.) Then, as you observe the plant for ten or more minutes, allow the following to become part of your awareness:

(1) Radio and TV waves, gamma rays and x-rays, microwaves, light waves, and many other kinds of electromagnetic energy waves—from the sun, from space, and from man-made sources—are streaming toward the plant, as you are looking at it.

(2) Many of the waves, like the x-rays and gamma rays, go right through the plant, sometimes hitting a piece of matter and getting slightly deflected on their path through.

(3) Some of the waves, including the light waves, bounce off the plant, and some of them bounce into your eyes.

(4) Because your eyes are sensitive to some of these light waves (those in the "visible" range), when they bounce off the plant into your eyes they activate all kinds of electro-chemical reactions.

(5) These electro-chemical reactions stimulate nerves at the back of each eye.

(6) The stimulated nerves send electro-chemical messages to your brain, with each nerve telling your brain its own unique electro-chemical story.

(7) Your brain listens to the different electro-chemical stories from your nerves, and translates them into a single three-dimensional colored picture.

(8) Somehow, you become aware of that picture created by your brain and you assume that your brain's picture is the same thing as the actual plant in front of you. But it is not. What you actually see is not the plant but a picture created by your brain out of fifth-hand information.

(9) The picture you actually perceive is sixth-hand information. It is Reality translated from an actual plant (whatever a plant really is),

to bouncing light waves, to electro-chemistry in the eye, to nerve stimulation, to brain stimulation, to the picture you become aware of. (And this is really a simplification, because many of these steps really involve several smaller steps, each one of which creates another translation of information.) Imagine how much information is lost when a plant is translated into light waves bouncing off it, which is translated into all these other mediums before you even become aware of it.

(10) Realize that, in addition to all this translation, what you are capable of seeing is limited to the pictures your brain is capable of making.

PART 2

Take a break if you like. Then continue to observe the plant, considering the following:

(1) You are only capable of "seeing" objects that glow with their own visible light (like the sun) or that are dense enough for light waves to bounce off them. For instance, unless air is polluted, you can't see it, because light waves go right through it. Similarly, if ghosts or fairies really exist and are dancing around the plant right now, you would not be able to see them.

(2) If your eyes were sensitive to infrared light (essentially heat waves) instead of the visible portion of the light spectrum, you would still see a plant, but it would look entirely different. You wouldn't see any color. You would simply see variations of glow or brightness, varying according to how much heat different parts of the plant were giving off. Changes in the temperature of the environment would change the appearance of the plant.

Be aware that what you would see, if you could see only infrared light, is actually present right now, except that it is invisible to you because visible light waves do not bounce off infrared radiation, and because you have not learned how to see infrared directly. Imagine all the other possible aspects of the plant's reality that are lost to your awareness. For instance, studies show that plants have emotional responses. Are you aware of them? How would your experience of the plant change if you were aware of them?

(3) If your eyes were sensitive to x-rays instead of light waves, you wouldn't see the plant at all, not even indirectly through a sixth-

hand brain picture, since the x-rays would go through the plant instead of bouncing back at your eyes.

PART 3

Take a break if you like. Then continue to observe the plant, and attempt the following:

Utilizing the awareness that what you are seeing is just a sixth-hand picture created by your brain, detach yourself from your "normal" perception, and then *directly experience* the plant's reality. In other words, even as you are looking at the plant, you are telling yourself that what you are seeing is not what is really there, and you are attempting to directly sense or be aware of what is really there. Something within you can reach out and directly experience the plant. If you have difficulty, relax for a minute and stretch, and then attempt it again. If you still don't succeed, try it with your eyes closed, and if you still don't succeed try it while touching the plant with your eyes closed. When you are successful, try it again with your eyes open. Be open to whatever you experience, even if it doesn't "make sense."

If you can't experience the plant directly, then periodically, as you go through this book, return to this exercise and try again.

PART 4

After you have succeeded in Part 3, practice shifting your awareness in that manner while you are walking outside; start by directly experiencing trees and grass, and then attempt to directly experience your outer world as a whole.

Also attempt to perceive other people from this state of consciousness.

2

The Role of the Body in Creating Physical Reality (Part II)

Our particular physical reality is not something that exists in some absolute sense, outside of us, ready to be perceived. It is constructed by—and mirrors—our own perception, so it cannot even exist without us. (As we will see later, this is the basis of modern physics.)

Earlier, I emphasized the fact that the nature of the physical reality we construct is determined by the narrow range of sensory data that our "bodies" are sensitive to and the kind of senses we have. Yet our world is not just a mirror of what we are capable of seeing, hearing, and so on. The reality we construct is much further from Reality than simply being a composite of specific slices of It, because our experience further depends upon what happens to the limited sensory data as it gets translated through different biosystems on the way to our brain, and even further depends upon what our brain does—and is capable of doing—with that limited, multi-translated data when it finally receives it.

This has enormous consequences for many other assumptions we make about our physical reality. For instance, even if a cat's eyes were sensitive to exactly the same range of light waves as our own, the cat's body and brain might do something very different with those bouncing light waves, making what the cat finally sees entirely different. We assume, since cats are responsive to the things that we see, that what they see is the same. But this is an immense egocentric assumption that becomes even more obvious when we consider the case of insects: a fly has two eyes, just as we do, yet each of its eyes is made up of thousands of tiny lenses, each one producing a separate picture. With thousands of simultaneous images and a pin-sized brain, how could the fly possibly create the same visual image we do? And consider the perceptual reality of monarch butterflies: tossed around by every wind and with almost no brain to speak of, they migrate by the millions from all over the North American continent to the same few mountains in Mexico and California that their ancestors did, mountains that the butterflies have never been to, since they were born in the north.

Human-physical-reality is definitely not the same as butterfly-physical-reality or even cat-physical-reality. In fact, just because butterflies look solid to us within our reality does not necessarily mean that butterflies experience the world as solid within their own reality. Since the solidity of the world is a perceptual illusion, it is logical to assume that some creatures aren't capable of creating—or don't choose to create—that illusion.

The question even exists as to whether we see what other people see. Because of our use of descriptive language, we know that what we see is similar, yet it may not be the same. For instance, when a friend of mine was tested for new contact lenses, the doctor put a different lens into each eye. To my friend's surprise, objects looked bigger through one eye than through the other. She asked the doctor which size was the "real" one, but of course there was no way for the doctor to tell. And any attempts to tell by measuring the objects with a ruler would prove fruitless, because the ruler itself would seem to grow or shrink in size, depending upon the eye viewing it. So although objects may look twice as big to you as they do to me, we could participate in the same consensus reality without ever noticing the difference, always assuming that we saw the same thing. In fact, in experiments in which people wore glasses that made the world look upside down, after a few days they completely habituated to functioning this way and they interacted normally with their environment and other people; no one else had any way to tell that they were perceiving the world upside down.

The physical reality we create with our perception intersects with the realities of all kinds of other creatures and human beings. Yet what we individually experience is always our own unique reality, constructed perceptually by our own individual human "body"—whatever that really is.

3

The Role of Emotions in Creating Personal Reality

Just as the point of view created by our body perceptually constructs our physical reality, our emotional point of view—consisting of our old emotional patterns as well as whatever depth of unconditional love and compassion we have developed—constructs our emotional reality.

Usually we think of our emotions as spontaneous responses to life, yet most of them are not caused by what happens to us; they are expressions of fixed, chronic emotional patterns that we project onto present life situations. They are actually old *emotional positions* or *attitudes* that we take toward particular kinds of situations. (I will use the terms "emotional position" and "emotional attitude" interchangeably.)

For instance, if in the middle of a thunderstorm a man says, "thunderstorms make me feel scared," his fear is clearly not a spontaneous emotional experience derived from that moment, but an old emotional position that he has about thunderstorms, that he is projecting onto the present. Ever since he first adopted this position, he has been "ready-to-be-scared" as soon as the next thunderstorm hit. And his emotional position prevents him from opening to the beauty or wonder or power of thunderstorms, for when a thunderstorm is happening, all he ever experiences is his old fear.

Another example is a woman who becomes angry whenever she is criticized. Her anger will seem spontaneous only to someone who shares this emotional pattern. Clearly, she is always ready-to-be-angry; she is always ready to project her attitude of anger onto the next person she believes is criticizing her. So although her old anger is *activated* by criticism, it is not really *caused* by these situations. And her attitude prevents her from opening up to situations in which she believes she is being criticized; instead of experiencing what is actually happening, she only experiences her old anger.

Our emotional attitudes make up the self-limiting aspect of our emotional point of view. They are self-limiting for four reasons: (1) whenever we project a fixed, pre-existing attitude onto a situation, our emotional experience will be limited to, and entirely comprised of, our attitude, (2) this prevents us from opening and responding *spontaneously* to what is actually happening in the present, (3) our attitudes create tension patterns in our body that block the free flow of our breath, constricting our aliveness, and (4) they keep us from love, from being our Self.

When we transform our self-limiting emotional positions we will still have an emotional point of view, but it will no longer be self-limiting because our present experience will be free of our past, enabling us to respond spontaneously to life. Our emotional point of view will then be comprised entirely of unconditional love, joy, and compassion, with "compassion" encompassing the infinite variety of inexpressible feelings that arise spontaneously in a truly open and fearless heart, as it experiences life. These are the only emotions that are not self-limiting, that are not derived from old positions, and that are spontaneous responses; these are the only emotions that can come out of a fully open heart. (We will explore this in more depth in later chapters.)

No matter how free or self-limiting our emotional point of view is (at this time), our emotional experience of life will always be determined by the emotional point of view that we bring to it. People who carry a lot of sadness will experience life with sadness; people who experience life with unconditional love will experience love everywhere. What we bring to life is always what we emotionally experience within it.

Yet our emotional point of view determines much more than the specific emotions we bring to life-situations. First of all, it also acts as a filter through which we *perceive* Reality. For instance, a woman who has the emotional attitude that "most people are selfish" will perceive the world through the filter of that attitude, and she will always notice and remember things that justify it. She has become so hypnotized with her perception that although she thinks she perceives Reality, *what she sees is really a reflection of the emotional point of view of her own attitude.* Even if such a woman lived alone in a cave, cut off from the rest of the world, she would feel that she is living in a selfish world. And she is, but her selfish world is her own creation, perceptually constructed by her own emotional point of view.

Secondly, because our emotional point of view affects our perception, it also affects the way we behave and the way others respond to us. This behavioral molding ends up creating a world that both mirrors and reinforces our original emotional point of view. For instance, because a violent, hostile person will see the world as being violent and hostile, he will tend to act in a way that brings out the violence and hostility in the people around him, thereby creating a personal reality that mirrors—and reinforces—his own emotional point of view. Another example is a man who goes to a party with the position that he's inferior in some way to this group of people; his position will show in his behavior and expressions, and most of the people who will be drawn to him will probably either share his position or enjoy feeling superior, either one of which will mirror and reinforce the man's position. On the other hand, a loving person will tend to evoke lovingness in other people, reinforcing his experience of love.

Thirdly, because our emotional point of view will determine what we want to experience (and avoid experiencing), due to our identification with our desires, it will lead us to consciously seek out (and avoid) particular situations—situations that reflect our emotional issues and desires. (We will explore desires in more depth in Chapter 23: "The Reflections of Desire.") The result, again, will be the re-creation of our emotional point of view in our life and the reinforcement of that viewpoint.

Yet we do not simply *have* an emotional point of view; we are also *attached* to it. We have seen that our attitudes prevent us from opening up to and experiencing what is actually happening, yet this is not an accidental consequence of our attitudes, this is their purpose. Our emotional attitudes and positions are actually *postures of emotional resistance.* We use them to resist opening up to and experiencing life-situations that we consider threatening (as did the woman who used anger to resist being criticized), and so we are attached to them; we believe they make us more safe. (We will explore this in depth in later chapters.) In addition, we are attached to our attitudes because we identify with them, and this identification leads us to believe that letting go of our attitudes means losing our self.

An important consequence of being attached to our emotional positions is that we will try to prove they are right so we can feel justified in keeping them, and we will be drawn—mostly unconsciously—to situations that reinforce, support, or enable us to validate them. A woman with the position "I can never do anything right" is actually attached to her position, for it enables her to resist being responsible for herself (which she is afraid of) and justifies her in having someone else—someone who *can* do things right—do them for her. So she will be drawn to situations that she really can't handle and make a mess of situations that she could handle. Even a man with the emotional attitude "no one loves me" will be attached to his attitude and make sure that no one disproves it—even though this condemns him to emotional isolation—because his attitude, by keeping people at a distance, helps him resist dealing with intimacy (which he is afraid of) and helps him to maintain his "poor me" identity. This does not mean that he will not form relationships, even sexual ones, just that he will be drawn to people who will reinforce or validate his attitude—or at least let him be comfortable in it—for he believes it keeps him safe. In addition, if as a child he copied this attitude from one of his parents so that it was something he *shared* with that parent, then this attitude—even though it keeps him isolated—helps him to feel connected to that parent, which gives him some sense of security. So, although our emotional attitudes limit our experience of life, a single attitude can have many "payoffs," many seductive reasons for us to maintain our attachment to it and unconsciously try to validate it in our lives.

In general, we can reinforce/support/validate our positions directly or indirectly. An example of indirect support is a man with the position that he is unlovable being drawn to a woman with the same position, even though the woman's position has nothing to do with the man. Direct support with this man can happen in two ways: if the man befriends someone who *agrees* with his position (that he is unlovable) or he befriends someone whom he can perceive as causing his position, someone who acts rejecting.

Ironically, although we are drawn to validate our emotional positions (because we think they keep us safe), we usually prefer to blame outer situations or other people for them rather than to assume responsibility ourselves. This is because we don't want to recognize that the real problem is that we are emotionally "stuck." So, we are also drawn to situations that enable us to *camouflage* our positions. For instance, an angry man will be drawn to situations that "make him angry," because then he will be able to blame his anger on these situations and camouflage the fact that, regardless of what happens to him, he is always angry, he has an angry position toward Life. Or a woman who has a deep issue around sadness may be drawn to people who are suffering (either friends or a particular kind of job); then not only can she camouflage her sadness by blaming it on these people who "make her sad," but she can also try to pass off her sadness as compassion.

So, by determining what kinds of emotions we will experience as well as what kinds of situations we will be involved in, our emotional point of view always constructs for us an emotional world, both inside and out, that reflects the nature of our emotional point of view. Our positions re-create themselves into life situations, and situations that reflect major emotional issues get re-created again and again, as long as we hold the same positions inside. A man who has grown up with deep resentments may have three marriages that all end with resentment; he may even hold a job that he resents. A woman who has grown up with the position that her parents abandoned her will tend to create relationships in which abandonment is a major issue.

Thus, we get to see ourselves in the mirror of the emotional reality we create around ourself; this is part of the perfection of Life, for if we don't like what we see, we know through the mirror where and what the real problem is within ourselves, which gives us the opportunity to transform it.

Self-limiting emotional positions are part of the package of being human—until we transform them. Fortunately, our emotional point of view is not as deeply rooted as the physical point of view created by our bodies. As a result, we can share the same physical reality with people who have different emotional points of view, and our emotional point of view and the emotional world that we construct from it will be easier to transform than our body's experience of reality as physical. It is much harder to turn water into wine than to learn to drop our positions toward life.

AWARENESS EXERCISE 2:
RECEIVING THE BREATH
PART 1

Sit comfortably on a chair, with your back straight (not rigid) and feet on the floor, close your eyes, and let yourself relax. Allow yourself thirty minutes.

Begin to become aware of your breath. Usually, we think that we take breaths, but actually we receive them. So as you become aware of your breath, do not *try* to breathe, just *consciously receive* your breath. Receive it into the core of your being; receive it into every cell of your body; allow it to fill you with Life.

Every breath is there for you unconditionally—whether you are a saint or a murderer—giving you the gift of Life. This is an expression of Life's unconditional love for you. And because each breath transmits that love, infusing you with the essence of Life, each breath has the capacity to fill you with more joy than you can imagine; all you have to do is receive it.

Yet we receive only a very small part of the breath that is available to us. Whenever we resist life—with worry, anger, fear, holding on to what we think we need, or with other attitudes—we tighten our body and restrict our breath. Resisting anything outside of us always blocks the flow of Life and breath inside of us; and over time, the accumulation of resistance literally suffocates us. Yet there is so much Life to receive, if only we would let go and allow ourself to open and receive it.

So allow yourself to fully receive your breath. You don't have to try to force the breath in; just relax the resistance and control that blocks it. As you open and consciously receive your breath, you can actually feel it moving everywhere in your body. It will create a tingling—which is an expression of heightened aliveness—and a feeling of joy. Don't try to hold onto these sensations, for the holding will begin to limit your experience again; just keep receiving your breath deeper and deeper into your beingness. Be aware of where in your body you are not receiving it—there will probably be stuck emotions and beliefs there—and simply allow yourself to receive the breath in those areas. Do not "try to breathe into" those spots; rather, *bring your awareness inside the stuck place and receive your breath there.* Three places to check in particular are the heart area, the navel, and the pelvis; make sure that you are receiving your breath there, for these are key areas that must be open if you are to receive very deeply.

Sometimes, as you receive your breath, especially as a stuck area opens, you will experience old memories, which relate to what is releasing. Don't get caught up in these old dramas; stay with receiving your breath, and continue to go deeper. Allow yourself to receive—into the deepest core of your beingness and into every cell of your body—the gift of Life.

PART 2

This is simply a variation of Part 1. Experience your breath as love, as God, as God's love, or as Light, so that as you receive your breath you experience yourself receiving love, receiving God, receiving God's love, or receiving Light. Try each one for ten minutes.

This exercise—or the part of it that you like the best—can work very well as a daily meditation. Try it sometime lying on your back (on a firm surface). Use whatever works best for you.

AWARENESS EXERCISE 3:
THE MIRROR OF EMOTIONS

Sit comfortably and close your eyes. Receive a few deep breaths ... and let yourself relax.

PART 1: A COMFORTABLE MIRROR

(1) Bring to mind someone whom you feel close to, preferably someone with whom you share your day-to-day existence, even if this is shared by telephone. This could be a friend, a spouse, a lover, a child, or even a relative (but do not choose a parent).

(2) Meditate on this person for a few minutes. Become aware of this person's emotional nature, attitudes, likes and dislikes, interests, and fears.

(3) Notice the degree to which this person is like yourself; notice the way this person *mirrors* yourself.

(4) Notice ways in which your emotional positions are validated, reinforced, or made comfortable by this person.

(5) Notice ways in which you share love or joy with this person.

(6) Sense within yourself how the emotions and qualities within yourself that you find mirrored in (or reinforced by) this person have acted like a magnet to draw this person into your life.

PART 2: A PAINFUL MIRROR

(1) Bring to mind someone whom you encounter frequently but who consistently brings up negative feelings or attitudes in you, a person with whom you always end up experiencing anger, arrogance, uptightness, sadness, fear, or some other self-limiting attitude.

(2) Meditate on this person for a few minutes.

(3) Meditate on your reactions and your resistance to this person. Notice what you are reacting to and where these reactions originate from within yourself.

(4) Consider that the part of this person that you react to mirrors a place in yourself that is similar, and that you don't like. Find this similar place within yourself.

(5) Notice ways in which your emotional positions are activated and made uncomfortable by this person. Notice that, although this causes you suffering, it validates and supports your positions.

(6) Notice ways in which you resist sharing love or joy with this person.

(7) Sense within yourself how the emotions and qualities within yourself that you find mirrored in (or validated by) this person have acted like a magnet to draw this person into your life. ⸺

PART 3: PARENTS

(1) Bring to mind one of your parents.

(2) Meditate on this parent for a few minutes. Become aware of this person's emotional nature, attitudes, likes and dislikes, interests, and fears.

(3) Notice the degree to which this parent is like yourself; notice the way this parent mirrors yourself.

(4) Notice the ways in which this parent is exactly opposite from yourself. Notice the way this, too, mirrors yourself—how these two opposites are flip sides of the same coin, are opposite ways of dealing with the same issues.

(5) Notice what you react to strongly in this parent's emotional nature.

(6) Notice where these reactions originate from within yourself.

(7) Notice that your reactions are expressions of old emotional positions and that your reactions attempt to validate these positions.

(8) Notice whether these positions are similar to emotional positions held by either one of your parents.

(9) Notice where you are willing and unwilling to share love with this parent.

(10) Sense how the emotions and qualities within yourself that you find mirrored in this parent have acted like a magnet to draw you to this person to become his or her child.

(11) Repeat this exercise with other members of the family you grew up with.

AWARENESS EXERCISE 4:
OUR PROJECTED ATTITUDES

Sit comfortably and close your eyes. Receive a few deep breaths ... and let yourself relax. Then:

(1) Think of a recent time that you became very angry.

(2) Remember two other times in which you became angry in the exact same way.

(3) Notice that this anger was not caused by these situations, that it existed (and probably still exists) in you as a pre-packaged emotional pattern that you projected onto these situations.

(4) Notice that you felt threatened in some way by these situations and that your anger was the way you resisted them, the way you resisted opening to them.

(5) Get a sense of the "posture" of your anger, the way your body physically arranges itself to express the anger. Notice the tension pattern in this posture and that this tension is an expression of resistance. Notice how this tension blocks the flow of your breath, cutting off your life-force.

(6) Think of the kinds of situations you use this anger to resist.

(7) Think of something that you are still angry about, that you are still projecting this anger onto (it can be one of the situations you've remembered in this exercise). Notice again how the anger exists as a pattern within you and how you have attached it to the situation. Then attempt to detach it. This does not involve changing or letting go of your anger; you are letting your pre-packaged pattern of anger continue to exist inside of you, but you are un-attaching it from this situation. Allow yourself to experience what actually happened, without resisting the situation with your attitude. Remind yourself that since this situation exists in the past, it cannot threaten you—it can only symbolize something that you believe threatens you—so you don't need to resist it.

If you have trouble doing this, imagine that you want to examine more closely what happened in the situation, but that you can't see it clearly while your anger is projected onto it. Then see if you can remove your anger from the situation—even if only temporarily—so you can examine in detail what actually happened.

If you managed to un-attach your anger, what did you experience when your anger let go?

If you didn't succeed in un-attaching your anger, do not be concerned; this can be difficult at first. You will have many other opportunities to work with anger in other exercises, utilizing different methods.

If you did succeed in removing your anger, repeat this exercise using situations involving sadness, and then repeat it again using fear.

4

The Role of Beliefs in Creating Personal Reality

THE NATURE OF BELIEFS

A belief is simply an idea about Reality—and therefore a point of view of Reality—that we hold to be "true" or "real." Beliefs can be superficial or deep and can exist at many different layers of our consciousness, enabling conflicting beliefs to be held simultaneously. We usually think of beliefs only in terms of whether they are true or false, yet the nature of beliefs is much more complex.

As Einstein pointed out, all points of view of Reality—and therefore all beliefs, even scientific ones—can be only *relatively true.* This is because a point of view is a perceptual filter that limits Reality and distorts It. Reality, which encompasses all infinities, Being What It Is, cannot neatly fit into the boxes that beliefs create for It. Yet this doesn't necessarily make beliefs false.

Whenever we try to determine if a belief is "true," what we are really doing is comparing it to some accepted truth—which is just some other belief or set of beliefs—and seeing if the new belief is consistent (true) or contradictory (false). We can never determine if a belief is absolutely true; we can only determine if it is fundamentally *consistent* with the point of view we already believe in. And of course, the point of view we already believe in is created and maintained by other, more fundamental beliefs—beliefs that we have simply assumed to be true. Two people with different points of view may disagree on what is true—one person's heroic revolutionary is the other one's murderer—yet each one may be right within the context of their own point of view. This holds for scientific beliefs as well.

Our beliefs can be only relatively true, yet this does not in any way limit their importance. Because we perceive Reality through the filter of our beliefs (along with the previously discussed filters of our body and our emotional point of view), they play a very critical role in the creation of our personal reality. In addition, certain beliefs will even be necessary for us, in our normal state of human consciousness, to operate in this physical reality.

BELIEFS CREATE OUR EMOTIONAL ATTITUDES

Within every emotional attitude (and thus every stuck emotional pattern) there are one or more beliefs that create and justify it. Although not all beliefs generate emotional attitudes, all of our attitudes are generated from our beliefs. We cannot hold an emotional attitude about life or about particular situations without certain beliefs. Because our attitudes are designed to resist certain situations (or life in general), at the very least two beliefs are always required to maintain an emotional attitude: that the kind of situation involved needs to be resisted (a fear-belief that we are not safe) and that this particular emotional attitude is the best way to resist it. For instance, a woman who holds a position of fear about men who make sexual advances toward her must believe that this kind of situation needs to be resisted (because it is threatening) and that her fear in some way protects her from the situation. Together, these two beliefs form the belief that sexual advances are "something to be afraid of." In addition, to really *feel* afraid she will need the identity belief that she *is* afraid, and to manifest her fear she must believe that a man is actually making sexual advances toward her (as opposed to simply being friendly).

Because we cannot hold an emotional attitude without beliefs, an emotion that is not generated by beliefs is not an emotional attitude. The only emotions that are not attitudes, therefore, are love, joy, and compassion, for they cannot be created by beliefs (although beliefs can facilitate their manifestation); they are what IS spontaneously experienced when there are no beliefs creating self-limiting attitudes, when our hearts are fully open to Life.

The beliefs that generate our attitudes—and thus the self-limitations within our emotional point of view—will be referred to as either "emotional beliefs" or "attitude-beliefs," depending on the context. These may be conscious or unconscious, and they may contradict each other or contradict beliefs held by other areas of our consciousness.

Many of our emotional beliefs are learned from other people, especially parents. For instance, a boy may copy his mother who believes that depression is the best way to deal with not getting what she desires (which she believes is threatening). Later, to become free of this emotional pattern, whether or not he recognizes the depression for the copied attitude it is, he will need to change these beliefs.

Because our emotional experience is determined by our emotional point of view, and because the self-limiting aspect of our emotional point of view is made up of our attitudes, our beliefs (by generating our attitudes) are the key to our emotional reality.

Here is an example of a group of beliefs generating a self-limiting emotional reality: A woman has felt resentment and distrust toward men ever since her father divorced her mother when she was four. Her father saw her frequently, treated her well, loved her dearly, and carefully explained why he had left. But she chose to believe that (1) his leaving was a personal rejection, that he really didn't love her anymore, (2) the best way to relate to her father was as "someone to distrust and act resentful toward," and (3) all men were like her father. (These beliefs may also have been a copying of her mother's reactions.) She could have made other choices. But once she decided upon these beliefs and hypnotized herself with them, they generated fixed, self-limiting attitudes; they became part of her emotional point of view, which then determined the kind of men she attracted and the emotional reality she created with them. To transform her emotional reality the woman will need to transform her emotional point of view. In order to do that, she will need to discover and transform the beliefs that are creating it.

We often believe that our emotional reality is determined by what happened to us in our past. Yet the critical factor is not what happened to us but what we *believe* happened to us—what we *choose* to believe happened. In the last example, it is not what happened to the woman as a girl that creates her emotional reality; it is what she (both consciously and unconsciously) believes happened and what she believes this means about the world in general and about herself. (And the key is not simply what she believed when she was little but what she still believes today.) The woman needs to separate her beliefs and attitudes from her actual experiences; only then will she be able to see how her self-limiting beliefs are creating her emotional reality. (Awareness Exercise 5, "Separating an Experience and Its Story," explores how to do this.)

When we separate our beliefs about our experiences from what actually happened or is happening, it becomes easier to see which are primary beliefs and which are secondary. Differentiating them helps us to more fully understand how our beliefs are creating and supporting our emotional reality.

BELIEFS DEFINE MEANING

If a woman is driving down the road and a man cuts her off, what happened—What Is—is itself infinitely meaningful, yet the woman's beliefs can define that meaning in terms of "men are careless and reckless," or in terms of "driving is not safe," or in terms of "that man is an idiot." While the woman's body perceptually constructs her physical experience, her beliefs define what her experience *means* to her, both intellectually and emotionally, and by doing so they shape her personal world.

If three women walking down the street pass a flowering rosebush, one may feel nostalgic, remembering the roses in her backyard when she was a little girl; another may get angry, remembering how her divorced husband always brought her roses after he got drunk and beat her up; and the third may feel sad, remembering the roses she put on her mother's grave. The three women share the same physical reality, and yet their beliefs about roses, about what roses mean, have generated different attitudes and taken each of them into a different, personal world—happy, angry, and sad worlds that were originally created and made meaningful with other beliefs.

One of the most important ways that our beliefs define meaning is by generating "stories," especially about past events. These stories become obvious in relationships, for after an emotional conflict, each person usually has a very different story about what occurred. Although these stories are our attempt to define the meaning of our experiences, we end up using them to define what happened in such a way as to support and validate our emotional positions about these experiences. And because our stories pretend to be objective descriptions, we find them especially useful for supporting positions that blame others for our own attitudes.

Whenever we create a story about an experience, we tend to remember our story rather than what actually happened, and then we believe that what happened was what our story describes. So these stories become part of the fabric of our inner world and our emotional point of view. And every time we tell our story again, whether to ourself or others, we reinforce the particular personal world our story describes, including any emotional positions or other meanings contained in our story.

Beliefs that define the meaning of our experiences are our most powerful creative tool, enabling us to create and reinforce personal worlds; yet such beliefs are a double-edged sword, for they also block us from experiencing the infinite, undefinable meaningfulness of Life by reducing that to tangible, bite-sized pieces of meaning in pre-packaged form.

BELIEFS DETERMINE DESIRES

Our beliefs also determine what we desire. Desires—as opposed to actual needs for physical survival—grow out of what we believe we will experience if we have what we desire, what we believe we will experience if we don't have it, and what we believe about the significance of those experiences for us.

For instance, a man may believe that a new sports car will make it easier for him to get dates, and that without one he will spend a lot of Saturday nights alone. If he desires the sports car, his desire will have grown out of these beliefs, as well as his beliefs about what it means for him to have more dates and what it means for him to be alone. And other beliefs will almost certainly be involved. Perhaps his beliefs about what it means for him to be alone are partially based on his beliefs about what it meant for his father to be alone. Or perhaps, in addition to his conscious beliefs about what he will experience with a new sports car, he has the unconscious belief that his dead grandfather, whom he loved dearly, would strongly approve of this kind of car.

Usually, even a simple desire will grow out of a very complex network of conscious and unconscious beliefs, and those beliefs will completely determine the desire.

IDENTITY BELIEFS & OUR CONSTRUCTED SELVES

Although you are Real, the "you" that you think you are at any given moment is very much a belief-constructed self. It is created out of perceived characteristics—such as your particular body, emotions, personality, mind, strengths, weaknesses, occupation, past experiences, attitudes, beliefs, desires, and so on—and the identity-creating belief that you are some combination of those characteristics. The identity that you construct with this identity-belief seems Real only because you (whoever You really are) have identified your Realness with this identity; you have hypnotized yourself with it and you believe that it is you. Your identity, at any given moment, also includes all the characteristics you believe you are but repress, deny, or reject, pretending that you don't believe these are you. Although your sense of identity, of who you are, is constantly changing in subtle ways according to your situation and whom you are with, you are usually aware of only your most basic commonly-used identities, and sometimes just one or two of them.

Old identity-beliefs are at the core of many webs of limiting beliefs. Since our personal lives are always experienced out of the context of a personal identity, and since personal identity is always created with identity-beliefs, these beliefs necessarily play a critical role in our creation of personal reality.

In today's world of sex-change operations, even the fact of being born into a male or female "body" is not sufficient to give the being in that "body" a sense of identity with that sex. Although such people are often regarded as being a little crazy, they show us that even at very fundamental levels, identity does not exist without a belief to create that identity.

Whether we are willing to lie, steal, get married, or even get a job, depends entirely on who we think we are. In addition, each of our emotional attitudes requires an identity-belief for its existence. For instance, I cannot *be angry* unless I have the identity-belief that *I am angry;* I cannot be angry unless I identify with anger and believe that who I am is some angry "character." This angry character is a constructed self. (The nature of these "characters" will be explored in depth in Chapter 22, "Character-Trances.")

Research with multiple personalities has illuminated how deeply our identity beliefs determine our experience. In many cases, not only does the emotional makeup change radically from personality to personality, but the body does, too. For instance, one personality may have allergies while the others have none. One personality may even have diabetes while the others do not.

Our identity-beliefs are among our most important beliefs; they play a crucial role in both the creation and self-limitation of our personal reality.

RELATIVE "FACTUAL" BELIEFS

We have seen that we determine the truth of a belief by whether or not it is consistent with a point of view we already believe in. Therefore, once we identify with our "body" and believe in its point of view, any belief that is consistent with its point of view will be considered true. In addition, since the point of view of our body constructs and is reflected in our particular physical reality, any belief that is fundamentally consistent with the way our physical reality works will also be considered true. For instance, because the belief that things fall toward the ground is fundamentally consistent with the workings of our physical reality, we will consider this belief to be true. Some other examples of this kind of belief are: knives can be used to kill, fire burns the skin, and food is necessary for us to stay alive. Because our individual bodies have similar points of view and construct similar physical realities, these beliefs that relate strictly to physical cause/effect relationships are considered true by everyone, and so they are called "facts." I call them "relative factual beliefs" because they are specific to this particular physical reality and, although they are factual within this reality, they are still beliefs.

Relative factual beliefs—or simply "factual beliefs"—have nothing to do with our emotional point of view; any belief that is generating or supporting an emotional attitude cannot be a factual one. Our factual beliefs pertain only to our physical point of view, to the nature of our physical reality. They enable us to manipulate, predict, and understand our physical world.

Factual beliefs have certain problems associated with them. The most significant is that non-factual beliefs are usually treated as if they were factual ones. This is common with scientific beliefs. For instance, although it is a factual belief that, in this reality, things fall toward the earth, scientific beliefs about why they fall are just theories, which change constantly and are not factual at all. Because scientists share a very similar point of view of physical reality, they tend to agree on what is true and become tricked into believing that this is factual truth, rather than their own self-consistent, self-perpetuating truth. This is why acupuncture was such a shock to the western medical establishment: it is based on a completely different point of view of physical reality than western science, and yet it works.

The problem of non-factual beliefs masquerading as factual ones also arises with what I call "individual factual beliefs." If yesterday I saw two cars crash, today I will believe that this did in fact happen. This belief is based on a physical cause/effect relationship (involving time) that is consistent with the way our physical reality works. Yet unlike a factual belief, this is a fact only for me, and what I believe I saw is dependent upon how I interpreted what I saw—I may believe one driver made a bad turn when the fault was with the other driver. Individual factual beliefs are based completely on direct *individual* experience, and some of our perceptions are more accurate than others.

If a man who didn't see the accident believes my story or what he reads about the accident in the newspaper, his point of view would be based on a "second-hand belief." Amazingly, most of our beliefs about our world fall into this category. Because second-hand and even individual factual beliefs are not truly factual, they do not simply reflect physical reality; they are primary beliefs that create new personal realities, including emotional attitudes and the great divergence of world-views that people believe in. These are the beliefs that define meaning for us. And because these beliefs are not truly factual, people can justify disbelieving any stories about events they haven't personally experienced, disregard their own experiences, or accept someone else's story but change the meaning of it. Hence, there are people who believe that men never walked on the moon and that the holocaust of World War II is government propaganda. Although we usually hold an angry or arrogant position toward such people, they remind us that *most of our world view is based on non-factual—and especially second-hand—beliefs,* and they remind us that we will treat our more tenuous ones as factual ones if this will help us to support one of our emotional positions or to support other non-factual beliefs. Although some sources of second-hand facts are clearly more reliable than others, once we believe a source we usually make the mistake of treating its information as completely factual, which leads to the creation of a new point of view and a new personal reality.

The second most significant problem created by our factual beliefs is that when we become overly focused on facts we tend to believe that factual beliefs are absolute and that factual truth for this reality is Truth Itself. Yet factual truth is simply that which is self-consistent with our body's fundamental point of view. As we will see in Part II, people can change that point of view, and by doing so they can alter what is factually true for them within this reality—for instance, they can walk on hot coals without being burned.

We have to carefully examine what we believe is factual. Although our factual beliefs give us a certain power to operate in this physical reality, when we deceive ourself about the truth of our beliefs, we generate and keep ourself stuck in self-limiting personal realities. Even when we are honest with ourself, because our factual beliefs reflect and support the point of view that constructs this reality, if we get overly identified with them we will limit our experience of Reality to the reality these beliefs reflect.

BELIEFS CONSTRUCT PERSONAL REALITY

Just as our bodies perceptually construct an outer physical world, our beliefs—by keeping us focused in that world, generating our emotional attitudes, defining the meaning of our experiences, and determining our sense of personal identity and our desires—perceptually construct an inner world, a personal reality.

One consequence of this is that our personal reality will always be an accurate reflection—a mirror of our own beliefs. In addition, because our beliefs are generating our personal reality, they will naturally appear to be true within it. Thus, our personal reality will support, reinforce, and tend to perpetuate the beliefs used in creating it (and the attitudes those beliefs generate).

For example, a woman who believes that roses are sad will feel sad when she sees them. A paranoid, who believes that people are threatening, will perceive people as threatening, thus creating an experiential reality in which people *are* threatening, reinforcing his paranoid beliefs. And a man who believes that his wife has stopped loving him will look for and perceive justifications for his belief, proving to himself that his belief is true, even if his wife really does love him—and over time his attitude will turn his wife against him.

A more complex example is a man who feels rejected by women. Every time he meets a woman, his beliefs about women (whether the beliefs are conscious or unconscious) regenerate subtle feelings and expectations of rejection, which certain women respond to—those women who have similar emotional issues, perhaps similar beliefs about men. His relationships with these women end either with the woman leaving, validating his beliefs, or with his leaving/ rejecting the woman because he thinks she is too unloving or rejecting, which still validates his beliefs.

Because we assume that our beliefs about an experience—our stories about it—are what actually happened, the fact of our experience becomes proof of our beliefs. For instance, consider a situation in which a child believes his mother is rejecting him when she says he can't have something. (He may have learned this belief by watching his mother's response to his father.) He will grow up believing that he is always being rejected, and his proof will be that his mother often doesn't let him have what he wants. (See Awareness Exercise 5, "Separating an Experience and Its Story.")

The reality created by a belief (or story) will always tend to support that belief; and this, of course, will perpetuate the creation of that reality. So, both our beliefs and the realities we create with them tend to be self-perpetuating.

Even when we hold conflicting beliefs about a particular aspect of our reality, both sets of beliefs will tend to perpetuate themselves. For instance, a man may believe that he is competent and in control, yet another aspect of himself may believe that he is just a helpless, inadequate little boy. Both sets of beliefs will be reflected in the personal reality he creates, and they will both tend to be perpetuated.

I have been using the word "tend" to qualify the self-perpetuation process of beliefs and realities, for two reasons. First of all, as we will see in the next chapter, what we create is always being modified by deeper levels of our consciousness. If this were not the case, the perpetuation process would keep us forever stuck in our present form of personal reality, with no way to grow.

The second reason is that if we hold a belief that, at some point, proves to be inconsistent with more basic beliefs, we will drop the belief and it will stop perpetuating itself. For instance, I may believe that I am going to win Sunday's lottery, but if Monday arrives and I have not yet won it, because of my core beliefs about space and time I will drop the belief that I am going to win the lottery; the belief is no longer consistent with my world view. (Yet while I held the belief, I may have begun making plans for how I was going to spend this money, reinforcing the belief that I was indeed going to win it.) Event-specific beliefs are often dropped because of this kind of inconsistency.

ATTACHMENT TO BELIEFS

A critical factor in the self-perpetuation of our beliefs is our attachment to them. Since the root of attachment is fear, we become attached to our beliefs—and therefore to "being right"—because we believe they keep us safe. Even when we create an identity with our beliefs we will be attached to them only if we believe that this identity keeps us safe.

An example of our attachment to beliefs is a woman whose father died when she was three years old. She loved her father, felt devastated by his death, and was unable to deal with her experience. So she decided to believe that he was a mean person for leaving her, and as she grew up, her belief/story shortened to "he was a mean person." Although this belief effectively cut her off from loving memories of her father, it protected her from having to deal with her experience of loss and insecurity. And as long she is afraid of her actual experience, she will be attached to her belief, will use whatever she can to support her position, and will resist stories that portray her father in a better light.

Another example is a little boy who was insecure, had difficulty making friends, and often felt lonely. He decided that the reason he couldn't make friends was because the other boys were rejecting him (which they weren't), and that they were, therefore, the cause of his unhappiness. This enabled him to avoid being responsible for himself and helped him to camouflage his own insecurity. Yet as he grew older, his need to make other people the cause of his unhappiness led to him becoming a bigot, and he was very attached to the beliefs he formed about people of other races and religions.

Because of our attachment to our beliefs we will tend to create stories and beliefs about our new experiences that validate our old beliefs, camouflage our real issues, and perpetuate our old personal reality.

TRADING IN BELIEFS

In spite of the relativity of our beliefs, we can make this one distinction among them: although beliefs that open our heart, promote love, and expand consciousness cannot be absolutely true, they are more "in harmony with Truth" than those which limit our experience of Life. An analogy, taken from the Zen tradition, is that if we want to have a direct experience of the moon (a direct experience of What Is, of Truth, transcending all beliefs), then although a finger pointing at the moon is not the moon itself, it is much more useful than a finger pointing at the ground.

Since non-factual beliefs are ultimately neither true nor false but perceptual filters that create personal reality, the most significant questions we can ask about a non-factual belief are: does this belief limit me, does it support a stuck emotional position, or does it open my experience of Life and bring more love and joy into my journey? If our beliefs are limiting us, if they are creating a personal reality that is not growing into deeper experiences of joy, then the best thing for us to do with those beliefs is trade them in for new ones, for beliefs that are "more in harmony with Truth."

If you owned an automobile that was continually causing you trouble, you would want to trade it in for one that worked better. Your beliefs are your vehicle for journeying into personal realities. Although the idea of trading in your "bad" beliefs may seem strange at first, your only obstacles are: a belief that they are a part of yourself (if you have identified with your beliefs), or that they are "true," or that they keep you safe. Another obstacle might be a resistance to bringing more joy into your life (which will be caused by other beliefs). To trade in your self-limiting beliefs all you must do is take the time to discover them, to choose different beliefs, and to integrate the new beliefs into your consciousness. Of course, some self-limiting beliefs are very deep; these will take more time both to discover and let go.

Here is an example of how this kind of trade-in can work. A woman believes that she cannot open emotionally to men because she wasn't loved as a child. Her belief in not having a history of being loved maintains her in an emotional reality of inner isolation. In such a situation, I would have the woman go back, in her memory, to any such time when she was a child. Then I would have her imagine that there were divine, unconditionally loving beings around her all the time, but that her fixation on physical reality blocked her from perceiving them. Although I cannot prove such beings exist, I believe in them and experience them. If the woman is willing to "try on" my belief, she will begin to experience that she was incredibly loved as a child. And as she begins to experience the love that was and still is there, her beliefs about being loved will change, which will change her emotional reality and her ability to open emotionally to men. (The same effect could be had if the woman imagined that she was loved by deeper levels of her parents' consciousness even if they had unloving human personalities.)

The set of beliefs presented in this book constitute a model of Reality that can be used to replace whatever model you are currently using. As with all other models of Reality, this one is ultimately neither true nor false. Yet because this model—which I call the *Creative Trance Model of Personal Reality*—uses a set of beliefs that are more "in harmony with Truth" than most models, it should help you to transform areas in yourself and your life that are stuck, help you to bring more joy and creativity into your life, and help you to free yourself from your past so you can live more in the present moment. Only when we move deeply enough into love and into the present moment can we enter into that unique place where we experience Life without any models at all.

When we forget that beliefs are neither true nor false but tools that create personal reality, then we also forget that the personal realities we create from our beliefs are constructs and not Reality. It is this forgetfulness that again brings the element of "illusion" into our experience. And once we have gotten caught in the illusion, we become stuck in it, for we have lost the awareness that we can change our experience. This is like becoming so en-tranced while watching television that we become lost in the illusion that the show is Real, and then we forget that if we are not really enjoying it, we can simply change the channel.

BELIEFS & THE PRESENT MOMENT

Because beliefs are carryovers from the past, they cover new situations in old clothes, distorting our experience and limiting it to variations of our past. For instance, if a woman believes that men are untrustworthy, her belief—which is part of the old baggage that she has collected and carried with her from her past—distorts her present experience and limits it to being a new variation on an old theme when she is with men. In the example with the rosebush, the three women were oblivious to the actual living plant directly in front of them. Their beliefs created meaningful experiences for them, yet those experiences were reruns of realities they had already experienced, so their beliefs blocked them from having new experiences in the present and trapped them in the past.

Metaphorically, our beliefs give us a way to grasp Reality, but grasping is a fixed position that resists the flow of Life and blocks our experience of What Is, giving us instead the experience of what is grasped and thus creating a personal reality that reflects our beliefs.

All beliefs limit our capacity to be in the present moment, yet we usually need to replace limiting beliefs with ones that are less limiting before we can dispense with beliefs entirely. For instance, the woman who distrusts men may first need to use a less limiting belief—perhaps that her experience with men has really been created by her own attitudes—before she can learn to drop her beliefs about men entirely and simply experience men as they are.

As we use less limiting beliefs, we free ourself from the baggage and illusions of our past—including our identification with our personal history—and we begin to exist more in the present moment. This brings more love, freedom, joy and compassion into our lives, since these experiences arise spontaneously when we are open to Life. And as we allow ourself to go deeper into receiving this kind of experience in the present moment, our beliefs become superfluous and begin to fade into the background of our minds, creating a new kind of opening: a door to the Living Now. This is the transformation from personal meaning to beingness, from the perceptual construct of physical life to the timelessness of Reality Itself.

AWARENESS EXERCISE 5:
SEPARATING AN EXPERIENCE AND ITS STORY

You'll need paper and a pen. A comfortable armchair would be the best place to sit—or lean against a wall with pillows. There are two parts. I recommend experiencing them on different days.

PART I: TRAUMA

(1) Think of a past event that in some way was traumatic for you. Then write down (a) what actually happened, (b) the thoughts, feelings, and attitudes that come to mind when you think about it, (c) the attitude you present to other people (if you tell others about it), (d) the story you tell yourself about it, (e) the story you tell others (if this is different), and (f) any attitudes and positions about life that your story (or stories) validates or supports. Write all these down.

(2) Notice how your story makes someone or something other than yourself responsible for your emotional experience.

(3) Now put aside the paper, close your eyes, go back to that event, and remember it as vividly as possible. Remember any objects that were present, where they were, any colors, any other people, how they were dressed, what their faces looked like, any voices or smells. Remember what you were thinking and how your body felt. Even if it was painful, allow yourself now to remember how your body felt then. Allow the whole experience to be remembered as vividly as possible. And while you are remembering, just be with the experience without any judgments, preferences, interpretations, or positions about it. Allow yourself to experience what is happening without resisting or telling yourself that it is good or bad or painful. If you feel like crying, let yourself cry without thinking about what the crying means. Stay with the actual experience. If you stay with it long enough—open to the experience deeply enough—your inner resistance to the experience will let go, and all your trauma around it will dissipate.

(4) Consider the experience you just had and look at all the thoughts, attitudes, judgments and stories you have told yourself and others over the years about what actually happened. Be aware that any story you have about it is something you made up and added to what happened. Be aware that you used your story to define the meaning of the experience for yourself and to support a particular position about life. Then compare what you experience when you tell

yourself your story to what you experience when you remember the event without your story. Finally, allow yourself to drop your story, so you just have what actually happened as your memory.

(5) Imagine that what happened was designed perfectly for your own spiritual growth, and think of the purpose it may have served. Make up a new story about what happened—create a new interpretation of the event—that has as its central theme what you ultimately gained from the experience. For a traumatic experience this may be a difficult point of view to take, but it is as valid as the story you originally created. In fact, somewhere in the world today, someone who has had a very similar experience has chosen to accept the experience and feel grateful for what it has taught. So create a story that has more positive consequences—that supports a more loving position about Life—than your original one. Write down the new story.

(6) Imagine sometime in the future telling someone about this old event, using the new story you created. Be aware of the way you will now describe it. Be aware of your attitude, of how your body feels, of what your voice sounds like. Notice how the listener responds to this new story.

(7) Write down any new insights you have gained from doing this.

Repeat this exercise for all the major traumas of your life.

PART 2: PEOPLE

This repeats Part 1, but, instead of focusing on traumatic events, you focus on significant *people* in your life. Write down your thoughts, attitudes, and the basic story you tell yourself and others about these people, and then experience each person without any stories. Repeat each step of Part 1, substituting the person for the event.

I suggest doing this exercise with all the significant people in your life, both alive and dead, starting with your parents, and including stepparents if they have played any significant role in your life. Then repeat the exercise with any siblings you grew up with, any children, spouse, or lover you have, and any other significant people in your life with whom you need to become more clear.

Again, write down your experiences. Writing makes your awareness more concrete, helps you to get in touch with the emotional aspects of the experience, and prevents you from blurring the parts of the experience together in your mind. A few words to sum up a thought is sufficient.

AWARENESS EXERCISE 6:
ROOTING OUT SELF-LIMITING BELIEFS

You will need three pieces of paper and something to write with. There are three parts.

PART 1

Draw a line down the middle of a sheet of paper. On the left side, list whatever attitudes you tend to get caught in, leaving five lines between each one. Then, on the right side, list whatever beliefs you have that create, support, maintain or justify each particular attitude.

Take your time. To discover the belief-structure corresponding to each attitude will probably require some contemplation.

PART 2

On the second sheet, draw a line down the middle of the page. On the left hand side, list present situations that you react to, resist, or are having difficulty with, and past situations that you still haven't completed or resolved. On the right hand side, list your beliefs about each situation. Again, take whatever time you need to really ferret out your beliefs. Look for both conscious and unconscious beliefs, both obvious and subtle ones. Write them all down.

PART 3

Examine the beliefs you wrote down in Parts 1 and 2, keeping in mind that *any belief that keeps you stuck cannot be completely true.*

What are the flaws in your belief-structures?

What is it that you are leaving out?

Where do your beliefs describe only half-truths?

Where do your beliefs do nothing more than support self-limiting emotional positions?

Where do your beliefs keep you in the experience of being a victim?

On the third sheet of paper, write down what you find.

Then, examine the attitudes and situations you wrote down (in Parts 1 and 2) in light of any modifications you have made to your beliefs, and see if your experience of those attitudes and situations has changed. If they haven't, you need to examine your beliefs about them more deeply.

First Scientific Interlude

Modern physicists, in their quest to understand the basic nature of physical reality, have been forced to examine old assumptions about reality that had been embedded in the foundation of Western science—and Western civilization. What they have found was previously stated only by mystics, and is remarkably similar (but stated in scientific terms) to some of the material presented in this book.[3]

Until recently, modern science did not consider the world a perceptual construct. Of the major assumptions of Western science, the most basic was: physical reality has an absolute existence which is independent of and unaffected by our perception of it. This invisible assumption was a root belief that programmed all scientific inquiry as well as everyday experience. For instance, if a scientist performing an experiment saw a flash of red light and then a flash of green light, he automatically assumed that the order of those events was a fact that would be true for anyone observing them. But then came Einstein's Theory of Relativity. Einstein showed that "facts" about space and time are *relative* to the perceptual point of view of the observer. For instance, a second scientist zooming past the first one in a rocket, observing the "same" flashes of light, might very well have seen them flash simultaneously rather than consecutively. To ask what "really" happened—to ask which order is the correct one—is to assume that some real event existed independently of the perceptions of the two scientists. But Einstein showed that *space-time reality depends completely upon the point of view of the observer.*

Years later, Werner Heisenberg, with a mathematical proof called the Uncertainty Principle, further showed that *perception (or measurement) always alters the reality of what is being perceived.*

---

[3]Much of the information for the first two scientific interludes has been gleaned from three books that describe modern developments in physics in layperson language: *The Tao of Physics* by Fritjof Capra, *The Dancing We Li Masters* by Gary Zukav, and *In Search of Schrodinger's Cat* by John Gribin. The first two books also talk about the parallels between modern physics and Far Eastern philosophy.

This is because to perceive reality, we must interact with it in some way. But interacting with it changes it, making the "true" nature of what is perceived "uncertain." If the object being perceived is a moving car, the alteration is not large enough for us to notice it, but at a subatomic level, it poses major restrictions for scientists. For example, in any experiment that attempts to measure both the position and momentum of a single moving electron, the process of precisely measuring the position alters the electron so much that the momentum measurement becomes very imprecise and "uncertain." And this margin of uncertainty must exist regardless of how sensitive we can make the instruments used in the experiment; it is created by the very nature of physical reality and perception.

Because of the extent to which reality is determined by perception, scientists have been forced to define what is "real" in terms of what is perceived. Scientifically, it is now meaningless to say that an event is real if no consciousness has perceived it. (Scientists are still quibbling over what level or type of consciousness is required.) An unperceived event is considered a "possible" event, sometimes even a "probable" event, but not a "real" one. Consciousness and perception are required to create reality.

The experiments that scientists have done with light clearly illustrate on a macro level the extraordinary degree to which reality and perception are intertwined. The most famous and important of these is called the double-slit experiment (designed to determine if light is made of subatomic particles or of waves), and its peculiarities are the heart of modern quantum physics. The experiment is done with a light source shining at a screen with two holes in it. A few feet from the other side of the screen is a photographic plate that will show where the photons of light land. (A photon is the smallest possible unit of light; a beam of light, therefore, is composed of millions of these photons.) Now, if only one hole is open, the light makes a circle on the photographic plate, with the greatest intensity at the center of the circle, in line with the hole. This is as it should be, whether photons are particles or waves. When both holes are opened, though, we find a wave interference pattern on the plate (just like the wave pattern created on a pond by two stones simultaneously thrown into the water), indicating that the photons of light are a wave. (The interference pattern can be created only if the photon goes through both holes simultaneously, which it can only do as a wave.) If they were particles, we would have seen two simple circles of light intersecting each other without any interference (because the photons would go through only one hole at a time). But here is the crux of it: if we look for the photons as-if they are particles, and we trace which hole each photon goes through by placing special detectors on the far side of each hole, the photons stop acting like waves and behave like particles, making two intersecting circles on the plate instead of the interference pattern. *Our own shift in perception totally alters the reality-manifestation of the photons.*

Scientists concluded from this experiment that light is made up of neither particles nor waves, but that the perceptual framework of their own experiment causes light to seem to be one or another. And since we can never know anything more about light than what we can discover in our experiments, we can never know what light actually IS; all we can know is what light seems to be when we perceive it and interact with it in various ways. In addition, since all subatomic particles can seem to be particles or waves (and in double-slit type experiments behave just like the photons), this effect of perception on physical reality happens not just with light but with the whole subatomic world that ultimately makes up our macro reality. In fact, this phenomenon actually happens with all matter, not just subatomic particles. Even large macroscopic objects like a house will manifest as either matter or a wave depending upon how we measure it, but the wave is so stretched out, we aren't able to notice with our eyes that it is waving. In *The Dancing Wu Li Masters,* Gary Zukav says:

> *If we observe a certain particle collision experiment, not only do we have no way of proving that the result would have been the same if we had not been watching it, all that we know indicates that it would not have been the same, because the result we got was affected by the fact that we were looking for it.*[4]

This is the definitive conclusion of quantum physics: *the reality we perceive does not exist independently of our perception; how we look always determines what we see.* And therefore, our world must always be a MIRROR of ourself and our unique perceptual point of view.

---

[4]Gary Zukav, *The Dancing Wu Li Masters* (New York: Bantam, 1979), pp. 30-31.

For scientists, this mirror effect caused by our perceptual creation of reality pertains only to physical reality, since that is what they are investigating; yet it is true of all facets of our personal existence.

Scientists have begun to perceptually construct artificial worlds in their laboratories. They call such a world a "virtual reality." Working with computers, scientists have designed virtual-reality "suits" that, when put on, enable the participant to experience an alternate reality whose rules are determined by a computer program. Inside the virtual-reality suit, two tiny television-type screens placed directly in front of the eyes enable the participant to see the "world" that is portrayed on the screens by the computer program; and sensors that detect movement in the eyes enable the computer to change what is shown on the screens according to how the eyes move, creating the experience of actually looking around in another world. In addition, sensors attached to the participant's physical hands enable him to move the hands he sees in his virtual reality, and with those "virtual" hands he can actually pick up things that he sees there. According to the computer program, his hand might look like a human hand, or it could appear to be a lobster claw. In fact, the computer program can create the experience of having the body of a dog or a dragon, and can even change the rules defining how things work in the virtual reality. For instance, the program can be designed so that if we push hard against something with just our little finger, the object shrinks or even disappears, or if we play a musical instrument (a "virtual" instrument) the sounds generate colorful shapes in the air. The program can even be designed so that we only "see" infrared.

Virtual-reality suits are being used in laboratories today. And they provide a wonderful metaphor, for we can think of our bodies as highly sophisticated virtual-reality suits that we "put on" when we were born in order to have a certain kind of experience. By perceiving through this body-suit, we were able to experience ourself as living within a particular kind of physical reality, the nature of which was determined by the nature of our body-suit and its built-in "genetic program." Yet over time, as we became en-tranced with our perception, we got lost in it; we came to believe that the virtual reality constructed by our body-suits was Reality Itself.

PART II

The Creative Trance

5

Trance-Illusions

I once visited a brother in a mental hospital. I sat in a room with him and his psychiatrist. He thought he was Christ and the psychiatrist thought he was a psychiatrist, and each of them was convinced that the other one was insane.
— Ram Dass, *Grist for the Mill*

If a man in a hypnotic trance is told that he is a cat, he will *believe* that he is a cat and will *experience* himself as a cat. He is not a cat; yet he thinks he is one because he is lost in the trance-illusion created by his belief. If a woman believes that old age is sad and becomes sad whenever she sees an old person, her emotional experience is really a self-induced hypnotic trance created by her belief. *Any reality created by beliefs is a trance.* Trance-realities seem Real to us only because we believe they are Real; through our belief we project onto these trances our own inner sense of Realness.

Therefore, when we believe that the perceptual construct created by our human body is Reality, we experience the world (and ourselves!) as physical and become lost in a deep hypnotic trance. And because other beings have also created reality-trances with human bodies, our experience of physical reality becomes a group experience, a group-trance. We don't notice that we are in a trance simply because we are all lost in the same trance, agreeing with each other that physical reality is Real. The only reason we can tell that the hypnotized man, who thinks he is a cat, is in a trance is because he is in a *different* trance than we are.

In addition to the group-trance of physical reality, we all share and live within a cultural group-trance, as well as participate in smaller group-trances created with religious, political, or other shared beliefs. If the members of a religious group believe that God loves only themselves, they are lost in a religious group-trance. This is easy to notice when you're not part of that trance, but when a whole society believes that killing young virgins appeases the gods, or that diseases are caused by evil demons, or that being successful is more important than being compassionate, or even that anger is the "natural" response to being mistreated, no one notices the trance.

We also exist within our own individual-trances created with our own individual beliefs. A woman who is unhappy with her weight is lost in an individual-trance. When a little girl believes that no one loves her, regardless of how much love she has or hasn't received, she is lost in an individual-trance. All emotional attitudes and positions are self-induced individual-trances (many of which other people agree with) because they are all created and maintained by beliefs. In addition, our sense of identity at any particular time is an individual-trance, created with beliefs about who we are. (Our sense of beingness is not a trance, for it is not created; it IS.) Some of our identity-trances are actually our deepest, most significant trances, for they are the basis of all our other trances. For instance, without the identity-trance that creates a sense of identity with our individual human body, we could not even be born.

Our experience of life is a complex trance—a changing fabric of many overlapping group and individual-trances, all of which are personal-trances for they are all created through our own personal beliefs, even if some are also shared beliefs. And these personal-trances taken together, along with whatever awareness we have of our true Self, which exists outside of these trances, make up our entire personal reality.

The fact that our life is lived in a trance does not minimize the significance of our experience. All of our trance-experiences are meaningful and have purpose. Yet when we experience a trance as Reality, we are caught in an hypnotic *illusion*—the same kind of illusion that traps the man who thinks he is a cat; the same kind of illusion we enter while dreaming, whenever we forget that we are dreaming and experience our dream as Real. (In our trances and dreams, *what* we experience is an illusion, yet the experience itself is still Real, for it is always our Real Self that is having the experience, regardless of the particular constructed self that we are identified with at the time.) Although all of our trance-experiences have value and meaning, the idea is to awaken from the illusions that trap us so that we can have a deeper, more meaningful experience. Perceiving our life-experience as a trance does not negate life but helps us to not be so hypnotized by—and thus trapped within—our experience, and so it helps us to "wake up" within our trance. We have to learn to free our awareness so that our consciousness extends *beyond* our trance. Then we can participate in physical reality without any trance-illusions limiting our full experience of the Living Now.

Two questions naturally arise when we realize that our experience of life is a trance:

(1) To what extent is our trance malleable to our consciousness and beliefs? How much freedom do we actually have to create and *trance-form* our own reality?

(2) How can we awaken our consciousness so it becomes free of its trance?

6

Creating Our Trance

The trance of human life gives us the opportunity to encounter a vast array of experiences. As awful as these experiences sometimes seem to the constructed self within the trance, they are wonderful learning opportunities for the Self who chooses to enter the trance.

We are creative beings, growing by exploring our Self through human trance-experiences. We are like actors, freely choosing to play a part in a movie. Although many movies portray violent and depressing dramas, actors know that they are only acting, so they feel safe in becoming the characters they are playing. And for the actor, the value of playing a particular character depends not on whether that character's life is "good" or "bad," but on the degree of personal growth that can be experienced through playing that character. Often, more growth is possible in playing a character who has an emotionally painful life than in playing one who has the kind of stress-free existence our constructed selves usually want.

For the Self, the decision to be born as a human being, to make an *en-trance* into Life, must be freely chosen, since we cannot be hypnotized so deeply against our will. For the same reason, we freely choose our particular family situation and the particular body we want to trance-identify with and perceive through. And our individual emotional point of view is created by our choosing to en-trance ourself with particular emotional beliefs. So our entire human situation is freely chosen according to our own particular needs for learning, growth, and creative expression. And since it is impossible to learn everything about human experience that is necessary for our growth from one role, from one short slice of human life, when we are finished with our trance we begin to look around for another one to enter. This is commonly called "reincarnation," but since this term tends to reinforce the illusion that human reality is Reality, I will generally use the term "reentrancement" in my discussions.

Whenever we reenter a human trance, we take with us a blueprint, a general idea, of what we intend to learn. Our learning doesn't grow haphazardly out of the situation we have been born into; rather, we choose that situation because it fits into our own larger plan. And choosing our birth situation is just the beginning of the process of creating (of trance-forming) the events of our life. We choose *all* the events in our life. To the constructed self within the trance this may seem impossible. But not all of ourself is lost in the trance. Part of the actor still remembers that he is acting. And outside of the trance, we are not limited by time and space. *Time and space are aspects of physical reality so they only exist within that trance.* Therefore, our out-of-trance Self, which is the part of us that is outside of time and space, is aware of all the possible events that exist for us within our trance at any time, both physical events such as earthquakes, and shared experiences with other beings. We move toward the events that we want to be part of and conspire with the part of other beings that is not in trance to mutually create exactly the experiences desired. Therefore:

(1) We choose and create all the events of our life.

(2) We are responsible for everything that happens to us.

(3) Since we create events according to what we need to learn, our life perfectly mirrors that learning as well as where we are stuck.

Clearly, there are no accidents in life. Yet there is also no predestination. Although we enter the human trance with a general blueprint for what we are going to learn, most of the details need to be worked out as we go. This is like planning a long automobile trip: although we start with a general idea of what we'd like to experience, perhaps even draw up a rough schedule, the details of the trip as well as whatever learning we will have through our experiences needs to unfold as we go. If we could work out all the details of all the events in advance, there would be no spontaneity, no creative process, and no power in NOW. There would be nothing new for us to learn from the actual experience; we wouldn't even have a reason to go. But we enter a life-trance (or take a trip) to learn and grow and explore our creativity through new experiences. So, much of our life drama must be worked out as we go, and it will not always go exactly as originally intended—we may grow faster or slower than we anticipated, or decide to explore some areas more deeply than originally planned. Although the general blueprint we came in with embodies a strategy for creating the growth we know we need, it has to be updated frequently to accommodate our actual experience.

Just because part of us is outside our trance and not limited by time and space does not mean it should be able to know everything that will happen to us in our future. If time and space were unchanging, static things, like a book, we would always know how events turn out. But all the beings in our trance are creating experiences for themselves as they go, following their own general blueprint for growth. Time and space *evolve* as beings freely create experiences within it. And since we participate only in those events we choose to experience, no event can be absolutely certain until it happens—until our choice to experience it becomes irrevocable—or free will would not exist. Yet at any particular time, the part of us outside our trance can see what events are probably unfolding at that time and in the immediate future. The further off events are in time, the more uncertain they become (a spiritual aspect of Heisenberg's Uncertainty Principle), yet the nature of some events enables them to be seen with a good deal of certainty far into the future.

The fact that people have had precognitive visions tells us that our out-of-trance awareness of probable future events can be accessed from within our human time-space trance. These visions should never be regarded as facts but as possibilities that can be altered. What is often called the "Divine Plan" is not some rigidly laid out schedule of events that must or should unfold. Even on our human level, a good plan has a lot of flexibility and room for alternative possibility. The Divine Plan, being perfect, contains *infinite* possibility, giving our out-of-trance Self infinite freedom to plan probable events and to choose, according to its own creative free will, those particular experiences that would best serve its needs Now.

It is the *mutuality* of reality-creation that enables some events to be seen far in advance. Although we individually choose all the events in our lives, most of these events need to be created with other beings who are also choosing how they will be involved in them. This kind of mutual creation is one aspect of our group-trance. An event like a war that involves millions of beings does not happen simply because an official decides to declare war one night. Every individual affected freely chooses (out-of-trance) to mutually create both the event and his or her individual role within it. (As we will see in the next chapter, the complex dynamics of mutual creation are actually very simple.)

Another aspect of mutual creation is that all of our individual learning is automatically shared with everyone else through the connection of our out-of-trance consciousness. This enables us, as we individually explore different facets of the same basic human issues, to expand our Self-knowledge from the experiences that everyone else is having, too. For instance, whenever two people become angry at each other, there are two beings mutually exploring the issue of human anger (among other issues); and their learning goes out to benefit all of us as we learn, individually and as a group, to confront this emotional attitude and transform it. So we are always helping each other to explore the issues for which we have become human to experience and transform. Even a hermit, living alone in the woods, is continuously participating in everyone else's learning and growth, and everyone else is intimately involved in his. In spite of the appearance of our human trance, we are never really alone.

Our human reality is a group drama that is mutually planned outside of our trance. Yet we are still individually responsible for all the events and experiences we personally experience in our lives. What we end up creating with other beings depends entirely upon what we choose to create. Our lives grow out of our own free will. In fact, free will exists at every level of creation. If free will did not exist, then complete predictability would be possible. But Heisenberg's Uncertainty Principle (discussed in the "First Scientific Interlude") proved mathematically that a margin of unmeasurability—and hence unpredictability—exists around every manifested phenomenon; a sphere of freedom exists for every participant in every event, even for participants as small as subatomic particles. In fact, subatomic particles demonstrate their free will in every laboratory experiment that measures them. Even a car, within its own sphere, demonstrates free will (the combined free will of all the molecules in it), for no computer, no matter how advanced, will ever be able to predict exactly the moment it will break down. Yet, as we will see later, because of the Oneness of all creation, even a car must mutually create its breakdown with all the beings affected by the breakdown.

Nothing happens to us without our permission, without our free choice. This is the promise and meaning of free will: *we are free to create our own trance and our own experience.* Anything less would be a sham.

AWARENESS EXERCISE 7:
IDENTITY-TRANCES

You will need paper and a pen. It is better to complete the instructions in each paragraph before reading the next one.

PART I

(1) At the top of one sheet of paper write, "I am.../I like...". At the top of the other sheet write, "I am not.../I don't like...". Then on each sheet of paper complete the top sentences in twenty different ways. For instance, on the first sheet I might write: "I am a man; I like to hike; I am intelligent; I like apples..." On the second sheet I might write: "I am not greedy; I am not a woman; I don't like noisy people; I don't like violence..."

(2) Notice how these sentences—both the affirming and the negating—define you to yourself.

(3) Notice that all your self-definitions involve your body, your mind, your emotions, your personality, your attitudes, or your behaviors.

(4) Notice that each definition contributes to an overall identity-trance that becomes your experience of yourself.

(5) Notice that your identity-trance limits your experience of yourself, both internally and in your behavior.

(6) Now you are going to experiment with entering into different identity-trances. (Actors and actresses do this all the time.) Choose any five of the characteristics you negated, and imagine yourself to be a person with all five of these characteristics. You may think of this as an acting exercise in which you have to internally become a different person. Be aware of how your voice changes, how the way you hold your body changes, how the way you feel about yourself and others changes—allow yourself to really become this other person. To do this well, you may have to focus individually on each characteristic, becoming each one in turn, before you can be all five together.

(7) If being a member of the opposite sex was not one of the characteristics you chose in step 6, add this to the five you chose and experience yourself as this person.

(8) Imagine that somewhere in a previous existence you were exactly the person you just pretended to become. Imagine the kind of life you had—the kind of childhood and parents you must have had,

the way you grew up, what happened to you as an adult and in your final years.

(9) Choose someone that you know well, and imagine that for a day you can trade bodies and experience the other person's life *as the other person experiences it.* Then actually step into and become this person. Feel your body become his or her body, feel your personality become the other's personality, and as the other person, feel your emotions, be aware of your thoughts, and get an overall sense of your existence.

(10) Imagine that at one time, before you were born, you had considered becoming en-tranced with this other person's body, but at the last minute you changed your mind and en-tranced yourself with the body you now call your own.

(11) Imagine that you could have also have chosen to en-trance yourself in the body of a cat or any other animal, or even a plant.

(12) Become aware of the "you" that you were before you en-tranced yourself with your body, the "you" that could have become en-tranced in some other body or form.

PART 2

Think of an emotional attitude that you often get stuck in, and remember a recent situation in which you manifested it.

Then ask yourself:

(1) Who do you think you are while you are expressing this attitude? What kind of character or identity-trance are you caught in?

(2) What key beliefs are held by this character that are necessary for maintaining its trance?

(3) Repeat this with another attitude and situation.

(4) Repeat this the next few times you find yourself feeling or expressing an attitude.

AWARENESS EXERCISE 8:
THE HUMAN TRANCE

PART 1

Go for a slow walk at a time when the light outside is soft.

While you are walking, imagine that you are walking in a dream, that everything around you is a dream. If you allow yourself to, you can actually experience yourself as being awake in a dream. It may help to relax or slightly "defocus" your eyes, for we tend to "grab the world with our eyes" and hold it in a way that is familiar to us.

When you can sense that the world around you is a dream, slowly expand your awareness, one step at a time, as follows:

(1) Imagine that your body, too, is simply part of the dream.

(2) Imagine that your thoughts are simply thoughts you are having in this dream.

(3) Notice that your current human personality is simply another part of your dream.

(4) Notice your tendency to become en-tranced with the dream, to become so absorbed in the dream that you forget you are dreaming and treat the dream as Real.

(5) As you move deeper into the experience of all of this being a dream, try to sense the place the dream is unfolding from. Be aware of the Source of its creation.

PART 2

Sit comfortably and close your eyes. Receive a few deep breaths ... and let yourself relax.

Now, imagine that your life is a bubble. You are in the center of it, and everything you have ever done—which includes everything you have ever thought about, known, imagined, fantasized, experienced, or even dreamed about—is contained within this bubble.

For the most part, your conscious awareness has been limited to the *time-bound* events and experiences that are contained in this bubble. Get a sense of your life as this bubble. Imagine what might exist *beyond* this bubble—beyond matter, beyond emotion, beyond even thought. Stretch your consciousness beyond this bubble of your human life and time, and contact what Is Now, on the other side.

Before you return to your familiar bubble, look at it and examine it from the point of view of your awareness outside of this bubble.

7

⚜

Oneness

Within every trance-reality is the imprint of the deeper Reality that constructs it. If we explore deeply enough the nature of our physical world, we will uncover the workings of all creation. Therefore, it is not surprising that as scientists penetrate the nature of matter and energy, they describe the world in terms very similar to those used by mystics for thousands of years.

Compare these two quotes, one from the mystic Sri Aurobindo and one from modern physicist David Bohm:

> *One is led to a new notion of unbroken wholeness which denies the classical idea of analyzability of the world into separately and independently existing parts ... we say that the inseparable ... interconnectedness of the whole universe is the fundamental reality, and that relatively independently behaving parts are merely particular and contingent forms within this whole.*[5]

> *The material object becomes ... something different from what we now see, not a separate object on the background or in the environment of the rest of nature but an indivisible part and even in a subtle way an expression of the unity of all that we see.*[6]

Mystics and modern physicists agree that the universe is a unified whole and that the appearance of the separateness of things is just that—an appearance. In Part I, we saw that the reality we perceive does not exist independently of our perception. We also saw that our perception is determined by our beliefs and by our entrancement with

---

[5]Fritjof Capra, *The Tao of Physics*, (New York: Bantam, 1984), p. 124.
[6]Ibid., p. 125.

our body's point of view. Mystics and modern physicists tell us that even our experience of the separateness of ourselves and of all manifest objects is just another perceptual construct. Therefore, *our experience of separateness is just another part of our trance.* The self that we experience as being separate from everything else—our constructed self—is just an identity-trance. We are all One Consciousness, One Self; we are Conscious Beingness, and that is All That Exists.

Yet to explore Itself, this One Consciousness en-trances Itself into form. Every soul, person, animal, plant, and thing is an *en-tranced expression of conscious beingness,* which in Itself has no qualities or form. A human being, therefore, is Beingness being human; it is Conscious Beingness pretending to be human. Conscious Beingness en-trances Itself as a "soul," as a being with its own identity that still remembers its Oneness, and then as a soul it explores Itself through the trance-experience of being human. (Although the term "out-of-trance Self" technically refers to our One Source—outside of all trances, because our soul is outside of our *human* trance and experiences its Oneness with Self—this term will also refer to our soul-consciousness.) Most of the time, we are lost in our entrancement with being human, yet we do periodically experience our true Self, our Conscious Beingness, when we are so totally overwhelmed with joy or love that we completely lose our familiar sense of self in the bliss that is pouring through us.

Conscious Beingness has been called "God," "Spirit," "Life Itself," the "Inner Light," the "Self," the "Higher Self," the "Creative Source," "Divine Love," the "Living Now," and many other names (that I will use interchangeably), each of which points to the unlimited ONE by emphasizing a limited experiential aspect of It. Conscious Beingness always exists Now. It is the Now. It is everything that Is Now.

The unitary relationship between Conscious Beingness and its manifest creations is vividly captured in an ancient symbol of the universe—the Tree of Life. All the particular forms of Life are expressed from the Tree as leaves. As a human being, living within the Tree as one of those leaves, we can choose to perceive ourself as separate from all the other leaves, or we can remember that *we are the whole living Tree expressing our Self as this unique leaf,* that our Self is also the Self of every other leaf within the Tree.

Of course, expressing our Self in human form is more complex than in mineral forms, for more expressions of our Self have to participate to mutually create the more complex reality-trance. To become human we need a soul-expression of our Self to become entranced with a human-body expression of our Self, which is itself a very complex mutual creation of Self.

Because of the inherent Oneness of all creation, the dynamics of mutual creation—which requires that every event in our lives be mutually created by everyone and everything that participates in it—is very simple, for there is really only *One Being acting simultaneously and concertedly through all of its parts to create the events of life.* An analogy is that my ten fingers have no trouble mutually creating the event of getting my shoes tied, for although they seem to act independently, there is only One Consciousness operating in all of them.

Yet the more deeply embedded we become in our human trance, the more we forget our Oneness and experience ourselves to be separate from everyone and everything else. We become focused in the belief (and hence perception) that we are just a particular leaf on the Tree, and then all the other leaves seem to be separated from us by time and space. We become like the person who doesn't know, when he sees a clump of mushrooms growing, that they are all connected under the ground. He sees only the surface shapes, which appear to be separate.

In our emotional trances, we experience this as personal isolation and self-alienation. We feel cut off from our "connection" to the Tree, to our Source of Life, which creates a deep sense of lack and loss, leading to attitudes of neediness and fear, especially *a fear of annihilation.* Instead of thriving on the unconditional love of eternal Beingness, we feel abandoned by our Source, and we become dependent on changing external situations and connections to other people.

Yet forgetting Who we are is no accident. To explore the Mystery at the heart of our Beingness, we must stretch our Self beyond our Self, beyond our own knowing, into the Unknown. And to do this, we must lose our Self, we must en-trance our Self with not-Self, with identity-trances in which we experience ourself as separate from the Source of Life. Then within these trances, the immense void that is created in us by our separateness is actually that piece of Unknown and Mystery that we have stretched into and encompassed. So, becoming human is the cutting edge of this stretch into the Unknown within our Self. Yet whenever a human being, because of the suffering created by his separateness, learns to transform himself so that the part of his consciousness that had stretched into separateness remembers who he IS, what was Unknown becomes Known; what was Mystery becomes Self. In this manner, our Self enlightens Itself.

So, our Self forgetting Itself and then remembering Itself is the very process of both creation and unfolding Love through creation. When the Self forgets Itself in a new form (in a new trance), creation expands; when the Self remembers Itself within that new form, Love and Consciousness and laughter expand within creation.

Since our lives are the vehicle for this process of unfolding and enlightening our Self, we design our lives to enmesh us within certain illusions—those that represent the unenlightened areas of our Consciousness that we will be working on—giving us the opportunity to explore and transform them. Our goal is to fully unfold our Self within our human form, to completely *enlighten our experience of being human.*

When all of our en-tranced human awareness awakens to Who we truly are, we will be able to fully and consciously live within the Oneness of all Life while enjoying the form and creativity of being human.

8

Our Emotional Trances

Although we are One Consciousness, forever residing in the bliss of eternity, in our form as human beings we have the capacity to experience emotions that deny the reality of Love and our true Self. We experience this kind of emotion only within a self-limiting trance. When we are free of our trances, when we remember Who we are, our emotions are spontaneous expressions of Beingness Itself. Only love, joy, and compassion originate from this deepest level of Self, so the rest of our emotions are just old attitudes and positions created by trance.

Our emotional trances all derive from one fundamental trance-generated illusion: that we are separate from our Source of Life. The moment we experience ourself as separate, we feel a very deep sense of loss, and we experience ourself as lacking within ourself what we need to maintain our existence—*not just our physical existence but our very beingness.* If we have to depend upon something outside of ourself for our existence, we could lose or be cut off from this thing we need; we could be *totally annihilated.* This belief generates our basic position of fear: that we are not safe, that life is not safe to experience. And fear's position is that to make ourself safe, we must contract away from this experience of possible annihilation; we must contract into ourself, constricting our body and breath, so as to not-feel our vulnerability. *This constrictive stance of resistance, withdrawal, and self-paralysis (to make ourself safe) is the posture of our fear.*

Yet fear's position that we are not safe is false, for it is based on an illusion. And its position that it can make us more safe (through paralysis) is always a lie. In fact, our fear-posture starts a chain reaction, for as we constrict ourself, blocking the flow of our breath and paralyzing ourself, we experience ourself being cut off further from our Life-force, creating a deeper sense of lack, reinforcing our belief about the possibility of annihilation, and creating an even deeper withdrawal and paralysis—which is a posture of even more intense fear—cutting off even more of our Life-force, and so on. We feel as if we are being annihilated, falling into an inner abyss; yet what is strangling us, what we are running from, and the abyss we are falling into, is our own fear of annihilation. (Hence the expression, "There is nothing to fear but fear itself.")

We usually think of fear as a natural "instinct" and therefore assume it to be an automatic reflex, a spontaneous response. But fear is not the same thing as the instinctive adrenal response that happens when we need to deal with danger; this response is simply a state of excitement that facilitates rapid action. Hence, people have often said after surviving a crisis, "I didn't have time to be afraid; I just acted." Their action was instinctive, but the instinct was not fear, it was their instinct to preserve Life, which includes the animal instinct for self-preservation. *Fear is not life-preserving; it is life-destroying.* It blocks our life-force, weakening and paralyzing us; in the long run it destroys our immune systems, which we need for self-preservation. When our life-preservation instinct generates a lot of energy to deal with a situation, our fear will try to use that energy to paralyze ourself (for safety). In a very intense situation, we can become so paralyzed that we are "scared stiff." Our fear "petrifies" us, and although this kind of stiffness is an efficient way to resist experiencing life, total rigidity is *rigor mortis,* which is death. So, when we experience fear in a dangerous situation and manage to run to safety, we have saved ourself in spite of our fear, not because of it. What saves us is our instinct to preserve life, and this grows out of the same consciousness that creates life, which is Love.

Because our fear cannot succeed in making us feel safe but always makes us feel less safe, if we are not too paralyzed from it in a particular situation, we try to escape from or camouflage our experience of fear (to make ourself feel more safe), and we try to find ways to help our fear resist the situation (to make ourself feel more safe). We do this by generating other emotional attitudes. For instance, if a man who feels threatened by rejection is rejected, his initial reaction will be to resist the situation with fear. Yet because this position makes him feel less safe, he may become enraged to escape from his experience of fear and to support his position of fear in resisting the rejecting situation.

In this manner, our fear-trances generate all our other attitude-trances. Depending upon the situation, these attitudes will take the form of *resisting* what is perceived to be threatening, or of *holding on* to what is perceived to be safe. So our "holding patterns" are also attitudes. And they fit our original definition of an attitude because they are "postures of emotional resistance"; but these attitudes resist life by holding on.

All of our fear-generated attitudes, because they reinforce our fear and create added tension patterns, end up cutting off more of our life-force. So the position of our attitudes—that they can help us feel more safe—is always a lie. In fact, because these attitudes are based on fear, the inner abyss created by fear exists within them, and we will unconsciously feel this abyss whenever we are en-tranced in one of these attitudes.[7]

In spite of how much we suffer from our emotional trances, we have identified so deeply with them and we experience so much emotion with them that it can be difficult for us to fully recognize that they are not spontaneous emotional responses. Yet if we are to become free of these trances, we must make the effort to see them for what they are. Unfortunately, there are a handful of obstacles that we must overcome.

First of all, our attitudes have become quite automatic. We are so in the habit of experiencing certain attitudes in certain kinds of situations that we don't question what we are feeling. And we don't notice that in each situation we have made a choice even if it was by habit—to resist our present situation with a particular attitude. We don't realize that we can break the reflex habit of our resistance and choose to open to life instead.

Another obstacle is that we identify with our attitudes. We get so used to experiencing ourself in the posture, emotional tone, and point of view of our attitudes that we think they are ourselves, so we never question their validity. If someone tells us to stop being sad we think he wants us to deny ourselves or be false to ourselves. Yet our sad-

---

[7]Because our inner abyss is created by the contraction of our fear, it parallels the astronomical phenomenon of the "black hole," for the darkness of a black hole is not created by an intrinsic lack of light but by an intense contraction of matter that resists the free-flow of light.

ness is just an attitude we're holding and projecting, so we can stop using it to resist life.

A third obstacle is that many people share the same attitudes. If I have angry attitudes and someone else gets angry, even if I disagree with his anger in that particular situation I will not notice that his anger is an attitude; I will think it is a natural response.

A fourth obstacle is that we deny many of our attitudes and therefore don't recognize that they exist.

A fifth obstacle is that our emotional attitudes can be very subtle. Three examples are: (1) insecurity will often try to pass itself off as vulnerability and sensitivity, (2) when we love someone and lose that person, our fear and sense of loss will try to use the love to justify our fear and sense of loss, and (3) self-righteousness will always try to pass itself off as Truth. In addition, compassion can generate feelings that resemble some emotional attitudes, making it easier for these attitudes to try to pass themselves off as compassion. For instance, compassion may generate a feeling that seems similar to sadness when it opens its heart to someone else's suffering. But this is not sadness. It is not a fixed position based on fear that is resisting life; it is unconditional love opening to suffering. And if it is truly compassion, then it is a spontaneous response and will be gone as soon as the situation is over; anything that "holds over" is an attitude. Of course, when we feel compassion and sadness at the same time, it is easier for us to be fooled when sadness tries to pass itself off as compassion.

A sixth obstacle is that, although our attitudes ultimately make us feel less safe and cut off our life-force, we often experience a certain amount of pleasure with them, and pleasure is associated with love. Although the pleasure we derive from our attitudes is really a "booby-prize" compared to the much deeper pleasure of experiencing life with an open (attitude-free) heart, when we get sufficiently lost in our emotional trances it becomes possible to mistake the mirage for the real thing. Because we are feeling something intensely and identifying with our feeling, we don't notice that what we are feeling is just our own emotional resistance to life, which has nothing to do with love.

The last obstacle that supports us in thinking our attitudes are true emotional responses is that we want to believe they are, because we are afraid to let them go (because we believe they keep us safe, because we identify with them, and/or because we believe they are the only source of pleasure or feeling we believe is available to us).

So, it may be difficult at first to recognize that most of our emotions are just old attitude-trances, not spontaneous responses. In addition, when we are identified with our attitudes we often fear that getting free of them will lead to a loss of feelings (or to a loss of safety or self). But a loss of feeling occurs only when we suppress our feelings. When we free ourself from our attitudes all we lose is our attitudes.

In Part III, we will see that our attitudes can create very complex inner dramas. Yet no matter how complex our drama, there will always be the same three keys for transforming our emotional consciousness:

(1) knowing that who we really are is Love-Consciousness,

(2) remembering that all our attitudes are lies and trance-illusions, and,

(3) remembering that all our attitudes are created from and support our position of fear.

When we have freed ourself from all our emotional trances, then all of our experience will be derived from love instead of from fear and we will no longer be trying to make ourself safe; we will always know that we *are* safe and that life is safe for us to experience. This is the full enlightenment of our human experience, for there will be no trance-illusions left within us that resist life, and our fully open hearts will merge us into Life Itself, into the Oneness of the Living Now.

9

Returning to Oneness

When you make the two one,
and when you make the inner as the outer,
and the outer as the inner,
and above as the below,
and when you make the male and female into a single one,
so that the male will not be male
and the female will not be female,
then you shall enter the kingdom.
— Jesus, *The Gospel According to Thomas*

When we experience Oneness from within our human form, we are simply Being Now, receiving Life as It Is. Hence, anything that helps us to release our resistances to receiving Life—to release our illusion—helps to return us to the Oneness of Life, as It Is, Now.

In general, the most effective tools for this are: love, awareness, our breath, attuning directly to our Self or God, and any techniques that help us to be here Now. This is because wherever we are stuck (in self-limiting trances), our awareness is limited, our breath is restricted, our ability to give and receive unconditional love is hampered, and we are not being here Now. As we release any of these limitations, we become less stuck, and we move closer to experiencing All That We Are.[8]

IF WE WORK WITH LOVE, with merging into the experience of Universal Love, we need to increase our willingness to receive, in all the dark corners of our human consciousness, the infinite uncondi-

---

[8]In Judaism and Christianity, prayer is used as a vehicle for "atonement." Yet until the idea of atonement was distorted to mean repentance for our sins, it meant at-one-ment, the process of returning to the state of Oneness.

tional love that continuously emanates from All That Is and that always exists for us, Now. Although this will automatically increase our unconditional love for others, *the goal is not to become a loving person, but to become Love Itself.* If we can Be Love, then both our perception and action will unfold through the context of love. An awareness tool for this path is noticing where we don't experience unconditional love, because this will always point to some area within ourself that is not *receiving* love. A primary benefit of this path is that, since we are focused on the experience of love, we are always immersed in love. On this path, our fear-trances are transformed both through our direct experience of love (in which the part of us that is afraid remembers Who it Is), and through our willingness to trust that love is deeper than fear, and more Real.

IF WE WORK WITH AWARENESS, we need to learn how to bring it into whatever comers of our beingness lack it, and we need to increase our willingness to see our illusions and to see through them to Truth so that no illusion has the power to en-trance us or separate us from Oneness.

IF WE WORK WITH OPENING OUR BREATH, we need to increase our willingness to *receive* our breath into all the places where we resist life. (This is not the same as simply increasing our lung capacity.) The breath is also an awareness tool, for in most places where we notice we are not receiving our breath, we have made contact with both an emotional resistance pattern (an attitude) and an illusion. Using this tool, we release our fear-trances by receiving our breath inside them; since the breath is the Essence of Life—in its most subtle form it is Conscious Energy—as we receive our breath inside of our fear we remember Who we are in that part of our being, which dissolves our fear there. (In addition to Awareness Exercise 2: "Receiving the Breath," an excellent tool for opening the breath is a healing art called Rebirthing, well described in *Rebirthing, the Science of Enjoying all of Your Life* by Phil Laut and Jim Leonard.)

IF WE WORK WITH ATTUNING DIRECTLY TO OUR SELF OR GOD, we need to keep ourself focused on this Consciousness or Presence, so we can have this awareness be the context through which we experience the situations of our life, and so we can bring this awareness into the parts of our human consciousness that lack it. Common tools for this path are prayer, meditating on God or God's love or the Presence of these, and the practice of remembering Who we are, free of all trances.

IF WE WORK WITH BEING HERE NOW, which is also a way of working with awareness, we need to increase our capacity to stay present in this moment. This does not involve "trying to hold" the present moment in our consciousness or trying to hold ourself in this moment (which creates a rigid posture), but learning to *receive* the present moment as it unfolds out of Life. As we learn to receive the present moment, we let go of all our mental and emotional baggage, which keeps dragging us into the past and future, keeping us out of the present moment, which is the *doorway* to Now. Although the "present moment" is often equated with "Now"—and for convenience this book has sometimes used them interchangeably—these are not actually equivalent. The present moment is simply the moment that exists between the last one and the next one; it exists "here" within time. "Now" is the timeless eternity of our out-of-trance Consciousness; it exists nowhere and in no-time, encompassing past, present, and future, all of which exist Now. Yet the present moment is our doorway to Now, for within this human reality, we cannot free ourself from our trance—we cannot even drop a simple attitude—in any moment other than this one. We need to be here, Now. This is the only moment in which we can remember Who we are.

AN AWARENESS OF THE BREATH (different from receiving the breath) is often used as a tool for increasing self-awareness and learning to be here Now. Because our breath is not very "interesting," as we focus our attention on it we begin to notice the contents of our mind and to become freer of our entrancement with it. In addition, because in each moment we experience a new breath, as we learn to keep our awareness attuned to our breath, we learn to stay present, here and Now. Many meditation techniques utilize an awareness of the breath.

At different times of our lives, we will be drawn to use different tools to help ourself grow. (Therefore, if a particular awareness tool or exercise presented here does not seem to work very well for you, put it aside rather than discard it; it may prove very useful at some later time.) Yet regardless of the tools we choose on our path, as we move deeper into the flow of Life and the experience of Oneness, we eventually enter into a profound inner silence, a joyful Silent Beingness in which we experience creation as it IS, as it infinitely unfolds from our Self, and we are Home again, Being Now.

AWARENESS EXERCISE 9:
BEING LOVE

PART 1

This exercise is designed to enable you to experience Universal Love on all levels of your being, including your physical body. Unfortunately, many meditations on love leave out the physical body, which can lead to various kinds of inner struggles, instead of wholeness. Love is the essence of all manifest forms of creation. When the body experiences love, it remembers its own divinity, which is your Self; and then all the levels on which you exist, from Source to physical manifestation, receive and become integrated within love.

Sit comfortably and close your eyes. Receive a few deep breaths ... and let yourself relax. Allow thirty minutes.

This exercise is very simple. Imagine that, just as you have hugged other human beings, you can experience yourself sharing an embrace with all of creation, with the conscious Loving Essence of All That Is. Then allow yourself, with your body, your heart, and your spirit, to open to that embrace, to experience the love of all of creation for all of yourself, including those aspects that you don't like or deny. Allow yourself to receive and share this love, and to receive and share more and more of it, until you just melt in the love, becoming One with it, until you experience yourself as *being* love.

An alternative (and for some people, more powerful) way to do this, is to imagine receiving and sharing God's Love (or the love of a particular being that, for you, embodies this depth of unconditional love). Receive and share the embrace of this love with all the levels of your beingness. Melt into this love and become One with it. Experience yourself as being God's Love.

PART 2

Practice this on a different day than Part 1. This section presents another way to contact the universal love that is the Essence of our Being. Allow thirty minutes.

Sit comfortably and close your eyes. Receive a few deep breaths ... and let yourself relax. Then:

Receive your breath into the area of your heart. Simply allow this area to relax, and receive your breath there. Don't be concerned about your breath anywhere else. After a while, as this area opens, you should feel an experience of love opening from within you. Keep receiving your breath deeper and deeper into this area. Allow yourself to merge into this love; experience yourself as Being Love.

An alternative way to do this is to receive your breath as love or as God's love in the area of your heart.

Sometimes, the experience of love will push to the surface of one's consciousness the emotional patterns and beliefs that resist love. For this exercise, do not focus on these; note them if they come up but keep your awareness and attention focused on the experience of love.

Often, simply by surrendering into the experience of love, many areas of our emotional consciousness that resist love will let go. This happens because, as we consciously move deeper into the experience of love, our love begins to bump up against—and to some extent to "seep into"—these other areas of our consciousness; and to the degree that we are willing, within our emotional resistances, to open to this love, we wake up within these trances and release the attitudes and illusions that we have been caught in, that have been denying the reality of love.

Unfortunately, this seepage effect of love is not always sufficient to release en-trenched attitudes. Then, as with delinquent children, they need more individual attention. Awareness tools for releasing these trances are presented in Part III.

AWARENESS EXERCISE 10:
DISIDENTIFYING WITH THE WEATHER

Sit comfortably and close your eyes. Receive a few deep breaths ... and let yourself relax. Allow thirty or forty minutes.

We live in a world of experience that is filled with thoughts, emotional attitudes, sensory awareness, cognitive perceptions, and inner experiences of love, joy, creativity, and personal identity. Our entrancement with these experiences both creates and maintains our world, yet it also prevents us from experiencing our own pure Consciousness. So, in this exercise, we will stop identifying with everything that we normally identify with—we will treat it all as *weather* that is moving temporarily through the infinite silent space of our own beingness. This will create a doorway to Silent Beingness and our own true Self.

While you are sitting with your eyes closed, become aware of your breath: coming in and going out, coming in and going out. You are not trying to control your breath; you are allowing it to flow naturally, as it comes in and goes out. And you are also not rigidly concentrating on your breath or identifying with it; you are relaxed, and you are simply noticing your breath happening. This relaxed, detached awareness of your breath will help you to stay both open and present.

After a few minutes, you will find yourself becoming aware of all kinds of things: physical sensations, inner thoughts, daydreams, feelings, external sounds, and so on. Do not push any of these away; do not try to prevent yourself from noticing them or experiencing them. Rather, *notice that they are there, and experience them as weather that is moving through the infinite, silent space of your Beingness.* In this open space, there is nothing to resist the weather, there is no involvement with it, and there is no weather that can disturb this space. You are Infinite Silent Space, and so all weather, no matter how long it lasts, is just temporary. Although any passing weather system can have clouds that obscure the sun and stars, the sun and stars are still there, unaffected, and they become visible again when the weather system passes. In Silent Beingness you are even less affected by your weather than the sun and stars, for you are the Infinite Space in which even the sun and stars are a passing show.

So, be aware of the weather, yet remain detached from it. Even your thoughts can be there without you being the one thinking them.

If you can simply allow your thoughts to be there, without identifying with them, they will keep changing by themselves, yet the Conscious Awareness that you are will remain as it is: detached, aware, forever unchanged. Of course, as you sit there, noticing your breath, you will get caught up in some of the weather—happening in your mind, your body, or the world—in spite of your intentions. That's okay. That's part of the process. Whenever you notice that this has happened, just detach yourself from your involvement and perceive your involvement as just more weather. If you get angry at yourself for getting distracted—just more weather. And it's just more weather if you find yourself identifying with the body whose breathing you are noticing, or identifying with anything else. In this process, you are *doing nothing;* anything that is being done is just weather. And in this process, ultimately, you *are nothing,* for Infinite Silent Space has no form or shape or individualized identity; anyone that is being someone is just more weather. The Self is formless.

Awareness Exercise 11:
Your Life as a Tree

Sit comfortably and close your eyes. Receive a few deep breaths ...
and let yourself relax. Then:

(1) Imagine that it is late spring and that you are a tree.

(2) Feel your roots reaching out from the core of yourself,
reaching into the earth for moisture and nourishment, becoming finer
and finer, becoming enmeshed with the beingness of the earth. Experience yourself feeding through your roots, sucking the nourishment
up from the earth into your larger roots and into the whole of your
tree-body, even out into your leaves.

(3) Feel yourself reaching out as branches and leaves toward the
sky.

(4) Feel your leaves. Feel how your leaves open themselves to the
sun to receive its living abundance. Feel in the core of your beingness how the sun's living light is food that keeps you alive.

(5) Experience the joy of being a tree, drinking up the earth and
sun, feeling green and happy with the simple radiant joy of being
alive as a tree. There is no thinking to disturb you.

(6) Now, a group of human beings walk by. Notice how they look,
these human beings. As a tree, how do you feel about them? Do they
seem to be in an awful hurry compared to your plant-self? What do
you feel about the way they relate?

(7) Now these human beings have moved off, but another one
appears, the one you normally think of as yourself. But right now
you are a tree. And as a tree, you examine this human being. What
do you see? What is your response to this human? If, in your tree-wisdom, you could tell this human something, what would it be?

(8) Now, as a peaceful and radiant tree, you stand in the warm
sun, and as you once more examine this human before you, you have
a startling realization: a part of your tree-self is this human being!
You are *simultaneously* tree and human. Feel the Oneness of your
beingness in both forms of your Self.

(9) Realize that you are the Tree of Life, and that your tree-self
and human-self are simply two of your leaves.

(10) Go and find a living tree, become your tree-self, and
commune with the other tree.

Second Scientific Interlude

Einstein was the first scientist to realize that all the Energy of the universe forms an interconnected whole. He said that the universe is a Unified Field of Energy, and that all the seemingly separate forms of matter are simply dense variations of the Field, areas where "the field is extremely intense ... for the field is the only reality."[9] Of course, a conscious and intelligent human being is also a dense variation of the One Field; so the Field as a whole must possess the consciousness and intelligence that is evident in this denser aspect of itself. This means that *the universe as a whole is a conscious and intelligent Energy-Field.* The forms within it cannot be random; they can only be intelligent expressions of the whole Field. In addition, since no part or expression of the Field is separate from the whole, *each part of the universe and energy itself must possess the consciousness and intelligence of the whole Field.* This would mean that rocks possess consciousness and that consciousness plays a role in all subatomic processes. E.H. Walker, a physicist, wrote, "Consciousness may be associated with all quantum mechanical processes."[10] Eugene Wigner also noted, "It was not possible to formulate the laws [of quantum physics] in a fully consistent way without reference to consciousness."[11] Indirectly, scientists have always acknowledged the innate intelligence of the universe, for their fundamental belief is that the universe is not chaotic but behaves according to Natural Law. In fact, although "chaos" was originally considered "disorder," which means without order, scientists have found that even chaos contains order, which means that even chaos expresses intelligence.

From a scientific standpoint then, what we call "Life" is a Unified Field of Conscious Energy that evolves itself, expresses itself, and perceives itself through various forms of itself, with each form

---

[9]Fritjof Capra, *The Tao of Physics,* (New York: Bantam, 1984), p. 197.

[10]Evan H. Walker, "The Nature of Consciousness," *Mathematical Bio Sciences,* 7, 1970, pp. 175-176.

[11]Fritjof Capra, *The Tao of Physics,* (New York: Bantam, 1984), p. 291.

containing the consciousness of the whole Field. Of course, this is exactly what mystics have said for thousands of years. When Jesus said, "I am within the Father and the Father is within me," he was mystically talking about the relationship between the Tree of Life and one of its leaves; and he was, in scientific terms, talking about the relationship of each expression of the Unified Field to the Field Itself. (Different dimensions of Reality—mystically referred to as different "planes of Consciousness"—are simply different vibratory levels of the Field. This is similar to the way water molecules, at different vibratory rates, can manifest as water, ice, or invisible gas. Physical reality, therefore, is the shape that the Field takes at a particular vibratory level, yet it is never separate from the other dimensions or vibratory levels—or trances—of the Field.)

The idea that the whole of something can be contained in a part of it was too paradoxical for logical, scientific thought—until the discovery of the hologram. A hologram is a three-dimensional picture created by light from a holographic negative. You can walk around it, just as if it were a real object, and view it from any angle. For scientists, the startling thing about holograms is that every piece of a holographic negative is a point of view of the whole object. (Compare this to a photographic negative, where an eighth of a negative only gives you an eighth of a picture.)

Yet it is the phenomena discovered in modern laboratory experiments that have forced scientists into their new view of reality. For instance, when particles interact, their individual "identities" become lost and their combined energies transform into groups of other particles. The word "particle," therefore, is actually misleading for it falsely implies the continuity of a fixed form. Particles live at the cutting edge of creation where the only continuity is energy's self-transformation into new patterns of existence. Particles clearly dramatize the trance-illusion of separate forms and the Oneness of all creation. Imagine how you would perceive your "separate identity" if you were always turning into other people and other people were always turning into you.

Another laboratory phenomenon, now called the Einstein-Rosen-Podolsky effect, shows that particles separated in time and space can respond *instantaneously* to changes in each other. (That this could be possible was actually very upsetting to Einstein.) Within the trance of time and space, the speed of light is the fastest speed at which a cause can create an effect. The fact that these particles respond instantaneously points to a dimension of fundamental connectedness that exists outside of time and space. (And this dimension is simply a higher vibratory level of the Field; space and time exist as aspects of the Field only at certain vibratory levels, such as physical reality.)

The double-slit experiments described in the "First Scientific Interlude" give us another phenomenon that points to the Oneness of Consciousness outside of our trance. We saw that light changed its form of manifestation whenever a scientist "peeked" to see which hole it went through. This phenomenon, which happens with all the subatomic particles, illustrated how deeply our perception alters our reality; yet it also points to the fact that light and subatomic particles somehow "know" when we are looking at them and respond accordingly. Of course, this would be impossible unless they have a consciousness that, outside of the space-time trance, is fundamentally connected to our own.

Physicists and mystics have come to the same conclusions about the Oneness of creation. The only difference is that physicists are making a left-brained, logical deduction based upon rational thinking and laboratory experiments, while mystics are describing their actual living experience. (And the mystic bypasses the limitations on being able to know Reality that are formulated in Heisenberg's Uncertainty Principle because these are limitations of measurement and perception. The mystic knows Reality by *being* Reality and knowing what he is.) It is one thing to conceptually prove that everything is a Unified Field; it is another thing to personally awaken from the trance-illusion of separateness and directly experience the Oneness of Life as it IS.

IO

༄༅༅༅

Thought and Creation

"In the beginning was the Word..."   — St. John

Since the manifest universe unfolds as a trance-expression of
Creative Consciousness, the vehicle of creation must be Thought. All
realities, including physical realities, are created out of thought,
which is the most subtle expression of Conscious Energy. This is
consistent with the scientific view that everything in our physical
world is created through the workings of Natural Law, for Natural
Law is a set of principles, which is a group of ideas or thoughts. The
set of Natural Laws for our physical reality is simply the complex
group of thoughts created by Consciousness (thoughts can only be
created by Consciousness) to act as the structural blueprint for our
world. These thoughts define the ground rules for the way Conscious
Energy creates this reality. (This is consistent with the principle,
presented in Part I, that our body's point of view perceptually
constructs our physical reality, because our body's point of view is
itself an expression of Natural Law for this reality—it is an
"embodiment" of Natural Law.) Utilizing these thought-rules, Conscious Energy evolves more and more complex thoughts, and It
enlivens these thoughts by entrancing Itself with them (by believing
in them); thus, Conscious Energy evolves itself into photons and
subatomic particles (the simplest expressions of Conscious Energy
that we can detect with scientific instruments), into atoms, and into
all the substances and forms of life that exist in our world, each with
its own mode of perception and experiential reality. (How a
particular enlivened thought-form *appears,* though, will vary according to how other enlivened thought-forms perceive it.) The unified
energy-field that is the scientist's description of Life, is really an

enlivened, unified thought-structure, since thought is the most subtle form of energy.

This process of thought-evolution is most evident in all the complex manmade things that have become "natural" parts of our reality. An automobile, for instance, represents thousands of years of thought-evolution—it required the idea of the wheel, of the use of rubber, metals and other materials, of harnessed combustion, and so on. In fact, most of the things in our daily reality were created through human thought-evolution, utilizing Natural Law and the "physical" materials on hand. Yet the physical materials were created in exactly the same way—by Creative Consciousness working through its expressions of Earth and Sun, utilizing its ideas of Natural Law for this reality, and the Conscious Energy of Itself. It is rather hard to imagine conscious, self-replicating, intelligent life-forms evolving from simple, supposedly dead, chemical elements without conscious intelligence and thought-evolution at the heart of the process.

Until recently, natural evolution was considered a random process and was, therefore, thought to proceed at an even rate throughout history. But scientists have found that large evolutionary shifts can occur extremely rapidly, which reflects a species' innate ability to adapt itself genetically to rapid environmental changes and indicates that intelligence—as opposed to randomness—is the key to evolutionary change.

In daily life, we see many indications that our bodies are complex, enlivened thought-forms: in psychosomatic disease, in the placebo effect, and in all situations where worry, fear, anticipation, and other thoughts physically affect a person's body. If the body were not a thought-manifestation, then thoughts could not interact with it and affect it. (Different foods as well as drugs affect the body because these are thought-forms, too.)

When a being en-trances itself with a body, it enters into a *relationship* with it. The body, as a deeply held set of beliefs (enlivened through the entrancement of Consciousness), creates a new point of view for the being (a point of view that changes as the body changes), affecting the being's experience. The being's thoughts and beliefs also have a profound effect on the body, continuously altering it. If one's beliefs are sufficiently deep, one can even alter the workings of Natural Law in the body. This is what happens with "fire-walkers"—people in many different cultures around the world who walk on red-hot coals without getting burned. Normally, fire burns the body because Natural Law for this reality says it should, and this Natural Law is embedded within the body's thought-structure, so the body follows it. But firewalkers temporarily suspend the workings of particular Laws in their body by believing deeply enough that the hot coals will not burn. Their belief alters the thought-structure that their body is a manifestation of, and their body then manifests according to a different Law and constructs a different reality.

Firewalking usually occurs as part of a religious ceremony, which acts as a catalyst, helping the firewalkers to create with their beliefs a trance-state that is deep enough to alter the thought-structure of their body. When the firewalkers emerge from the pits of red-hot coals, their feet are actually cool. Firewalking is not a trick created by rubbing special fire-retardant substances on the feet, for the phenomenon has been well-documented, and there are many reports of onlookers from non-firewalking cultures who suddenly *believed* that they could walk on the hot coals too and did so without harm.[12]

Natural Laws Operate For Us Only Because On A Very Deep Level We Believe In Them. Yet because these beliefs are embedded in the thought structure for our body, and because we en-trance ourself so deeply with these beliefs in order to be born as human beings, we cannot usually affect them unless our self-awareness has evolved to an extraordinary degree. Hence they become common beliefs used by all of us, helping to create a consistent group reality. But because they are beliefs, it is possible to alter them. Therefore, it is not surprising that, in addition to the phenomenon of firewalking, there are many stories throughout the world of other aspects of Natural Law being altered in dramatic ways. There are stories of yogis and Kabbalistic masters being able to fly, defying gravity; yogis have been known to manifest or transmute objects; and Jesus reportedly walked on water and turned water into wine.[13] In fact, the basis of Christianity is the belief that Jesus did not die but transmuted his body, defying Natural Law and showing us that physical reality is just a trance. And he said that we could do everything he did, and

---

[12]For more on firewalking, see *Firewalking and Religious Healing* by Loring M. Dansforth, and *The Anatenaria, Tracian Fire-Walking Festival* by Ann Anthony.

[13]A collection of modern stories about a man named Neem Karoli Baba, who performed many of these kinds of trance-formations of physical reality, can be found in *Miracle of Love* by Ram Dass (E.P. Dutton, 1979).

more. In light of the well-documented fact of firewalking, these ancient stories are probably not myths but recorded evidence of the power of our Consciousness to alter physical reality—by altering the thought-structures of Natural Law in our body, which constructs our body, which constructs our world.

Thought-evolution is the basis of all creation, yet the creation process also needs to "densify" thought to produce manifest reality. Since the experience of density can only be a trance-experience, it must be created through *entrancement with the idea of density*. In our waking human reality, the idea of density is built into the thought-structure that is our human body, so that the body will perceive itself and its world as physical. When a soul-expression of Consciousness en-trances itself with a body, it focuses on and *believes* in the point of view of that body; and this "body-trance" then creates for the soul (and therefore for the Self, for Conscious Beingness) the experience of a physically dense reality. (Although the illusion of separateness is facilitated by a body-trance, a body-trance does not in itself separate us from our Oneness; we can be aware of our Oneness while we are inhabiting a body.)

The trance-creation of the experience of density is easily observed with dreams. When we dream, if we utilize the belief that our mental images are dense, then as we en-trance ourself with our dream-thoughts, we experience them as physically solid. Although dreams don't use a body-trance to create the experience of density (we can observe a solid dream without having a body in that dream) they are still utilizing an entrancement with the idea of density.

This is how all realities are densified. The differences lie only in how the idea of density is embedded into the reality, how dense a reality is manifested (not all densified realities are physical), the complexity of the creation process for each reality, and restrictions on what may be manifested, in keeping with each system's Natural Law. For instance, Natural Law for our waking reality requires a continuity in space-time that usually prevents the kind of instantaneous thought manifestation that happens in dreams. In addition, because our waking reality is a much more complex system, the trance-creation process is more complex, involving *mutual entrancement* among the participating beings, and utilizing a body-trance as part of the process. Yet, whether the reality being densified is simple or complex, dream-reality or waking-reality, the vehicle of its manifestation is always a trance.

Awareness Exercise 12:
Thought-Manifestation

Sit comfortably and close your eyes. Receive a few deep breaths ... and let yourself relax. Allow thirty minutes.

Now, as you relax, become aware of your breath. Coming in ... going out ... coming in ... going out ... just feel the sensations of your breath ... and every time you become aware that you have fully gone off into a thought or daydream or feeling or inner dialogue, just notice for a moment (1) where you went, (2) how you densified your thoughts into an experiential daydream-reality, and (3) that while you were focused in the trance you had no conscious awareness that any other reality, including your waking reality, existed. Simply notice this without getting caught up in thinking about it, and then return to feeling and watching your breath, starting the exercise over again. The more deeply you can focus your awareness on your breath, the more dramatic will be your shift into other trances, making your trance-creation process more visible.

In addition to providing insight into the process of thought-manifestation, this exercise may give you a sense of the outer layers of your daily consciousness.

AWARENESS EXERCISE 13:
CONSCIOUS ENERGY

PART 1

This part of the exercise is to be done outside, preferably while walking. It can help you to free yourself from your trance and experience your Oneness with all of creation.

(1) Notice your environment while you are walking. Usually, your mental programming makes you see much of your environment as filled with lifeless "things." Yet this is just a trance-illusion. Allow that point of view to drop from your mind.

(2) Realize that everything you see is made of energy. Get a sense of the way energy has assumed all these different shapes.

(3) Allow yourself to be aware that this energy is *conscious.* Allow yourself to experience everything you see as being made of Conscious Energy and as being a form of it.

(4) Recognize that you, too, are a form of this Conscious Energy, and experience your connection with all the other forms of it around you.

PART 2

Sit comfortably and close your eyes. Receive a few deep breaths ... and let yourself relax.

(1) Become aware of your breathing. Then notice how your breathing *feels* and experience how your body feels as you breathe.

(2) When you are relaxed in feeling your body, then imagine you can feel the space outside your body as if it were part of your body. Just extend your awareness of feeling so that it extends into and fills the space around your physical body.

(3) Open your eyes yet continue to feel the space outside your physical body as if it were your body.

(4) Look at an object in the room and imagine you can feel the object as if it were part of your body.

(5) Repeat (4) with some other objects.

(6) Feel yourself in several objects at once.

(7) Attempt to feel yourself in the space of the room and in these objects at the same time.

AWARENESS EXERCISE 14:
THE WORD, "GOD"

We have developed many different words for the Oneness that was always called "God." We call it the Creative Source, our Self, the Light, and so on. The advantages of these names is that each emphasizes a different aspect of the One, reminds us that the One is not some separate being outside of and separate from us, and enables us to talk about God in terms that are nonsectarian, non-religious, non-disturbing, and universal. The disadvantage of these names is that when we use them, we often forget that what we are talking about is what we have always experienced as "God"—not as some separate being, but as the deepest experience we know. The advantage of the word "God" is that every cell in our body and every fiber of our human consciousness resonates with that word. When we almost get hit by a car or have some other sudden fright, the word that most frequently first jumps out of us is "God!", no matter what our religious beliefs, no matter whether we believe in God or life after death or believe that the universe is just some big machine that somehow created itself, plugged itself into itself, and began running. The word that still leaps out of us is "God!", because in those critical life-and-death moments, when we are in touch with the core of our being and all of our awareness is focused to a point, we remember what is truly Real (independent of whatever we have been taught or believe), and "God" is the English-language word that we have always associated with that experience.

Because of the connection of the word "God" to the experience that the word represents, we can consciously use the word to connect to that experience. What follows are two ways to do this. Try each one for at least thirty minutes. (The second way may be done at a different time.)

PART I

Sit comfortably and close your eyes. Receive a few deep breaths ... and let yourself relax.

Then simply say the word "God" in your mind, with the intention of having the word connect you to what the word represents. After a while, a response should automatically begin to happen in your body and consciousness. Allow yourself to notice that response, and then follow it inside yourself. (If there isn't a response, try saying the word louder—even very loud—in your mind.) Allow yourself to follow the movement of your own beingness as it responds to the word "God." The movement will take you toward the place within yourself where you already know and experience God. Allow yourself to relax and surrender into the experience that unfolds.

PART 2

This is a more passive variation of the first part. For some people, though, it will be more effective (and what works best for you now may not be what works best for you later). This time, as you sit and repeat the word "God," you will not have the intention of having the word connect you to the experience that the word represents, and you will not try to follow your response to the experience of God within you. Rather than attempting to guide your experience, you will simply relax and allow whatever happens to happen of itself (this includes allowing any stuck emotional places that may get activated to move through you). As you repeat the word "God" in your mind, simply relax into the sound and allow yourself to become intimate with it. To help you do this, you can imagine that your mind, your head and body, and even your emotions form a musical instrument, and every time you think the word "God" the sound of the word resonates inside you; then you can relax into this resonance and become intimate with the sound of it. Notice any places where you feel yourself blocking the sound, preventing yourself from opening to the experience of it. If you come across such a place, simply relax a little deeper, surrender a little deeper, and allow yourself in that place to become intimate with the word "God." Allow whatever you experience to happen.

Third Scientific Interlude

Most scientists believe that the physical universe is currently expanding, and that this expansion began when the universe exploded into being with a "big bang." Until recently, scientists believed that what originally exploded was an intensely compressed ball that contained all the matter and energy that exists today. (Matter is simply a dense form of energy.) This seemed logical enough, for the law of conservation of energy says that energy can neither be created nor destroyed (it can only change form) and, therefore, the energy/ matter that exists today had to have existed in the beginning. Yet as scientists probed deeper, they discovered a more exciting possibility: *the entire universe could have been created from nothing.* Matter, which is positive energy, generates gravity, which in physics equations represents negative energy; so when matter is created, the total amount of energy in the system stays the same. (The amount of positive-matter-energy created is canceled by the amount of negative-gravity-energy it generates.) And this means that no energy is actually needed to generate the new matter, which means that matter—and the entire universe—can actually be created from *nothing*.

Although this idea is a mathematical consequence of Einstein's Theory of Relativity, its cosmological significance remained hidden until Alan Guth, a physicist, discovered a model of creation for the physical universe that is now called the "inflation" theory. In this model, in the initial fractional moments after the big bang, the universe expanded (inflated) much more rapidly than was previously thought and the amount of existing matter and energy inflated as well. This model created a precise mathematical scenario in which the physical universe could have been created from nothing. Alan Guth said, "The universe might be the ultimate free lunch."[14] Most physicists today believe that this is what happened.

What could the nature of this nothing be that it could produce everything? What kind of shift or change or stimulus could happen

---

[14]*OMNI* magazine, "Interview with Alan Guth," November 1988, p. 96.

within that nothing so that, at some non-point, nothing begins to generate what seems to be something? Scientists have just begun to explore these questions. Yet ultimately, these kinds of questions cannot be answered without reference to consciousness, for only consciousness can simultaneously exist and yet be nothing—really no-thing, requiring no-time and no-space for its existence. (The Einstein-Rosen-Podolsky effect, discussed in the "Second Scientific Interlude," at the very least proves to scientists that there is a realm of connectedness beyond time and space.) Consciousness also has, within its nothingness, infinite variation, thus enabling the universe manifesting out of it to have variety, too. And ironically, since the smallest visible manifestation of energy possible in our physical universe is a photon, a unit of light, what else could have started the original big bang manifestation of matter/energy out of no-thingness but a thought like, "Light!" or more poetically, "Let there be Light!"

These physics theories of creation tie in very neatly with the concepts we have been exploring. First of all, if the no-thing that gave rise to the universe was consciousness, then the universe is really manifested thought. In addition, if everything was created from nothing, then the essence of our universe is also nothing, and the physical nature of our reality necessarily contains a certain element of "illusion." The natural conclusion from these two ideas is that the universe is a thought-illusion, or in other words, a trance. And the idea that the manifest universe could have grown from nothing parallels the way our consciousness works. For instance, if someone asks you what comes to mind with the word "red," out of nowhere you will begin get some kind of image, and that will generate other images, which will generate other images, and if you keep thinking long enough, you will generate a whole mini-mental universe, all growing (exploding/inflating) out of nowhere in your consciousness, triggered by the single thought, "red."

One other consequence of Guth's "inflation" theory is that there are many other universes (not galaxies, but universes) existing simultaneously in nothingness with our own. Since ours was created from nothing, there is no reason that billions of others wouldn't have been created from nothing as well. And since each universe would, as Guth says, "create space inside itself," each would exist in its own space and time and not impinge on or bump into any other universe. And again, this is how we have seen consciousness works. If we create a fantasy about the dinner we are going to have and another one about a trip we are going to take, although they both exist in the nothingness of our consciousness, each one exists in its own time and space and doesn't interfere with the other.

In human life, we see universes created out of nothing all the time. Every book you read, every song you hear, is created out of nothing but the individualized river of consciousness that manifested it, that brought it into time and space from the no-time/no-space of inner beingness.

PART III

Awakening Through The Mirror

11

⚜

The Journey Through

We are all on a journey, exploring our Self. We create souls out of
our Self to journey with and create worlds out of our Self to journey
through. Along the way, we pretend to forget Being Oneness and
enter the trance-experience of separateness. Yet we never really
leave our Self; every moment of our journey is lived within the
eternal beingness of Self.

Our journey has taken us into the trance-reality of being human.
As described earlier, we have entered this particular trance to explore
our Self in human form and fully enlighten our experience of being
human. Part of this process involves exploring the joy of our human
creativity—through such forms as art, music, mathematics, and
poetry; through less noticed forms of our creativity, such as fixing a
broken toy or machine, finding the perfect gift, or even preparing a
delicious meal; and simply through creating and experiencing unique
human situations, such as being born and growing up with an identi-
cal twin, or having the experience of being a traveling salesman, or
sitting alone on a mountain top in a human body, watching the stars
and smelling the night air. We have become human to experience all
these forms of our creativity, as well as to enlighten our human
emotional experience, and to explore and transform all the self-limitations which block us, within our human form, from experiencing
the joy and creativity of our Self.

Yet to enlighten all facets of our human experience, we need to
take the "time" to immerse ourself in them. To be able, *while we are
being human,* to fully receive Life and be One with it, with all its
apparent rage, hate, violence, and suffering, we need—at the very
least—to have been through all those trance experiences, discovered
for ourself the trance-illusions within them, and gone beyond them,

so there is no longer anything in our human experience that can limit our awareness or love. And this requires more "time" than is available in one "lifetime." So, we keep re-entrancing into human form, creating many different kinds of lives and opportunities.

And wherever we journey as human beings, we have a mirror that reflects back to ourself our own inner situation, enabling us to see how and where we are stuck: the experiences that we create in the trance of our lives.

12

Life in the Mirror

The trance of human reality enables us to represent—*to re-present*—the dynamics of our inner consciousness as human experience. Although we live in a group trance, because our personal reality is determined solely by what we choose to create, our life will *mirror* the point of view we create it with and the issues that we are exploring through being human. Our point of view necessarily encompasses both our soul's point of view and our human one, and therefore includes our identity beliefs, our belief structures for our body-trance and for Natural Law, our emotional attitude beliefs, all the rest of our conscious and unconscious human beliefs, and our different levels of awareness of Self.

Although certain issues and beliefs will always be more in the foreground, our life reflects every belief and awareness within our point of view and every issue that we have chosen to explore. The areas within ourself that are free, that give us pleasure and fulfillment, as well as those in which we are stuck in trance-illusions, causing ourself suffering, will be reflected back to us; they will be re-presented to us through our experience. This is part of the perfection of the design of Creation, for we can always see exactly where we are stuck, simply by noticing where in our life we are suffering, and by noticing what issues are surrounding our suffering.

The mirror that we find in our life experiences is, therefore, a powerful tool for own transformation. All we need to do is learn how to use it, and learn to remember that the reflection we see in it is always our own.

13

The Role of Suffering

It is not *what happens* to us that makes us suffer, it is *how we experience* what happens. Whenever we are stuck in an illusion, whenever we believe in fear and limit our experience of love, we suffer.

Although all of our suffering is based on an illusion (the illusion of our separateness), suffering itself is a Real experience. Hence, if a child begins to cry because a little birdie got knocked on the head in a cartoon, although we know the child's suffering is based on illusion, we still feel compassion for the child who is actually suffering.

It is our creative urge to explore our Self that takes us out of Oneness, yet once we become lost in a trance of separateness, it is our suffering that urges us to return Home again. And because our life always comes with us, there is nowhere to hide; if we don't deal with an issue, we maintain the illusion within it, and this forces us to keep re-creating similar kinds of situations to re-present it, causing a stuck pattern in the mirror of our life. (These patterns are especially visible in relationships.) Of course, sometimes we do need to repeat situations, or variations of situations, to complete the learning needed to release a trance-illusion that has kept us stuck; yet when we avoid dealing with an issue, the events in our life-mirror that reflect it tend to become more ominous or painful, encouraging us to stop avoiding ourself. Eventually, in this life or another, to relieve the suffering we are creating for ourself, we are forced to transform the illusions and self-limitations that are creating it. Our suffering, therefore, plays a critical role in our journey: in addition to letting us know exactly where we are stuck, it is Life's way of ensuring that we will eventually free ourself from the trance-illusions that limit our experience of Life.

Unfortunately, we don't usually recognize that our suffering is helping us to see where we are stuck, that these outer, painful situations are actually *gifts*. Instead of receiving these gifts we deepen our resistance; instead of acknowledging responsibility for how we are stuck we blame everyone and everything else. Of course, this creates less openness with which to receive, forcing us deeper into the illusion of separateness, making us feel more frightened and increasing our suffering. This then gives us another opportunity to become aware of what is going on by looking at our life-experiences as a mirror—as a representation—of our inner situation, but usually we don't. We have become too much like a wild animal in a house of mirrors who doesn't recognize and is afraid of his own reflection. The animal runs, barks, and even tries to attack his mirrored image, yet the more aggressive he becomes the more intimidating his mirror-image seems, frightening him even more. Eventually, he ends up in a panic, for he cannot scare off or overwhelm his reflection and there is nowhere to hide; his reflections are everywhere. It is only when he finally gives up and surrenders in defeat that his reflection stops looking frightening, and he realizes that he is safe.

In the exact same manner, either we choose to confront our illusions and fears, or our suffering finally gets bad enough that it forces the transformation. For instance, a man may be terrified of poverty, which means that he has projected his fundamental fear—his fear of annihilation—onto this issue. He avoids dealing directly with his fear and spends his life accumulating wealth to protect himself from being annihilated. Yet when his soul-consciousness decides that it is time to transform this issue, he is no longer able to avoid dealing with it for things start to go wrong, increasing his suffering. Eventually, perhaps all his investments go bad and he ends up with nothing. At this point, his fear will begin to give way to despair. The despair is the recognition that, for all his grabbing and pushing, he has ended up in the very situation he was terrified of. There is nothing he can do to prevent the annihilation that he expects. Yet this despair is a door, for it is a disillusionment, a breaking up of the illusion that fear and control could help him stay safe. With attempts at control now useless, his grip on his life loosens, creating a space in which he can now receive. And if he doesn't numb or kill himself, at some point he will receive an odd little awareness: *he has not been annihilated; he still exists.* The trance-illusion that poverty would annihilate him had caused him much suffering, yet it was his suffering from this illusion which eventually bought him to free himself from it.

Of course, it is possible that, when the man lost everything and found he wasn't annihilated, he still held onto his belief about poverty, thinking that annihilation would occur at any time now. He might then have begun stealing to forestall this as long as possible. In this case, there would be other lessons to come. Perhaps in his next entrancement another lesson would be created around this issue, but from a different angle. Perhaps he would be enormously rich and yet, for all his money, he would not be able to save his daughter—whom he loved more than anything—from cancer.

Our suffering will keep forcing us into our abyss so we can discover that it is not the infinite hole we fear will annihilate us, that it hides a false bottom which gives way to Light. As a result, our suffering ensures that (in this entrancement or another) each of our layers of fear and illusion will finally be faced and transformed, including our core illusion—that we are separate from our Source of Life. Whether we allow our suffering to lead us, or force it to drag us kicking and screaming, it eventually guides us to completely enlighten our experience of being human.

(When we think we have transformed an issue and then find it mirrored once again in some event in our life, we often become frustrated, thinking we have deluded ourself, that we're "still stuck in the same old issue"; yet we did transform either a layer or an aspect of the issue—we freed some part of our consciousness from its trance—and this allowed deeper layers or other aspects of the trance to become visible to our awareness. Sometimes, a lot of learning, in a lot of different situations, must take place around an issue before we are ready or willing to transform it completely. We can never be where we were; we are always growing.)

At some point of our journey, we do recognize that wherever we are suffering we are stuck in an illusion, and we do learn to see these situations as gifts for becoming aware of the illusions that keep us from Oneness. Yet we cannot return to Oneness in a state of suffering; we must be filled with joy and laughter, and with pleasure so intense it can only be called ecstasy.

14

Acknowledging Responsibility

In order to free ourself from the illusions that trap us and cause us to suffer, it is absolutely necessary that we acknowledge responsibility for creating our experience of Life.

We are clearly responsible for our own responses, reactions, and behaviors, and for all the choices we make; so in this area, we can either deny what we know IS our responsibility, or acknowledge it and experience it. Yet most of us do not consciously experience responsibility for manifesting the events in our life (even if we believe we are responsible), because most of us are not in touch with our unconscious human intentions or the out-of-trance part of our consciousness that is creating these events. Therefore, with these situations, when we do not consciously experience our responsibility, choosing to acknowledge it involves an assumption, based on belief. In time, working with this belief, experiences will occur that will transform the belief into knowledge; until then, acknowledging responsibility for events will require *assuming* responsibility. And assuming responsibility is not some weak substitute for direct experience; neither is it a burdening, a "taking on" of a responsibility that wasn't ours before we "took" it. Rather, *choosing to assume responsibility for all the events in our life is a powerful act of personal transformation that enables us to feel safe and to consciously receive all of our experience.*

Even in models of Reality in which God is experienced as a separate consciousness rather than as Self and is perceived to be the sole creator of events, since these events have been perfectly created for us, we must still acknowledge responsibility for: being the mold which determined what events would be needed for our growth, receiving what has been created for us, and transforming whatever our experience shows us is stuck—whatever within ourself is not unconditional love.

If we acknowledge responsibility for some aspects of our life but not others, a problem arises around where to draw the line. For instance, a man's wife runs off with a traveling salesman. He may acknowledge responsibility for his anger yet deny responsibility for being in that situation.

When we do not acknowledge responsibility for the events in our life, it is difficult to let go of our reactions—which are resistances—to these events, even when we acknowledge responsibility for our reactions. The event is perceived as something that is happening to us rather than for us. When we assume that an event has been created for us by our own higher consciousness, our attitude toward the event is automatically different and we become much more willing to open to the experience and seek out its lessons.

When we choose to acknowledge responsibility for every facet of our life—including the events in our life and our responses to them, our family situation, our feelings, our attitudes, and our beliefs—we are consciously adopting a particular relationship to our life that puts us in harmony with what IS, helps us to receive Life, and commits us to transforming our experience of being human.

Acknowledging responsibility does not mean that we blame ourself for what we don't like in our life. Self-blame is really a way of avoiding responsibility; it only leads to guilt and anger, not to transformation. Acknowledging responsibility simply means that we recognize our Self as the source of an our experience in Life.

Acknowledging responsibility for our life also does not mean that we cannot hold other people accountable for their actions. Although we have chosen to have these people and their particular behaviors in our life as a mirror, they have also chosen to manifest their behavior. Therefore, we hold them accountable/responsible for their actions—not the same as blaming them—so they can learn to acknowledge responsibility for their experience of life, too.

When we forgive someone we are not absolving the person of responsibility—in fact, no one can be absolved of responsibility. Forgiveness, when not distorted, is simply an expression of unconditional love. Unfortunately, most forgiveness is distorted. When we say, "I forgive you for what you did to me," we usually still blame the other person, and the act of forgiving becomes an arrogant position that attempts to elevate us over the other person, deny our own responsibility, and punish the other person by withholding real love. Such forgiveness is really a power play, not an expression of love. Love never blames; yet it would also never want to deny someone his or her responsibility, for that responsibility is a critical vehicle for the person's growth.

There is nothing "wrong" with not acknowledging responsibility. Yet there are consequences. To not acknowledge responsibility we will have to deny our responsibility, and this will trap us in our illusions and keep us resisting our life. We will also blame others (or Life Itself) for whatever we don't like in ourself and our life, and by making them the cause of our experience, we will camouflage our own stuckness, feel powerless to transform our experience, and reinforce our attitudes of fear, resentment, and self-pity. In addition, when we make other people (or Life Itself) the cause of our experience, we take the position of victim, and as long as we hold that position we will not be able to let go of our suffering.

Disowning responsibility will especially affect all our relationships, making them difficult. The problem with our relationships will always be the other person, so we will feel powerless to make our relationships work except by trying to control the other person. Our blaming the other person will also tend to turn the person against us (the person's outer hostility will reflect our inner resentment and hostility), creating war in the relationship.

When we disown responsibility for our life, we are choosing to stay en-tranced with fear, paralyzing us, inhibiting our response-ability. Without response-ability we lose our sense of spontaneous aliveness and can only react to situations with old attitudes.

In general, when we do not acknowledge responsibility, we do not deal with the source of our problems, so we stay stuck and re-create situations—usually more painful situations—to mirror the stuckness, increasing our suffering.

Acknowledging responsibility for our life grows out of an awareness of the way things are and our commitment to transforming our experience of being human. At some point, we *will* acknowledge responsibility for our experience of life. We will have to. For nothing else will work.

15

Reflections of Our Soul & Human Points of View

Because we are souls en-tranced as human personalities, the trance-experiences we create in the mirror of our lives necessarily reflect both the point of view of our soul-consciousness and the conscious beliefs of our human form. For instance, two men believe that the easiest way to make a living is by breaking into private homes and selling whatever they can steal. One man gets caught and goes to prison while the other one, after reading a magazine article about life in prison, decides to stop stealing. The one who goes to prison thinks that he is simply unlucky; yet whether or not his human, emotional consciousness purposely acted self-destructively to get himself caught, the event of his getting caught was intended and created by his soul,[15] whose point of view is that some years spent in the trance-experience of prison would, at this time, be the most effective way to explore—and ultimately enlighten—the issues and attitudes that are most pressing in its human situation. For the other man, the decision to stop stealing reflects his conscious beliefs; yet the event of coming across the magazine article, which catalyzed his decision, reflects the intentions of his soul.

Because our human consciousness usually has many more issues to transform than we can explore at one time, only those issues that our soul decides are the most important for our growth right now will be reflected back to us strongly in the mirror of our life. For

---

[15]Whenever I refer to our "soul" as the creator of events in our lives, it is always with the understanding that I mean our "Self in the individuated form of our soul," for the Self is the only Creator.

example, a woman may be afraid of intimacy, but if her soul-con-sciousness does not consider this an important issue for her growth right now, it will keep situations that re-present that fear to herself more in the background than in the foreground of her life. And issues may be moved back and forth between foreground and background as our learning needs change. While some issues will be prominent for only short periods, others will be central themes running through our entire life, or several of our lives.

There are times when we will notice that an event has been manifested into our life from the soul-level of our consciousness. Sometimes the timing of the event will point to this "divine intervention," sometimes it will be the miraculousness of the event, and sometimes it will be the realization of how much the event affected our future life. For instance, perhaps your car mysteriously broke down on your way to the airport and you missed your plane, which later crashed. Sometimes though, it will be a minor event whose absurdity catches your attention. For instance, perhaps you are driving at three miles over the speed limit, other cars are passing you with several going dangerously fast, it is a quiet Sunday morning, and a policeman pulls *you* over for going too fast but only gives you a warning. In a situation such as this one, it would be wise to meditate on what this "warning" is really referring to in your life. In addition, because the situation is screaming out that it is an intervention, it will be easier to sense the deeper level of your con-sciousness which manifested the event, so it is an opportunity for you to become aware of, and to make contact with, this level of yourself.

Although the role of our soul-consciousness may seem to be the most significant factor in unfolding our Self and creating our personal reality, the role of our human consciousness is just as important. While our souls direct the larger stream of events flowing into our lives, our human consciousness, through its responses to those events, forces them in specific directions and determines how we grow from them, which in turn affects the kind of events that will be necessary for our growth in the future. In the example of the two men who were stealing, when the second man consciously decided to stop, he forced future events into a different direction; in addition, the personal transformation he created affected the kind of learning-events that his soul would bring into his life later on. And the first man's path of growth will not be determined simply by the fact of his being in prison, but by how he responds to what he encounters there.

This general situation applies to us as children, too. The fact that we create our own reality does not mean that a little girl chooses to be sexually abused by her father; it means that her soul level of consciousness has chosen to be born to this particular man in order to force certain issues to be confronted in this human life. And some of these issues will have nothing to do with sexuality *per se*—issues such as rage, fear, helplessness, and resentment. For a soul that wants to confront the helplessness within its emotional point of view, sexual molestation provides a stage upon which the helplessness can be projected with great emotional intensity. Without such dramas, it can be very difficult for the soul to explore these issues and transform them. Of course, other kinds of dramas could be used to explore this issue; and they *are* used—in other lives. In each life the soul chooses what best serves its growth at that time. And with the molested little girl, as with all our life-experiences, the larger situation is not simply what has happened but how she chooses to experience and to deal with what has happened.

Our soul consciousness and human consciousness have different spheres of influence, yet it is important to remember that both levels are expressions of our Self, so as human beings we are never a "victim" of the creative inclinations of our soul—its intentions and decisions are always our own. Our Self is always both the creator and experiencer of our human lives, and the only One who is responsible for effecting transformation.

As souls and as Self, we grow from our human experience regardless of whether we seem to learn anything consciously as human beings; yet at a certain point of our growth, our human consciousness must grow too, for we cannot fully enlighten our experience of being human unless our human consciousness transcends its trance-limitations and recognizes its Oneness with our Self.

16

Utilizing the Mirror

We don't need to search our souls in deep meditation to discover which of our issues we are working on right now; all we need to do is look at our lives. For instance, a woman who always ends up in abusive relationships is clearly exploring issues of human self-love and violence (among other issues). A man who is always angry does not need to stare very hard in his life-mirror to see where he is stuck.

Our life-mirror will always tell us where and how we are stuck. When we are observing our reflections, there are several things to look for. First of all, it is important to notice our emotional reactions—our attitudes—to our life situations, which point to issues and self-limiting beliefs that need to be transformed. The bottom line is that wherever we don't respond to life with unconditional love and compassion, we are stuck in a trance-illusion. Therefore, our reactions and attitudes tell us very directly what we need to work on within ourself—what is blocking our unconditional love—and give us an opportunity to transform these areas before they become major painful events in our lives. For example, if a woman gets angry at her husband for forgetting her birthday, her reaction points to issues about anger, insecurity that she camouflages (as well as supports) with anger, various trance-identities, and limiting beliefs that create these trances. Seeing this, she would then have the opportunity to explore these issues and begin transforming them. But if she feels justified in her anger (thinking that her husband's negligence is the whole problem and ignoring the fact that her life-experience is a mirror of herself), she might have to experience a larger event, such as a divorce, to force her to deal with her issue of insecurity (if this issue is up for her at this time). If she still managed to avoid it, she might have to experience an even larger event, or a pattern of events, that would continue to deepen her suffering, until she finally acknowledged her responsibility for what was happening and began to transform herself.

Our life-situations are never the cause of the emotional attitudes that we direct at them; rather, our attitudes already exist within us as issues that we are exploring, and when a suitable situation comes along, we attach our attitude to it and blame the situation for our experience. Thus, we try to alleviate ourself of responsibility, using outer events as an excuse for having our attitudes and as a camouflage for the fact that we are—and have been—stuck; yet the outer situation simply *activates the expression* of our pre-existing inner attitude. A common expression for this is that the outer event "pushes our buttons," which points to the awareness that our attitudes are machine-like, push-button reaction patterns. It doesn't matter what kind of event is pushing our buttons; our buttons were there before the event, so the event cannot be the cause of the reaction inside the button. The event is actually a gift, for it enables us to see what kind of trance-illusion we are stuck in, giving us the opportunity to explore and transform it.

Once we have utilized the key of noticing our reactions, we can also notice what it is that we are reacting *to*. Because we react to situations only when they activate pre-existing emotional resistance patterns within ourself, whatever we react to is always a mirror of our own issues and self-limiting beliefs, including our identity beliefs. For example, if a man gets angry at a fellow worker at an office party because the person is making himself the center of attention, the self-centeredness that the man is reacting to is as much a mirror of himself as his anger, whether he expresses his anger or not. If the angry man were willing to examine himself, he would find that he is self-centered, too, and he is jealous of the attention being given to the other man. It is his own trance of self-centeredness, along with his own beliefs about anger and attention, that are the cause of his anger in this situation, not the behavior of the other man. (Although the man who was successfully being self-centered existed in the reality of each person at the of office party, he was only a mirror of something stuck for those individuals who reacted to him. For individuals who genuinely had fun with him, he mirrored some fun-loving, creative part of themselves.)

In the example of the woman who was angry at her husband for forgetting her birthday, the woman's anger mirrored certain issues within herself; yet her husband's negligence, which she reacted *to,* is also a mirror—possibly of some way in which she neglects herself, of a belief that she is not worthy of loving attention, and/or of some important way in which she neglects her husband.

Whatever we react to in a situation is always a mirror, a re-presentation, of issues and self-limiting beliefs within ourself. Yet we never react to a situation as it is; we are always reacting to what we *believe* is happening in the situation, what we believe this signi-fies for ourself, and what this reminds us of within ourself that we are already reacting to. For instance, the woman with the negligent husband was not already reacting to her husband's behavior—which may or may not have been negligent—but to what she believed about his behavior, what she believed this signified for herself, and what this reminded her of within herself that she was already reacting to. If she were willing to consciously look at her reaction, it would help her immensely to specifically name what she is reacting to. At first, she might simply say that she is reacting to his negligence, but as she becomes more specific, she would have to name what it was about the negligence that she was reacting to. This might lead to statements like, "When he's negligent I feel he doesn't love me," or "When he he's negligent I feel like I don't really matter to him and that I am all alone." These statements enable her to see more clearly the beliefs and attitudes that are the real cause of her unhappiness.

If we look deeply enough in the mirror and examine what we seem to be reacting to, we will discover that we are really reacting to something within ourself. This is congruent with the idea of One-ness: *since everything is an expression of our Self, whatever we react to is something within our Self that we are resisting.* In fact, whatever other people do in our life situations is what we our Self are doing for ourself in order to grow.

In addition to our reaction and whatever we are reacting to, many situations present a third mirror: the nature of the situation itself. Sometimes, this is the most important mirror being presented. For instance, a woman whose husband lies to her has created a mirror with this situation. Even if she is not lying to him, most likely there is some significant way that she is lying to herself or others. Sometimes, though, it is a different issue that is being reflected. For instance, the husband's lying may simply be a way of keeping her at a distance, in which case the issue he is reflecting back to her—the issue she is re-presenting to herself with his lying—may be one about emotional distancing and walls to intimacy. In relationships, the situation-mirror is usually very significant. Sometimes, though, the reflection in it is subtle. Another example is a quiet, scared, dutiful woman who is married to a violent, irresponsible man. Where is the mirror? Whenever we find two opposite or complementary attitudes in a relationship, the mirror will always be some single issue that both positions are an expression of. By looking deeper at this situation, we may discover that the posture this woman has taken toward life is her way of resisting the experience of violence. Yet the violence she avoids is a mold she shapes herself around, so it is definitely part of her nature. And given the right circumstances, she will manifest that violence. So both she and her husband have violence as a central issue in their lives. Although they manifest this issue differently, they are definitely mirrors for each other. In fact, the woman's fear is a reflection for the man, for without some similar fear he would never have become violent.

The situation-mirror is found in many areas of our life besides relationships. It is especially noticeable whenever we find that we have created a pattern with a particular kind of situation. Patterns always make the significance of events visible. Yet because the timing of events is never accidental, even first or one time occurrences that seem to coincide suspiciously with other events should be examined for deeper significance. In general, the more emotionally charged or disturbing a situation is, the more significant the issue that is being mirrored in it.

The fourth mirror a situation can provide is of the conscious and unconscious *intentions* of our human consciousness and of our soul. We simply ask ourself why (as a human being or as a soul) we would have created that particular situation. This kind of questioning will often generate new revelations and point out patterns that we may otherwise miss. For instance, a woman who has divorced her husband, after finding out that he had been having a long affair, would notice many issues directly reflected in this mirror, yet if she also asked herself why she (as a human being or as a soul) might have created a situation in which she was married to someone who acted like this, she might become aware of some other issues. For instance, she might have unconsciously created this situation to validate an attitude-position that men are untrustworthy, or because she wanted to camouflage her own unhappiness by having someone else to blame for it, or because she had entered a marriage that she really didn't want to be in.

To become aware of our intentions, we simply (1) look at what we can see resulted from the situation, including the validation of pre-existing attitudes, the camouflaging of attitudes, and/or whatever personal growth was generated, (2) acknowledge that we must have intended (from somewhere within our Self) both the event and all its consequences, and then (3) ask ourself: for what purpose could I (as a human being or as a soul) have created this experience? Usually there will be more than one purpose involved, both because different areas of our consciousness will usually create the same event for different purposes, and because the learning ultimately intended from a situation will invariably encompass a lot more than we can possibly become aware of or understand. Yet knowing all the intentions behind our creation of a situation is not necessary; becoming aware of just the most prominent issues—and acknowledging responsibility for them—will powerfully feed our growth.

Sometimes the events in our lives will reflect contradictory beliefs or intentions. We have little trouble simultaneously holding opposing viewpoints. We often refer to this kind of situation with statements like, "Part of me agrees and part of me doesn't." A woman who believes that her rational mind is the best judge of how to act, yet also believes that she should always trust her feelings, is an example of this inner division.

Whenever there are conflicting beliefs or intentions, a life-situation that reflects one point of view will usually also reflect the other, as well as the struggle to work out the contradiction. A soul exploring conflicting human beliefs about love and rejection might en-trance as a boy into a family in which the mother tells him that she beats him only because she loves him. Later in his life, all situations about love will reflect his beliefs about rejection as well as his creative struggle to work out his inner contradictions.

The most visible events in the mirror of our lives are those which are most traumatic. As souls, we usually create traumatic events to force us (as human beings) to deal with an issue that we have avoid-ed, to create a strong focus for an issue so we can contact it more easily, to create a sudden transformation, and/or to alter the direction of our life. Accidents, near-death experiences, and emotional losses are the most common vehicles for this. The intensity of such events reflects the importance of their message, so these mirrors should always be given special consideration.

Unfortunately, even when we look in our life-mirror and see exactly how we are stuck, we nevertheless may resist allowing a transformation because of our fear, which is generated by our beliefs about what will happen to us if we open up or let go. Fear is the inner fabric of all our resistance to growth. Yet our fears are also vehicles for our growth. When we realize that our life is an expression of our learning needs, then all experiences become gifts, from our Self to our en-tranced self, giving us the opportunity to grow and experience more love. Fear is just another experience in the mirror of our life, another gift and opportunity for our growth, as we unfold our Self, enlightening our experience of being human. Some of our most powerful gifts initially create the most suffering as we receive them, because of our fear, yet in the end, these also unfold the most love. Ultimately, *all of our major lessons in life are about transforming our illusions of fear and separateness into experiences of Oneness and Love.*

Learning to use our life-mirror to see where we are stuck is one of the most valuable tools we can acquire for transforming ourself. In general, we need to pay attention to:

(1) the nature of the situation, including what the situation may symbolize and how intense our experience is;

(2) the particular emotional attitudes that we react with, that we resist our experience with;

(3) what we are reacting to, both generally and very specifically;

(4) the nature of our trance-identity—who we think we are or what kind of "character" we are being—in the situation;

(5) what we consciously believe about the situation, and ourself;

(6) what we think we intended by creating the situation;

(7) the fact that the situation has been created by our Self, and that it has been created from Love.

If we look carefully at our life, we will find mirrors everywhere. Even when they seem filled with nothing but darkness, by showing us where we are stuck they illuminate our path, and so they are expressions of our Light and Love, guiding our way Home.

17

Decisions

The fact that our life mirrors our point of view has important consequences for the way we make decisions. As might be expected, situations that result from a particular decision will tend to mirror the point of view which chose that decision.

If we make a decision from a position of fear, what grows out of that decision will tend to reflect that fear. If a decision is based on greed, the resulting situation will tend to reflect that greed and create lessons for us about it. On the other hand, decisions which are based on love and awareness will tend to create life situations which reflect and reinforce that love and awareness. This idea is especially important for relationships, because many relationship decisions are decided from emotional neediness or fear of loss, and then what is created embodies these issues.

With important decisions, therefore, it is very important to consider your state of awareness. If you are not in a clear and loving state of consciousness, WAIT. Put aside your worries, relax, and get yourself into a more harmonious state.

Then, after you have sifted through all the possibilities in your mind, realize that there are two ways to make decisions. You can "decide" with your intellect, or you can align yourself with that place within you that "knows," that is beyond the changing, thinking mind and is, therefore, certain. In this latter case, you don't "decide," you "hear what is."

So, after you have relaxed and opened your heart, reach very deep within yourself, and when you feel that you are touching the center of your being, allow your knowingness to manifest in your awareness as a decision.

AWARENESS EXERCISE 15:
WHAT WE PUSH AWAY

Sit comfortably and close your eyes. Receive a few deep breaths ... and let yourself relax. Then:

(1) Bring to mind someone whom you strongly dislike. (If you can't think of anyone, use someone whom you strongly dislike when they are acting in certain ways.) Focus on what in this person you are reacting to. Get a very clear, specific sense of it.

(2) Ask yourself, what is it about this person or their behavior that you find threatening? In some way, you must find it threatening, or it must remind you of something that is threatening; otherwise you wouldn't push it away so strongly. What are you afraid to experience here?

If you have trouble discovering what is threatening, focus on the place within you that is reacting to this person and merge into this part of yourself. Feel how your body tenses, how your breathing changes, feel the posture you take on, and notice what goes on in your mind. Then, aligned with this part of yourself, ask yourself what is threatening about this person? What does this person's behavior remind you of? What are you afraid to experience?

(3) Instead of blaming the other person and making this person the cause of your reaction, recognize that the real problem is that you find this person's behavior threatening. Acknowledge responsibility for your fear and ask yourself how you would perceive and experience this person if you were able to stop feeling threatened.

(4) Recognize that, if you still have a reaction to this person, he or she is now a tool for you, because you can think of this person and use your reaction to make contact with some place within you that is stuck, that is ultimately caught in a fear-trance.

(5) Recognize that any tool that helps you to encounter and transform your fear is a gift, and acknowledge to yourself that this person you strongly dislike is a gift for your spiritual growth.

AWARENESS EXERCISE 16:
A SITUATION IN THE MIRROR

For this exercise, you'll need paper and a pen.

PART 1

Remember a recent situation in which you had a strong emotional reaction. Then write down:

(1) The nature of the situation;

(2) Your reaction to the situation;

(3) Specifically what you were reacting to;

(4) Your identity-trance—the kind of "character" or constructed self you experienced yourself as being in the situation;

(5) All your beliefs about the situation—including beliefs about its cause, its meaning, what you were reacting to, the "validity" of your reaction, the intentions of the other people involved, how the situation affected your life, and any other beliefs that relate to what happened, even if some of your beliefs are contradictory; and,

(6) Any intentions—for either validating a stuck position, camouflaging an attitude, or for generating growth—that you can see expressed, or possibly expressed, in the situation.

PART 2

Each paragraph below refers back to your answers in 1 through 6, in Part 1.

With (1), ask yourself if this kind of situation forms a pattern in your life. Look at the situation as a mirror to see what it reflects about yourself and the issues you are working on. If an artist had painted this scene, what would the painting tell you about the artist? Write down what you find.

With (2), ask yourself if this kind of attitude/reaction occurs frequently in your life. Note whether you usually justify your reaction or usually recognize that it is just a place that you are stuck. Note the particular kind of fear that this attitude/ reaction represents. Ask yourself what beliefs exist in your consciousness when you are in the middle of this kind of reaction. Look very carefully for these beliefs and then write them down.

With (3), be willing to see what you were reacting to as a mirror of yourself. Then look for what it is within yourself that you were pushing away, afraid to experience, or disowning. Write down what you find. If there are any beliefs operating here that are not already listed, write them down.

With (4), ask yourself if you can be in this kind of situation without pretending that who you are is this character.

With (5), look at your beliefs as *beliefs*, not as truths. Then step back and look at these beliefs as a portrait of a particular person. What do you see? What kind of person do these beliefs reflect? What kind of issues is this person working on? Write this down. Then, once again, examine your beliefs as beliefs and ask yourself which beliefs are self-limiting. Which beliefs block your experience of unconditional love? Which beliefs lead to suffering? Which beliefs create fear? Write down what you find.

With (6), if the situation was created to validate or camouflage a stuck position or attitude, ask yourself if you are willing to stop validating or camouflaging what you know is false. If the situation was created as an opportunity for a particular learning, ask yourself if you are willing to receive that learning deeply enough so that you won't need to create a similar situation later. Write down what you find.

AWARENESS EXERCISE 17:
THE MIRROR OF UNCONDITIONAL LOVE

Wherever we resist experiencing unconditional love, we are stuck. Therefore, for the next week, or month, or for the rest of your life, have the intention of experiencing people from a place of unconditional love, and notice when you have difficulty and what gets in your way. Examine what you believe gets in your way very carefully and very honestly.

And remember, unconditional love does not need to be created, for it already *is* inside of us; we simply have to allow ourself to experience it.

18

Reflections of Need

Once we believe that we're separate from our Source of Life and therefore lacking *within* ourself what we need for survival and wholeness, in addition to resisting this situation with a posture of fear we look for security and wholeness *outside* of ourself. We look for an *external source of Life*. When we think we have found one, we attempt to hold onto it and control it (to keep ourself safe); we develop holding patterns that, later in life, sometimes manifest as addiction patterns.

Whenever we believe we have found an external source of Life, we are projecting our own inner Source of Life onto this outer thing. As infants, our projected, external sources of Life are people (especially our parents) or situations or things that remind us of our forgotten connection to our Self—that remind us that we are safe— by giving us love or approval, by enabling us to have fun or express our creativity, or by giving us some kind of sense of security. Later, our projected sources of Life may become anything that we perceive to be a vehicle for obtaining love, approval, fun, or security, or even things that control our connection to this vehicle. So, what began as a simple fear of annihilation becomes a maze of projections in which we struggle with and try to control our projected sources of Life and feel threatened by anything that may resist or interfere with us.

Our life experiences will always mirror back to us our fear-generated beliefs about our projected sources of Life. If we spend our lives chasing money, afraid of whatever seems to threaten our financial well-being, either we have turned money into a source of Life, or else we believe that money is a critical vehicle for obtaining a source of Life, which may be love or power or one of many other possibilities. In addition, we will believe that poverty is a source of danger, a trap-door leading to our abyss and annihilation. If the major issues and fears in our life come up around our experience of love in intimate relationships, we know we have probably made someone else's love or approval a source of Life, and we have probably made rejection the trap-door to our abyss. In addition, if we believe that beauty or fame or money or youthfulness is necessary to ensure this love, then we will feel threatened by any lack or potential loss of these, and often we will feel threatened by those who have more of these than we do.

Independent of what we have made sources of Life for ourself, they will always match our identity beliefs, because who we think we are will determine what we think we need, and who we think we are will determine what we believe threatens us. For instance, if we identify with our particular body, threats to it will bring up our fear of annihilation—not just our fear of physical death. Most of us have some sense of identity tied to our body, emotions, and mind. Yet our identity may be tied to many other things: our country, our religion, our creations, our children, and so on. If a painter's sense of identity is tied to the paintings he creates, then problems with his eyes or painting hand will bring up fears of annihilation. In general, whenever we identify with something, some other thing can threaten us; to be free of fear we must be no-thing; we must be our Self. (This idea of "becoming nothing" exists in most religions, but usually is presented with great distortion and equated with self-denial, self-worthlessness, and self-deprecation. This only gets us more stuck.)

Another way to look at what happens when we set up anything outside of our Self as a source of Life is to perceive what we are doing as *practicing idolatry*. From this point of view, all the suffering we experience in these situations, including the hurt and rejection we feel in relationships, may be considered to be a consequence (not a punishment) for transgressing spiritual law. In the Old Testament, the first (and most important) commandment says: *Thou shalt have no other gods before me.* Breaking this law will always have painful consequences.

Of course, in spite of our behavior, we unconsciously know that an external source of Life cannot give us what we think we need, and this knowledge, although unconscious, always threatens the false sense of security we try to create. In addition, no matter how tightly we hold onto an external source of Life, no matter how much we try to control it, our position is never entirely secure, because the possibility of losing this external thing, which we believe (in our projection) would either lead directly to our abyss and annihilation or leave us vulnerable to it, is always just under the surface of our consciousness. It can take us a long time to learn that there is nothing we can *do* that will make us feel safe, and there is no-thing we can *have* that will make us feel safe; we experience ourself as being truly safe only when we recognize that we *are* safe. Even the incredible suffering created by our fear and our sense of separateness is safe for us to experience.

Whatever maze we construct for ourself out of our belief that we need something outside of ourself will be reflected as learning situations—usually painful ones—in the mirror of our life. Yet it is enlightening to look back on our life and notice that, in spite of the millions of times that we felt we needed the support of an attitude to keep ourself safe from annihilation, in spite of the constant impending possibility of annihilation, we are still here; we have always survived. And although we tend to believe that we have survived because we held on and resisted Life (reinforced every time we resisted Life and found that we survived), we have survived in spite of the paralysis of our fear, not because of it.

19

Freeing Ourself From Attitude-Trances

In our experience as human beings, we have gotten caught up in many different kinds of self-limiting trances. Yet *all that maintains any trance is our belief in the reality of it.* So, whenever we see through the illusion of a trance, we free ourself from it; and there is always a sense of laughter, love, unburdening, lightness, space, or freedom, for we come back to our out-of-trance Self, which is filled with the joyous, spacious beingness of Now, and we see how funny and foolish we were, forgetting our Self and getting so lost and carried away in believing we were something that we are not.

For instance, if a man who believes he is angry suddenly frees himself from his trance, he may laugh at how funny he was, experiencing himself as if he were some angry character. At the very least, he will momentarily feel a sense of release and opening, even if he almost immediately manifests another attitude, such as shame or unworthiness for having gotten lost in an anger-trance. With attitude-trances, instead of being grounded in our Self, we identify with our constructed selves and their attitudes. We think, "I am really sad," or "I am better than those people," or "Teenagers are irresponsible," and we believe that who we are is a particular "character" with a particular attitude. From our point of view out-of-trance, this kind of self-deception is hilarious. This is why in Carlos Castenada's books, the Yaqui sorcerer don Juan, who easily accesses his out-of-trance consciousness, always finds Carlos' emotional posturing so outrageously funny. When we are lost in our emotional trances, we are like children who have gotten so caught up in a game, we have forgotten that it is not Real.

Yet we can free ourself from our trance. Since our attitudes are always illusions, and since who we are is always the loving Consciousness of our out-of-trance Self, when we are stuck in an attitude-trance we must be *pretending to believe* that we are that particular character and its attitude. "Pretending" is really the correct word here because no matter how deep our trance, we always know who we really are; we can never entirely lose our Self. And, since it is only this pretense of belief that maintains the trance, *we can free ourself from any attitude-trance by having the part of our Consciousness that has en-tranced itself in it stop believing in the illusion of the trance.* This can be accomplished by getting the part of us that is in the trance to remember the Self it really is, or to *recognize* (which means re-cognize, or know again) that its attitude is just a self-induced, illusion-generated trance. (All beliefs that generate attitudes are illusions.) Either awareness will dissolve the whole trance because, with attitude-trances, the false identity and its attitude are inseparable—the constructed self that is used in an attitude-trance believes that who it is, is the attitude it holds. Without the attitude, that particular character-identity falls apart; without the identity, there is no way to hold the attitude. For instance, a man with a poor-me attitude will identify with this position, and when he is manifesting it he will actually believe that he is some poor-me character. He can get free of his trance by having the part of him that is caught in it either remember Who he is or see his attitude as a trance. (We do have constructed selves that do not have attitudes as part of their construction. For instance, the trance, "I am a man," or "I am Chinese," can be constructed without any attitudes. Yet eventually, *all* our separateness-based identity-trances must be released for us to become centered in our Self.)

Freeing ourself from attitude-trances can be very simple, yet we must be careful not to fool ourself. We can say, "I know this attitude (or identity) is a trance," and then avoid experiencing it or dismiss it as being unreal, instead of doing what is necessary to actually free ourself from the trance. In such cases, we are *denying and suppressing* our attitude instead of transforming it, and we are dismissing the Real part of ourself that is caught in the trance. The first step, therefore, when we recognize that we are caught in an attitude-trance, is to allow ourself to continue to feel whatever it is that we are feeling, even though we know that it is a trance. This enables us to maintain contact with our trance yet keeps part of our awareness free of it.

Only then do we have the opportunity to bring a more enlightened awareness into this en-tranced part of ourself.

Although we recognize a trance with a part of our awareness that is outside of it, it is the part of our Self that is in the trance that must recognize the illusion of the trance for it to let go. (From the point of view of free will, the part of our Self that chose to en-trance Itself and forget Who it is must choose to remember Itself.) Otherwise, no matter what is going on in the rest of our awareness, the part of us that is in the trance will still be caught in it, and the trance will still exist. So, *we must bring into our trance, and into the part of ourself that is stuck in it, a conscious awareness that is deeper than our trance;* then it will no longer en-trance us and will cease to exist.

Of course, trances that are rooted in deeply held beliefs—especially our fear-trances—are always more difficult to be conscious in, and we will have more difficulty with trances that are indistinct, or those which are just poking up from beneath layers of other trances. With difficult trances, we simply need to go deeper in our awareness. And sometimes we need to recognize that this deepening of awareness is a "project" that will take commitment and time.

We also need to recognize that we often recreate trances after we seem to have released them. This occurs for two reasons. The first is that a deeper trance which has not been released is recreating this more superficial one to support its position. In this case, we just have to go deeper. The second possibility is that we are simply so in the habit of using that attitude that we unconsciously revert back to it. This kind of unconscious reflex can continue to occur for a long time, and then we have no choice but to repeatedly recognize our trance and release it again. As we will see in Chapter 21, "The Role of our Physical Body," after we release a chronic attitude we still have the pattern of it embedded in our body, and this takes more time to change. Yet, as we repeatedly release our trance, releasing it becomes easier, and over time, the trance loses its power: we stop identifying with it and the reflex itself simply becomes a passing thought.

In practice, there are various ways to bring a more conscious awareness into our trance. In the next awareness exercise you will be introduced to ten of them. And, using these techniques, it will be obvious when you get free of a trance, for it will dissolve in that instant and you will experience a sense of release, contact with your real Self, and a moment of inner love or laughter. When you try to fool yourself or don't quite effect the real transformation none of this happens at all.

There is only one kind of situation where a trance will let go and a sense of release will not be experienced. This happens when, immediately after the trance lets go, another attitude-trance emerges to take the first one's place. For instance, arrogance may give way to an attitude of worthlessness. Whenever a deeper, more emotionally intense attitude immediately replaces a more superficial one, the superficial trance may be considered a camouflage or support for the deeper trance, which contains the real issue involved; and it is this second, deeper trance that needs to be released for laughter and contact with our Self to emerge (unless yet another trance emerges).

It is important to realize that there are many ways to significantly alter an attitude-trance without actually releasing it. This kind of trance-*modification* (which is the goal of most forms of psychotherapy), can be very useful, but it is not as powerful as freeing ourself from a trance and dissolving it completely. This is the difference between change and true transformation, between feeling better and becoming filled with love or laughter.

As an example of trance-modification, a woman has generated hurt-feelings due to her belief that her husband has been inconsiderate. If a more conscious part of herself convinces the hurt part that her husband is simply tired, not inconsiderate, she will stop acting hurt and will feel better. She has now changed her trance, but the part of her that was en-tranced with her hurt feelings still believes in the reality of this attitude; that constructed self still holds the attitude but it is no longer being projected onto this particular situation. It would have been more powerful for this part of her to remember that Who she is, is Love—not some character that feels hurt—and that feeling hurt is just a self-induced attitude-trance. Then she would come back to the joyous love that is her Self.

The true goal is not to modify our trances but to see through the illusions within them so they *cease to be Real.* Yet, over time, if we repeatedly modify an attitude-trance, letting go of its projections, we will eventually realize that the attitude itself is just a trance, then we will laugh at how funny we have been, believing that who we were was some character with that attitude.

Metaphorically, since all attitudes grow out of a fear of annihilation, when we free a part of our consciousness from an attitude-trance, we are *resurrecting* it from its entrancement with death and restoring it to Life.

Learning to dissolve our attitude-trances is a little bit like learning to ride a bicycle: difficult at first, and then pleasurable and easy, with a sense of amazement that there was actually a time when we didn't know how to do it. What could be simpler than releasing an attitude by perceiving that our experience of it is a trance?

AWARENESS EXERCISE 18:
RELEASING ATTITUDE-TRANCES

Sit comfortably and close your eyes. Receive a few deep breaths ... and let yourself relax. This is a long exercise, so you will probably want to break it up into several sittings. With each part, practice the technique for fifteen minutes or longer, or until you experience your attitude-trance let go.

(1) Since any part of us that is en-tranced in an attitude has stopped believing in Love, believes in fear, and thinks it is a particular character with an attitude, if we can get that part of us to receive Love, it remembers that it is Self and not a character, its beliefs in lack and fear disappear, and its attitude and character-trance cease to exist.

To utilize this, first notice your breath for a few minutes and notice any sensations your breath makes you aware of in your body. See if any of these sensations are tied to an emotional attitude. If no attitudes come up, simply become aware of an emotional attitude that you still have in connection with a particular person or situation. This can be an anger that you still hold toward someone, a sadness that you still feel about some situation, a guilt, a fear, and so on.

Then receive Love into the part of yourself that is holding this attitude. There are several ways to do this. You can simply receive Love in that part of yourself, you can receive your breath as Love or as God's Love (as in Awareness Exercise 2) in that part of yourself, or you can have that part of yourself receive an embrace from the Loving Essence of All That Is (as in Awareness Exercise 9).

(Releasing a trance may bring to the surface a deeper, more basic trance. When this happens, there will sometimes be a momentary sense of release or letting go, but then the deeper attitude will emerge. If that happens, simply repeat whichever step of the exercise you were doing, working with the new attitude.)

(2) If you didn't succeed in releasing your attitude, then work with it again here; otherwise let your breath and body sensations make you aware of another attitude, or choose another attitude that you know you are holding.

Align yourself with the emotional quality and posture of the attitude, and then reach out with your consciousness and make *direct contact* with the part of yourself that is en-tranced in the attitude. You can imagine that you are trying to wake this part of yourself out of a bad dream. If you can contact them within their dream, they will realize that they are dreaming and wake up. If you make contact and the trance doesn't let go, open yourself more to this part of yourself and attempt to make contact from a deeper place within yourself or with more love.

(3) Use the same attitude if it didn't release; otherwise, as before, become aware of another one.

Align yourself with the en-tranced part of yourself and notice the fact that its attitude is a trance. Then make direct contact with the en-tranced part of yourself as you did in (2), but when you make contact, attempt to communicate your awareness of its trance. Sometimes it will help to say in your mind, "This is a trance," and direct the statement, along with the awareness it contains, to the en-tranced part of yourself.

If the attitude doesn't let go after a while, notice the "story" that the entranced part of yourself is telling itself to justify its attitude. Then again make direct contact with the en-tranced part of yourself, but now communicate your awareness that this story is just a position about what happened (or about many events) and that the meaning it describes is not really what happened.

If this doesn't work, notice the particular illusion—the core belief—that is running this trance, and then communicate your awareness of this as illusion to your en-tranced self while you are making contact with it. If the illusion is not immediately obvious, ask yourself, "What belief would be necessary for this part of myself to have this experience, to hold this attitude?" You can safely assume that the belief you will find is not true, that it contains an illusion, because it is generating an attitude.

(4) Use the same attitude if it didn't release; otherwise, as before, become aware of another one.

Move as deeply as you can into the experience of Being Love (using one of the methods in Awareness Exercise 9). Then, while you stay centered in this experience, extend your awareness and experience of Being Love into the awareness of the en-tranced part of yourself. Directly *share* your experience, your love-consciousness, with the part of you that is stuck, that has forgotten love.

(5) Use the same attitude if it didn't release; otherwise become aware of another one.

Align yourself with the emotional quality and posture of the attitude, and with the inner character—the constructed self—that is holding it. In this part of the exercise, you will simply *become one* with the en-tranced part of yourself and its experience without identifying with it and losing your larger sense of Self. Go as deeply into this oneness as you can. Be willing to *inhabit* and become one with the emotional charge this en-tranced self is experiencing. Just don't get lost in it—maintain an awareness of your Self. The more deeply you can do this, the more your conscious awareness (your *out-of-trance*, Self-consciousness) will seep into your en-tranced awareness. There is nothing you need to communicate to this character; simply be conscious within its consciousness, experiencing its sense of identity and attitude without being lost in it

With this method, you must be prepared to feel—sometimes very intensely—whatever emotional charge this inner character is holding. But you need to allow yourself to continue to open to this and to mold yourself to wherever the experience takes you. Sometimes the experience will take you from one attitude into a completely different one, perhaps with a different set of memories. Whatever comes up, just maintain oneness with it, continuing to bring conscious awareness into the trance.[16]

(6) Use the same attitude if it didn't release; otherwise become aware of another one.

Inhabit and become one with your en-tranced self as in (5), yet now, as you experience being this part of yourself, open to whatever your attitude is resisting. Because this attitude must be based on fear, its essence is to resist whatever it perceives as threatening. If you can, as this part of yourself, open to what you are resisting, you will recognize that you are safe, that the fear is an illusion, and that there is nothing that needs to be resisted, dissolving the attitude.

(7) Use the same attitude if it didn't release; otherwise become aware of another one.

Align yourself with the emotional quality and posture of your attitude, and with the inner character that is holding it. Become aware of the particular kind of body-tension created by the posture and holding pattern of this attitude. Then *receive your breath* into the core of your being, and into the tension/holding/resistance pattern that maintains this attitude (as in Awareness Exercise 2).

---

[16]Arnold Mindell, in his excellent books on "process psychology," explores this technique in great depth (from a somewhat different context.)

When your en-tranced self receives the breath, it receives Life and remembers that its true identity is the Essence of Life, not a character with an attitude. At the very least, since its attitude is based on fear, on a belief that it is not safe to fully breath (to live), when the en-tranced self receives its breath it realizes that it *is* safe to breathe, dissolving the fear-trance generating the attitude.

(8) Use the same attitude if it didn't release; otherwise become aware of another one.

Align yourself with the emotional quality and posture of your attitude, and with the en-tranced part of yourself that is holding it. Then open yourself to receiving the experience of this part of yourself. This is similar to receiving your breath, except that you are receiving the emotional experience of a stuck part of yourself. Be willing to let all of the experience in. Be willing to integrate all of this walled-off emotion back into yourself.

(9) Use the same attitude if it didn't release; otherwise become aware of another one.

Recognize that the consciousness of your Self exists within any part of yourself that is caught in a trance. You can, therefore, assume responsibility for creating this trance and refuse to do so any longer. Simply reach into the core of your being and have your intention be to refuse to become the character in this trance; refuse to believe in its attitude. If you can reach deeply enough into the core of your Self with this refusal, your intention will contact your Self-within-the-trance, awakening it and dissolving its trance. (The danger with this method is that you will simply suppress the attitude. In your heart, though, you will know if you have done this or released the trance.)

(10) Think of someone who once acted hurtful toward you and whom you have never forgiven. Then align yourself with the place that still holds some attitude *against* this person, enter into that trance, and from within the trance completely (with no secret hold-outs) forgive this person for whatever was done.

Practice using these ten awareness tools as attitudes come up in daily life. Discover which ones work best for you. Additional tools will be introduced later.

20

Tools for Releasing Fear-Trances

Fear is simply False Evidences Appearing Real.
— Mary Burmeister, teacher of Jin Shin Jyutsu

We live within a physical body that can be harmed or even killed. Yet we have died a thousand times in other lives, sometimes with great pain and terror, and we are still here. Our beingness, our core Self, has always survived. This is because who we really are is Free Spirit, and so we are, always have been, and always will be *safe*. If this were not true, then we could learn to handle fear but would never be free of it. The only reason we can get free of fear is because it is based on a trance-illusion. And therefore, the only methods that can help us to get free are those that help us to break free of this illusion—by helping us to remember who we really are and that we are truly safe. The awareness tools presented in this chapter, therefore, are really different strategies for stirring our memory and recognition. These tools are designed specifically for fear-trances, yet they can also be used to work on other attitudes if we isolate and focus on the position of fear embedded within those attitudes. Here are eight awareness tools for releasing fear:

(1) In general, when we are caught in our fear-trances, it helps to peel away the layers of projection that keep putting the causes of our fear—and the source of our security—outside of us. When we are afraid, anxious, feeling attachment, or thinking we *need* something, we can remember that our fear really has nothing to do with the outer situation, that the outer situation is simply activating our basic position of fear, which we are then attaching to the situation.

If we have difficulty seeing our projection, we can uncover it by asking ourself *why* we are really afraid—or *what* we are afraid of—in this particular situation. Then, whatever answer we give, we again can ask why we are afraid of this, and so on, until we come down to the root. In this manner, we can peel away our projections and recognize that our fear really has nothing to do with the particular situation. Although this recognition does not in itself deal with our root-fear, it will often release its projection onto that particular situation, and it will put us in contact with our root-fear, giving us the opportunity to deal with it. Another way of seeing our projection is simply by asking ourself if either our physical, emotional, mental, or spiritual survival is really threatened by the situation. If it is not, then there is no reason for fear. Although we may *desire* for the situation to be a particular way, we don't *need* it to be. Whenever we realize that what we thought to be a need is really a desire, we release our projected fear-trance in the situation.

The situation might be something as simple as going into a panic because we will be late for a dinner engagement. Perhaps we have made the person we are going to meet into a source of Life for ourself, and so the possibility of this person's becoming angry at us or rejecting us activates our fear of annihilation. If we ask ourself why we are in a panic, we will answer that it is to avoid this person's anger and rejection. Yet if we ask why we are afraid of this, we will sense the more fundamental fear of annihilation that we have projected onto the situation. We could have also asked ourself if either our physical, emotional, mental, or spiritual survival was really at stake in the situation; and if we consciously looked at the situation, we would have to answer "no," exposing our projection. Although we desire to be on time, we don't need to be, so we can stop projecting our fear of annihilation onto the situation. Again, this technique will not work when we believe that our survival—which is the survival of whatever we identify as our Self—is really at stake.

(2) We can remember that fear does not help us to survive, that it paralyzes us and cuts off our life-force. As much as we may try to make ourself feel safe by becoming numb, we will never feel safe this way; so fear defeats its own purpose and is superfluous; we can feel safe in letting it go.

(3) We can remember that all fear is an attitude. There is nothing in the universe that is inherently something-to-be-afraid-of unless we decide that it is; a situation simply is what it is. When we say "That

was scary," we are using language to disown our responsibility for our fear. A situation cannot be scary; a situation is simply a situation; the fear comes from our own attitude. The thought of annihilation is scary only because we have decided that it is something to be afraid of. *Since we have never experienced being annihilated and don't know anyone who has, we really know nothing about it.* We may be assuming that it will be horrible because situations that we believe were close-calls we experienced as being painful; but our assumption is just a projection. Actual annihilation, if it were possible, might be quite pleasurable—we have no way of knowing—so we don't have to take the attitude that it is something-to-be-afraid-of. We can drop our attitude and simply experience what is happening, even if we think it is annihilation.

(4) We can remember that all fear is based on fantasy. Since our fear will always be about future annihilation, which couldn't have happened yet, it is really based on fantasies about the future and fantasies about annihilation (which are actually *old* fantasies—old "horror movies"—that we keep re-projecting onto new situations). We generate these fantasies, perceive them as if they are real events happening now, and then resist them with fear. (Hence, fear is based on False Evidences Appearing Real.) So, simply being here now, experiencing what IS, will always eliminate our fear. In addition, since fear is based on fantasy, it can be dealt with *through* fantasy. Simply imagine how you would feel if you were in just this exact situation, but you were capable of experiencing it without fear, feeling safe. Imagine how you would feel. As you imagine this, you begin to feel it. Then you have a choice: you can imagine yourself in this situation feeling afraid or you can imagine yourself in this situation feeling safe. What you imagine you will feel.

(5) Another way of dealing with fear is to simply let it be there without trying to do anything about it and without identifying with it or believing in it. Fear is just there, to be observed and appreciated for the unique trance-experience it is. Fear becomes a form of emotional weather moving through the infinite space of your consciousness (as in Awareness Exercise 10). It is simply another experience.

(6) Perhaps the easiest way to deal with fear is simply to BREATHE. Just receive your breath. Fear paralyzes your body by paralyzing your breath, which is the Life-force enlivening your body. To the extent that you can receive a full breath, you are experiencing your aliveness and your Self, and you have eliminated fear's holding

pattern, which is all that fear is. It may help to acknowledge to yourself that it is *always safe to breathe.*

(7) We can also deal with fear by remembering that it is simply a trance-illusion, which was derived from the trance-illusion of being separate from our Source of Life, which was created by a trance-belief. In other words, we can remember that all fear is a lie because life is safe to experience. With this awareness, we can choose not to believe in our fear; *we can directly challenge our fear by being willing to experience what fear insists isn't safe.* Even if we feel as if we are falling into an abyss, we can allow this experience knowing that it, too, is safe, that our abyss is just a long tunnel leading back to the Light. Every time we allow ourself to experience something that our fear insists isn't safe, we catch fear in its lie, proving it wrong, and our belief in its position weakens.

With the awareness that fear is a trance-illusion, we can also focus our consciousness on remembering Who we really are, and enter into that experience. This will peel away the illusion of our separateness from our Source of Life and thus free us from the fundamental trance that has created our fear. In Oneness there is no fear of annihilation; in Beingness there is no fear of nonbeingness; in Love there is no fear. (Use one of the exercises presented in this book—or any other method you know—that helps you remember Who you are.)

Alternatively, we can remember that we are Spirit having human experiences. *What* we experience is not *who* we are. In spite of the infinite variety of our changing experience, our Self—that which is having the experience—never changes. When we are lost in a fear-trance, we have identified with what we are experiencing and have forgotten that we are the experiencer. Therefore, we can unhook from fear simply by asking ourself: Who is afraid? This puts us in touch with our Self and reminds us that the fear is just another experience that our Self is having.

(8) The last way of dealing with fear is by simply remembering that love is deeper than fear, and so *we can always choose to experience love instead of fear.* Emmanuel (channeled by Pat Rodegast) says:

> *In every circumstance, as your life unfolds minute by minute, recognize: at any given moment you are choosing fear or love; there*

is no other choice to make in Life. All other choices stem from those two basic choices. You choose fear or you choose love. [17]

When we choose love, we experience love and feel safer, making it easier for us to believe in and choose love; when we choose fear, we experience fear and feel less safe, making it easier to believe in and choose fear. So whatever we choose reinforces itself. Yet as deeply as we choose and believe in fear, it is always a trance-illusion; love is always deeper and more powerful because love is Real.

Choosing love is really choosing to *allow* love, for love is what IS; love is what we spontaneously experience when we are not resisting Life with fear. And when we choose to allow love deeply enough to remember Who we are, we will be very amazed, especially at how funny we've been: we have been standing with our backs to the Sun, hypnotizing ourself with the blackness of our own shadows, and feeling afraid because we don't see any Light.

[17]Emmanuel (channeled by Pat Rodegast), "Dealing with Loneliness—A Search of Identity," taped 1986.

AWARENESS EXERCISE 19:
RELEASING FEAR-TRANCES

Sit comfortably and close your eyes. Receive a few deep breaths ...
and let yourself relax. You may want to break this exercise up into
several sittings.

PART I

Remember a recent situation in which you felt you *needed* something
or needed events to unfold in a particular way. Then:

(1) Ask yourself what you were really afraid of in the situation—
what you were resisting—and keep tracing your fear back to its root.

(2) When you come to the root of your fear, ask yourself why you
were (or are) afraid of this and carefully examine any reasons you
come up with to justify your fear.

(3) Ask yourself if you really needed what you thought you
needed in this situation—was your physical survival really at stake?
If it wasn't, ask yourself if you are willing to release your sense of
need from this situation and replace it with *desire.*

(4) If you did not get what you thought you needed in the situation, recognize the fact that you survived. You were not annihilated.

(5) Imagine yourself in a similar situation sometime in the future,
but without projecting your annihilation fears onto it; imagine being
in the situation with desire instead of need.

PART 2

Remember another situation in which you consciously experienced
fear. Then:

(1) As you observe yourself in this situation, notice the point at
which you decided that there was something to be scared about.

(2) Realize that the situation was not scary until you decided that
it was.

(3) Realize, therefore, that your fear was an attitude you attached
to the situation.

(4) Notice that you chose your attitude of fear based on your
fantasy about what you expected could happen. Notice your fantasy.
And notice that at the moment you chose to react with fear, you were
still alive, you were still okay.

(5) Notice that the moment you chose to react with fear, you
projected an old horror movie—one of your favorite annihilation

fantasies—onto the situation to reinforce your position of fear, and notice how well this worked: you watched it and became even more frightened of the situation, even though this old horror movie really had nothing to do with what was actually happening.

(6) Imagine yourself in a similar situation in the future without creating a fantasy about what might happen in the next moment or later on.

PART 3

Remember another situation in which you consciously experienced fear. Remember this as vividly as possible. Then:

(1) Ask yourself whether your fear made you feel more safe or less safe in that situation.

(2) Recognize that any belief or attitude that supports the belief that you are safer with this fear must be a lie.

(3) Ask yourself why you are holding onto this fear.

(4) Since your fear is really a position of self-paralysis that resists experiencing the situation, go into the situation and be willing to experience it. Simply allow yourself to experience what your fear-belief insists is not safe.

PART 4

Again, vividly remember a situation in which you consciously experienced fear. Then:

Go into the experience, and imagine yourself in that situation but choose to believe in love instead of fear.

PART 5

Find a place inside yourself where you hold fear. Then:

Go into the place you hold this fear, and receive your breath there.

PART 6

Notice that while your experience always changes, the Self having these experiences does not. Notice that although your self has had many experiences of fear, none of those experiences have affected or changed this Self at all. (If you think it has, then you are confusing your Self with your personality, which is an identity-trance your Self is experiencing.)

Then imagine some future situation in which you might experience fear. Imagine in that situation asking yourself who is having this
experience. Notice what happens to the fear.

PART 7

Practice utilizing these awareness tools in life situations while you
are experiencing fear. Develop a reflex that automatically challenges
the voice of fear when it insists that you are not safe, that you must
resist life with fear and other attitudes to become safe. You can
refuse to believe in fear. You can believe in being safe.

AWARENESS EXERCISE 20:
TRAUMA MIRRORS

This exercise is not an easy one to do because it confronts deeply held emotional beliefs and attitudes. Confronting real trauma tends to activate deep fear, as well as all the attitudes and beliefs which support that fear. So, you may even find yourself getting angry at my suggestions. If you do, I suggest you stop and recognize that your anger is simply your own protective attitude. Then ask yourself why you feel the need to protect yourself from whatever suggestion triggered your anger.

When you are ready, sit comfortably and close your eyes. Receive a few deep breaths ... and let yourself relax.

Now, remember a traumatic event in your life. Remember the feelings that the event brought up in you and the issues that came up around the event. Then look very deeply within yourself and:

(1) Find where, within your consciousness, you hold the belief that you survived the situation because you emotionally resisted it— either through direct resistance or through the indirect resistance of holding on. (Being numb and passive is also a form of resistance.) Then see the illusion, the lie, within this belief. Recognize that you survived *in spite of* the fact that you constricted your breath and blocked your life-force with your resistance. Recognize, too, that since you actually did experience what happened (in spite of your resistance) and you survived, it would have been safe for you to have *consciously* opened to the experience. Allow the place within you that has always resisted this experience to open to it now; allow yourself to let go of your resistance and receive the experience, knowing that it is safe to do so. Open to it with your body and feelings, remembering that you were, and still are, *safe*. (Take all the time you need for this.)

(2) Find the places in yourself where the emotional attitudes and positions that you have about this situation existed *before* the event. Then allow yourself to acknowledge that the event didn't create these emotions you associate with it but activated them strongly into your consciousness or brought them into a sharper focus.

(3) Imagine that you have completely transformed these emotions. What happens when you imagine this? What do you feel?

(4) Ask yourself how you would perceive this event if you believed it was not an accident but was purposely designed by your

own soul-consciousness to activate these particular feelings and issues, because it had become necessary for your growth. Can you perceive the event in this way now?

(5) Ask yourself what you denied, or lied to yourself about, in connection with this event.

(6) Unless your body was severely injured, allow yourself to recognize that the real trauma was not what happened to you but your resistance to the event and the holding patterns that your resistance created within you.

(7) Allow yourself to recognize that the emotional trauma that you still have about this event exists not because of the past but because you still hold it in your posture of resistance to the event and with your beliefs about it today.

(8) Receive your breath into whatever physical/emotional tension you still hold about this event, and allow yourself to relax your holding; allow yourself to receive Life and Love in this place where you have denied it for so long.

(9) If there was someone involved in this situation who acted hurtfully toward you, allow yourself, from within the core of whatever hurt or fear you may still feel, to forgive this person.

A traumatic experience is completely healed when and only when there is no longer any inner resistance to what happened, no attitudes about it, and the situation is fully received with an open heart, just as it was. (Awareness Exercise 5, "Separating an Experience and Its Story," is an excellent complement to this exercise.)

21

*The Role of Our
Physical "Body"*

Our physical "body," which is an enlivened thought-form of Conscious Energy, plays many roles in the process of our Self-enlightenment. Here are six of them:

(1) It enables us to have the trance-experience of physical reality (which includes the experience of ourself as physical beings). This alone is a wonderful gift, yet becoming physical also gives us a stage for enacting and working out the areas within our Self that need enlightening.

(2) Because in physical reality our bodies seem to be separate from everything else, identifying with a body intensifies our experience of separateness, and thus intensifies all the attitudes and issues that grow out of our experience of separateness. This brings these issues into a sharper focus, helping us to become aware of them and to explore them.

(3) Because bodies are created with incredible variety, as well as with a rich assortment of possible disorders (genetic and otherwise), we are able to have exactly the kind of body-experience we need for our spiritual growth. A crippled body may be a painful experience, yet it presents a particular kind of opportunity for growth.

(Physical accidents that traumatize the body can have many purposes. Some of the most common are: to bring to the surface a deep physical/emotional holding pattern; to create a physical re-presentation of a holding pattern that was visible but was being ignored; to break up—to smash—an old pattern, which will usually create a dramatic change in the person's experience of life; or to force the person to deal with new or old issues that the physical trauma will make unavoidable.)

(4) Through the gift of sexuality, our body gives us a powerful vehicle for exploring intimacy, emotion, love, relationship, sexual violence, the depths and subtleties of our human physicality, and all the other issues and experiences that arise around our sexuality.

(5) Our body, through its ability to give us the experience of pleasure, both through sensation and the experience of physical creativity, can help us to remember that we are not our emotional attitudes but the infinite joy and creativity that is at the core of Life. (And therefore, keeping our body in good health can help our spiritual growth.)

(6) Because our emotional holding patterns imprint themselves as postures and breath restrictions in the body, the body acts as a special kind of stage and mirror, enabling us to explore, become aware of, and make *contact* with these emotional patterns through physical tension and disorder. And this gives us an opportunity to assume responsibility for the stuck patterns that we have avoided dealing with. For instance, if a woman develops ulcers at work, her body, by accepting the imprint of the emotional distress, acts both as a stage on which she is exploring her distress and as a mirror that enables her to see it; and this also gives her the opportunity to acknowledge responsibility for the emotional patterns that are causing her ulcers.[18]

Because all of our life-situations are designed for our growth and self-exploration, all chronic dis-ease will re-present some issue, and that issue will have a corresponding emotional pattern that expresses itself in the body as an emotionally charged "dis-ease posture." (This includes hereditary disease.) A clear example of this was a man I met who had cancer in his back. The emotional attitude that creates cancer is resentment, generated by grief, hurt, and self-pity, and this man was obviously stuck in that place. When questioned, the reason he gave for his feelings was that his best friend had slept with his wife; and the phrase he used repeatedly to describe his experience was, "I felt like he stabbed me in the back." So, being stabbed in the back and feeling resentment, hurt, loss, and self-pity was his inner posture, and his disease manifested as cancer in his back. His body,

---

[18]A tiny book by Louise L. Hay, called *Heal Your Body,* lists many physical diseases and symptoms, and the most common emotional positions that cause them.

by manifesting this cancer, gave him the opportunity to make contact with his emotional posture and transform it.

Many forms of therapy utilize direct work with the body to help in making contact with emotional patterns.

(7) Through its womb experience, the body also provides us with a way to bring particular attitudes within our emotional point of view into the foreground of our experience in this life, so we can more easily explore them. It does this by accepting emotional "imprints" from the mother, and sometimes to a small extent from the father, while it is in the womb. For instance, if the soul wants to focus on an area of its consciousness that is still caught in human anger-trances, it may choose a mother who holds a lot of anger. Then in the womb, the new body will be imprinted with this anger, and the anger will then become a strong element in the new human being's emotional point of view. (These imprints are different from "genetic" patterns, which represent the body's original thought-structure.)

It is important to recognize, though, that womb imprints are designed to amplify and help focus upon attitudes that *already exist* within the incarnating being; they are not the original cause of these attitudes. Parents are always carefully chosen so they correspond to our own learning needs. Yet even if we could "inherit" new attitudes, the problem would still be our own entrancement with them (not where they came from), which we are always responsible for, creating it out of the darkness of our own illusions.

COMMON MISCONCEPTIONS

One common misconception about the body is that it is healthier to "let our emotions out" than to hold them in. Yet letting our self-limiting emotions out is not the same thing as letting them go, or even bringing awareness to them. For instance, a man can spend twenty years crying about his wife's death or acting angry because his life didn't work out the way he wanted it to; yet all this emotional "letting out" never lets anything go. And it never changes his aware-ness or experience. The holding pattern that is destructive to the body still exists. So neither holding our emotional attitudes in nor letting them out is beneficial to our body; to help our body, to enable it to become more alive, we need to become more aware of our emotional holding patterns and let them go.

Another common misconception is that since all body disorders mirror learning-issues, working out those issues will heal the body. Yet this is not necessarily so. For instance, a man may totally transform himself through the experience of cancer or AIDS and still die of the disease. In fact, for someone who is terrified of dying of cancer, the spiritual lesson may simply be learning to have that experience without fear. *Ultimately, the only disease that we need to heal is our experience of fear and separateness.*

A second example is a man who is born with one arm. Although he will be exploring a variety of issues and emotional attitudes, enlightening those issues will not heal his physical body; the man will still have only one arm. He cannot assume any responsibility for changing this "permanent" condition. Yet he cannot blame any of his emotional attitudes on his condition; he is still responsible for these. (I do believe that at some future time, when scientific advances enable an arm to be regenerated out of cellular DNA, people will have spontaneous healings of these kinds of conditions, for they will then believe that limb regeneration is possible, and they will manifest trance-realities that reflect the new belief.)

This misconception about body-healing sometimes applies to simpler body disorders as well. This is because, when our emotional postures stay imprinted in our body for a long period of time, they literally get "glued" into our body tissue. As a result, even when we emotionally transform a chronic issue, the old pattern of it in our body can give us a sense of still being emotionally stuck in it. For this reason, I recommend working directly with opening the body to create space in it for old holding patterns to release. Deep massage, Rolfing®, Jin Shin Jyutsu®, yoga, cranial-sacral therapy, Vortex-Healing®, FasciaUnwinding®, and meditations that open the breath are some popular methods for doing this.

A third misconception is that since we are not really our bodies, we don't really need to pay attention to our bodies to evolve spiritually. Yet breaking our identification with our body is not the same as *resisting* our experience of it. (And an action that is resistance for one person may not be resistance for another; for instance, a man who chooses to be celibate may or may not be denying his sexuality.)

Sometimes our resistance can be very subtle. For instance, people who are consciously working on their spiritual growth often distance themselves from their bodies in their attempt to let go of or "get above" the emotional issues that are manifesting there. When they do this they often feel better, leading them to believe they have trans-formed what was stuck; yet they feel better because their conflicts have been forced into the background of their consciousness and because now it is easier for them to remember their Self. Although pushing away our body and our drama to make better contact with our Self can be very valuable at times—and even necessary when we have gotten lost in our emotional stuff—we still need to transform what we pushed away. And although we may feel "lighter" and more loving in this position of distance-from-our-stuff, this position prevents us from making contact with and setting free those areas of our consciousness that we have pushed away. In addition, this position will also manifest as distance from other people, and we will be less able to make emotional contact with them. So, if we need to push away our body and our stuff to recenter ourself within our Self, we must intend to bring our restored awareness of Self back into the areas of our consciousness that are still not free.

Our physical "body" is both our vehicle for human experience and one of our most powerful tools for Self-enlightenment while we are here. And no matter how well or poorly we treat it, no matter whether we acknowledge responsibility for our experience with it or not, it will still serve to enlighten us.

22

Character-Trances

THE NATURE OF CHARACTER-TRANCES

We have seen that every attitude-trance is dependent upon an identity-trance, upon our believing that who we are is a particular "character" who holds that attitude. For instance, when we are being arrogant, we are identified with being an arrogant character. In this chapter we will see that our inner characters are not independent of each other; they are tied together in an *inner drama*. Yet before exploring this drama, we must examine the characters themselves.

Most of our characters have very familiar faces. Many of them have the expression, as well as the attitude and posture, of one of our parents. These are "parental character-trances" (or for abbreviation, "parental-characters" or "parental-trances"), and we acquired them by copying, identifying with, and/or resisting our parents' characters (many of which were our parents' parents' characters, and so on, back through the generations). If we focus on our experience when we are in one of these trances, we may feel as if we have actually turned into our parent. For instance, if a boy's father acted like a particular angry character whenever he felt insulted, and if the boy, for reasons that will be outlined shortly, copied his father's attitude, then whenever the boy is insulted he will tend to act and feel as if he is his father, after his father has been insulted. And the boy may creatively expand the use of that angry character to other kinds of situations. If we used people other than our parents as the pattern for our character-trances, these will function exactly like parental-characters, so I will refer to these as parental-characters as well.

Parental character-trances are at the root of all moral systems, of Freud's "superego," and of what we generally consider to be "conscience" (as opposed to compassion). Wherever internalized authority and precept replace love and true compassion, we have a parental character-trance.

In addition to our parental character-trances, we have "child character-trances" (or simply "child-characters" or "child-trances"). Our child-characters were not derived from anyone else; they are rooted in the emotional point of view we brought with us into this entrancement to experience and transform. Their roots precede our birth and conception. (In the womb, though, if the mother has a similar enough attitude, the child-character will often identify with it so deeply that the mother's emotional experience becomes incorporated into the child-character's psychic structure. This is the deepest kind of womb-imprint. All other womb-imprints form the beginnings of parental-characters, some of which become major inner characters in our future life-drama.)

When we are in a child-trance, we are identified with being the child we were, at some particular age, holding a particular attitude. Within this trance, we believe that child-character is who we are. Yet although we identify very deeply with these trances, the identity we experience in them can never be who we truly are, both because of the attitude and because we are no longer a child; they are always trances.

As we will see shortly, our child-characters are really the key to our inner drama, for they hold our oldest and deepest fears and needs. An example of a child-character is a man who begins to act needy, looking and acting as if he were three years old when his wife tells him that she is going to have to be out of town for a week on business. In this trance, he is experiencing himself as one of the child-characters he was stuck in as a child, and the part of his consciousness that is generating this trance identifies with being that child-character and *believes* that this is who he is. If this man's neediness had actually been patterned after a parent, regardless of the age at which he patterned it, his expression and posture would be different—it would have the feeling-tone of a parent—and an astute observer would be able to see (whether or not he had met the parent) that it was a parental-trance.

Child-characters can be more difficult for us to recognize within ourself than parental-characters because we identify much more deeply with them. These child-characters always *feel* like ourself, yet they always hold attitudes, and so they never represent the open, spontaneous, child-like consciousness within us, which is our true Self manifest in human form, sometimes referred to as our "Original Child" or "Free Child." Our Original Child consciousness is what is en-tranced *within* our characters, which act like cages for its spirit; our path is to see through the illusion of these cages and fly free.

Sometimes the character in a child-trance will look (or feel) older than a child. Yet regardless of the age of the character, if it wasn't derived from a parent (or someone else) then it must still be a child-character.

Although we usually recognize our characters (both child and parental) because of the emotional attitudes they are expressing, some of our characters can be very "reasonable." Yet when a character is being reasonable, its intent is usually to manipulate reason to support its own stuck position. For instance, a woman with a character that feels sorry for itself when left alone may use reasonable arguments to convince her husband to stay home with her. Although the woman will seem reasonable, she is simply allowing her inner character to use reason to support its emotional position.

Similarly, some characters will seem to be kind or to express love instead of emotional attitudes. Yet if the source of the behavior is a character, then the love is not completely genuine; it is at least partially a *posture* of love, which will always have some hidden, manipulative purpose. Genuine love has no purpose; it IS.

Because parental character-trances can be copied from anyone and then again passed on again to the next generation, and because the attitudes they hold are issues that most of us are dealing with, many of them are common enough that they have become part of our group-trance. Some characters will predominate in certain cultures, and some will be more universal. Myths are actually symbolic descriptions of these universal inner characters. The myths delineate common relationships formed between the characters, and the better myths point to the way of their transformation, which was their original purpose.

Because myths reflect our inner characters, sometimes our characters may seem to wear the expression of some particular mythic persona. In addition, some of our characters may seem to be patterned after animals, as in "he gets angry like a bear." It is likely that when we lived closer to nature, we copied not just our parents and other people but animals as well, and these character postures are still being passed on through the generations. It is also possible that a few of these—such as crab or reptilian characters—are lingering vestiges from our prehistoric genetic history and memory.

As much as we may dislike our characters, they are ultimately *tools* created out of Love for our own unfoldment; we use them to explore certain areas of our inner darkness that are limiting our experience of Light.

THE EVOLUTION OF CHARACTER-TRANCES

All of our character-trances begin with our trance of separateness. As soon as we experience ourself as separate, our sense of being Self shifts to a sense of being a particular self; and as we generate various attitudes out of our loss of Oneness, we experience ourself as being a scared self, an angry self, and so on. When we en-trance with a particular human body, we identify with it, and we express these attitude-selves through it; our new human body then takes on the expression and posture of these attitudes. These are our child character-trances. They are our deepest, most emotionally-charged characters, both because they are direct expressions of the emotional point of view we took with us into this entrancement, and because they formed around our deepest fears of separation and annihilation.

Although parents do not cause the attitudes these characters hold, these characters will usually blame the parents for their own experience; and since our parents are usually far from perfect, it is never very difficult to find a parental behavior or character to blame. This is also facilitated by the fact that we chose our parents because of the way their attitudes and behaviors mirrored our own learning needs.

Because all the attitudes we take with us into this entrancement are ultimately futile attempts to make ourself safe, wherever we are stuck in one, wherever we are caught in experiencing ourself as a child-character, we will always try to use whatever is happening to us to support our emotional position. Soon after birth, this leads to the creation of our parental-characters.

In our early infancy, we both *differentiate* ourself as being separate from others and mistakenly *identify* ourself with others. This identification is not purposeful; it is caused by the fact that our personal boundaries are not well-defined at that age. Yet when we identify with those around us, we believe that these other personalities are our self. (This is how we received womb-imprints.) This process has the advantage of enabling us to directly absorb survival behaviors, including language, yet as we will see, it also enables us to create what I will call "undifferentiated" parental-characters.

As we become more able to differentiate ourself as a separate being, we let go of most of the identifications we made in our less differentiated state. Yet wherever we resist becoming more differentiated and separated, we attempt to maintain that oneness by not letting go of our identification with our parents. We incorporate their personalities into our sense of self and "hide ourself" within them; we thus stay merged with our parents, experiencing them *as our self* and experiencing their emotions as our own. These incorporated parental personalities then become, as we learn to express them, our *undifferentiated parental-characters.*

Hidden within these undifferentiated characters we use their attitudes to support our own emotional positions and to camouflage the fact that we are stuck. In general, the key to our undifferentiated parental-characters will be our scared and needy child-characters, for this is where we resist becoming separate. (Our resistance to being separate can also lead us, in intimate relationships, to try to become undifferentiated with our partner, leading to the creation of a new undifferentiated character, which will function just like our parental ones.) We can have undifferentiated parental-characters based on personality aspects of either our mother or our father, but those based on the mother are almost always first formed in the womb.

(The state of being undifferentiated from a parent is, of course, very different from true Oneness with that parent, for undifferentiation is always maintained by a scared, needy child-character who experiences itself as separate but doesn't want to be; the parent has simply been incorporated into its identity of separateness. We must be willing to become entirely separate from our parents—we must become fully *born*—to be able to fully enter into Life and the true state of Oneness.)

As we grow through infancy, the areas of our consciousness that have differentiated are learning many skills to help the new, differentiated self function in its world. And one of the things that every child quickly learns how to do is to copy its parents' behaviors and points of view. This is important to learn, for it enables us to copy behaviors that are necessary for socialization as well as for survival, and it enables us to see the world through our parents' eyes, which gives us both a new understanding of our world and a way to comprehend our parents. Yet when we copy our parents, along with what we need to learn, we also copy their "negative" attitudes and behaviors. At first we internally copy everything, including both their own child and parental-characters, yet the only ones we end up holding onto are those corresponding to pre-existing positions held by our child-characters. Over time, we become en-tranced with what we have copied, and we finally end up identified with (and hidden within) the copied character, at which point we end up believing that the character is ourself, just as with the undifferentiated parental-characters. Yet because we are now identifying with something we once felt separate from, the en-trancement or identification is not as deep as with undifferentiated parental-characters, and it is easier for us to recognize that these characters are not our self. But this does not make releasing these characters any easier; to release them we usually have to release the foundational child-character that is hiding within them, using them to support and express that child-character's positions. And child-characters are very deeply rooted.

When we copy our parents, we can copy their attitudes toward the world in general, toward particular issues (like money, sex, and so on), toward particular people or situations, or toward ourself. *And we will always copy what we strongly resist*—what we fear—in our parents, because this will always support our position of fear, and sometimes other positions as well. In general, we have at least ten incentives for choosing to copy and hold onto a parental-character:

(1) We perceive its attitude-posture as containing information we need for relating to and manipulating our new world (including our parents);

(2) The parental-character supports, directly or indirectly (this distinction was described in Chapter 3), a position held by one of our child-characters;

(3) We want to get the same responses that this parental-character gets, either from the other parent or other people;

(4) Experiencing our parents' characters internally helps us to feel that our parents are with us and that we are connected to them (and also, therefore, that we are not alone);

(5) Internal parental-characters can provide us with a sense of approval for our behavior and feelings, or they can be copied to provide us with disapproval, whichever better supports our position;

(6) We are afraid that if we don't support our parents' position by copying their attitudes, or if we don't use their attitudes as an inter-

nalized directive to control our own behavior, they will reject or condemn us;

(7) We already have a similar character and attitude, yet by copying the way our parent presents it, we can pretend that our attitude is really theirs and avoid responsibility for it;

(8) We love our parents and want to please them or be like them;

(9) We believe we need this character in order to "fit in" with our family, usually to provide what is expected of us;

(10) By copying our parents, we get on their "wavelength," and we believe this will make it easier for us to relate to them.

One interesting side-effect of copying a character is that we always get more than we bargained for. This occurs because, in addition to its most visible attitude, the character always harbors at least one supporting or foundational attitude, and when we copy a character we acquire its whole pattern. For instance, because every character is ultimately based on fear, every character contains an inner abyss; so whenever we copy a character, regardless of what we intend to use it for, we acquire the character's abyss as well (which, of course, has power only because it mirrors our own abyss).

As children, we are aware of both the characters our parents actually express as well as the ones they have suppressed yet act out in their thoughts, and so we can copy any of them to suit our purposes.[19] Sometimes we will even copy two that are completely contradictory. For instance, if a father expresses a self-righteous character when his little girl tells lies and yet shows her, with a deceitful character of his own, that it is both useful and acceptable, then she may copy both attitudes and use whichever one is most useful at any given time. This kind of contradiction may also occur if the characters and attitudes of the two parents conflict.

Parents, of course, generally become upset when their children act out what they themselves have suppressed or denied, and so they try to suppress these behaviors in their children, with varying success. Yet even when characters are suppressed, they have not disappeared, and they still actively affect the child's emotional point of view and the personal reality he creates with it.

---

[19]When a parental-character seems to jump a generation, resembling a grandparent rather than a parent, then, unless that grandparent had a lot of interaction with the grandchild, the character was probably copied from the parent, even though the parent was not actively expressing it.

CHARACTER DYNAMICS

Our inner characters will interact with other people's characters. Sometimes they will be drawn to these characters, sometimes they will resist and react to them, and sometimes they will interact neutrally. In addition, our characters will react to each other, within our own psyche, creating inner dramas. For instance, if a girl copies a judgmental parental-character from her mother, then regardless of the reason why she copied it, whenever she does something that this character would disapprove of, the character will become activated in her own psyche and the little girl will probably react to its disapproval by feeling rejected or guilty—by manifesting a rejected or guilty child-character. This will usually, in turn, activate an angry parental-character—most people have one—that will express its anger at the judgmental character that is making the girl feel guilty (regardless of which parent the angry character was copied from).

The internal dramas we create with our characters usually reflect certain aspects of the outer drama that existed in our early family. In the last example, the little girl would have observed these character dynamics either entirely within her mother, between her mother and father, or both. (For most people, once these kinds of dramas are established, they continue for life.)

Character dynamics clearly have the potential for great complexity. Hence, reading about them may be a little confusing at first. Yet people who are working on transforming their emotional issues are likely, at some point, to encounter these kinds of inner situations, and at those times the kind of model presented here will prevent them from getting lost in their drama. So, just to illustrate how entangled these dynamics can get, here is a more complex example: a little boy learns that he can get his mother to stop being angry at him by whining. Whining then becomes a means for controlling his projected source of Life, his mother; it becomes an emotional position that he believes makes him more safe. Even though his father gets angry at him when he whines, he is too attached to his position to give it up; and his mother will placate the father when this happens, supporting her son's position, even though the father then gets angry at her, too. More than likely, the child will blame his whininess on his mother's and father's anger, and he will copy their angry characters to support his position in being whiny (among other reasons). He will also copy his mother's placating character, for this is his defense against the angry father-character. Now he has created three inner dramas. One involves just the whiny child and angry mother. In the second, he uses the angry father-character to get angry at and to control the angry mother. And the third involves the whiny child-character, the angry father, and the placating mother. When this drama is activated, all the characters in it will become activated, regardless of which one is expressed. For instance, if someone is angry at him, then his child-character will whine (both toward this person and toward the internal angry father-character) and try to hide behind the placating mother-character, his mother-character will placate, and his father-character will become angry at the child-character (and possibly the other angry person). This will happen throughout his life if he doesn't transform this inner situation. And whenever this pattern is activated, his body will reflect the holding patterns of all three characters and their interaction. A sufficiently astute observer will see all this in his posture—the characters as well as the dynamic relationships between them—yet the boy-now-adult may only be aware of the particular character that he is identifying with at that moment.

As complicated as this situation seems, it only describes his *inner* drama. While this is going on, his inner characters will be drawn to create outer dramas with other people, especially those who have matching characters and dramas. For instance, as an adult, his whiny inner child will be drawn to women with angry characters, for these characters will support the whiny child's position, and they will form the kind of emotional environment the whiny child is comfortable in. In fact, for these reasons, the whiny child will actually try to trigger other people's anger.

The varieties of forms that our character dynamics can take are as diverse as the human psyche, and so it is too broad and complex a subject to detail here.[20] Yet our character dynamics can be greatly simplified if we recognize that *the key to our whole dramatic show is our scared and needy child-characters, because they hold our deepest fears and needs, which are the basis of all our other emotional positions.* And therefore, when our scared and needy child-character

---

[20]Many of our character dynamics are well-described in books by Dr. Eric Berne about Transactional Analysis, although his emphasis and context are rather different from what is presented here.

issues are dealt with, our parental-characters as well as other child-characters are no longer needed, and they fall away.

One interesting irony of character dynamics is that whenever we resist and react to a character in someone else, we reinforce its trance-reality and thereby strengthen the person's identification with it. In addition, our reaction to this character will make us look for it when interacting with this person, creating even more focus on it, and manifesting our dynamic with it even more strongly and more frequently into our relationship with this person.

In general, the advantage of understanding our character dynamics is that we can gain insight into ourself and learn to recognize what our real issues are, enabling us to focus on these instead of getting lost in all our secondary and compensatory issues that generate the maze of our inner drama. The disadvantages of focusing on our character dynamics are that (1) we can become so focused on our characters that we get lost in their drama anyway and forget the *I AM* that we are, independent of our characters, and (2) we can forget that the only attitude we ever really have to deal with is our fear, that the only key that will unlock all our resistances to life is the awareness that life is safe to experience because we are one with the Source of our Beingness.

It should also be pointed out that, when we are children and as we grow up, we do relate to our parents' beingness, not just to their characters. And what we learn from our parents that is a pure expression of love, we assimilate, and it enters into the consciousness of ourself as Self (just as food, when digested, becomes our body). Parental-characters, on the other hand, are always extraneous to ourself; since they are not pure expressions of love, they are unassimilable; they cannot become Self.

HOW WE HOLD CHARACTERS IN THE BODY

Because we are identified with our human body, our emotional positions become physical postures and positions; conversely, every physical holding pattern (that has not been caused by physical injury) will correspond to an emotional posture, an inner character.

Every character will have its home on one side of the body or the other. (Our "Free Child," though, inhabits our whole body, for it is not a character.) In general, the female aspects of the inner child will show up as characters held in, and expressed from, the left side of the body, while the male aspects will show up on the right. Paralleling this, female parental-characters will be found in left side of the body, while male parental-characters will be found on the right. I say, "in general," because while this is true on the "physical" level, there is an energetic level of the body where this reverses, putting the male energy on the left and the female on the right. But this energetic level will not often be encountered.

All children have both male and female parental-characters, and male and female aspected child-characters. Because the mother-characters will be held on the left side of the body, most of our womb-imprints will be found there, as well as the deepest needy/codependent part of the inner child that is trying to stay merged with the mother, that is afraid of separation. This child-character aligns itself with the female energy because it is trying to be like the mother in order to more deeply merge back into her. There may also be needy child-characters that are trying to stay merged with the father, and these will show up on the right side of the body.

Because our inner characters are involved in an inner drama, this drama will be expressed in the body as well. For instance, a character on one side of the body will often hold a belief structure or attitude that supports a character-position on the other side of the body. In general, every character will be emotionally, physically and energetically tied to at least one other character in the body. In the example of the whiny child, the whiny child-character will probably be found on the left side of the body, with the placating mother-character, and the angry father-character will be found on the right. (Hiding within that angry father-character will also be found an angry child-character who uses the father-character to express its own position of anger toward the mother.) When one of these characters becomes activated in the body, they all become activated, and the body will express the postures of all three simultaneously. Conversely, when one of these characters begins to change or let go, all the characters are activated and confronted. This is why a physical symptom on one side of the body may be tied to a whole complex of characters involving both sides of the body.

Our body plays an important role, not just in expressing our characters, but in reinforcing our identification with them. This is because of the holding patterns we develop when we identify with a character (child or parental) for a period of time. Once this happens, our identification with our body will reinforce our identification with these holding patterns and with the emotional attitudes they express. (As we saw in the last chapter, after we release a character-trance, we often still need to work directly on our body to free it from the emotional posture of that character; otherwise, our identification with our body will tend to make our entrancement with that character linger.)

FREEING OURSELF FROM CHARACTER-TRANCES

Freeing ourself from character-trances is similar to—and sometimes even the same as—the process of freeing ourself from attitude-trances, except we are usually more focused on the character that is holding the attitude than the attitude itself.

As with other trances, the part of our consciousness that is stuck in the character-trance must become free of its trance (must become "resurrected") for the trance to let go. When that happens, the en-tranced part of our consciousness remembers Who it is and returns to Love-Consciousness, which is our Self. As Self, we still manifest personality, yet our personality is no longer trapped within the rigid limitation of a character structure. *Personality is a unique expression within Love;* it is not a holding pattern or character-trance.

Often, though, only part of our en-tranced consciousness will wake up and remember that it is Love. When this happens, the awakened part of our consciousness returns to Self, and the trance that part of us is still caught in becomes freer, less rigid. For instance, the consciousness within a "poor me" child-character may awaken enough to let go of the poor-me attitude, yet not enough to let go of its identification with being a child. The character may thus evolve into an "I'm okay" child-character, which isn't as limiting, but is still a character. We can even have happy characters, but the happiness they manifest will not be entirely free or genuine; there will be some holding in it, some resistance to Love or to experiencing life, for a character always holds some attitude, some posture of resistance. (The experience of expressing ourself through a body is not in itself a character-trance; it's our identification with postures of emotional resistance that create character-trances.)

To transform our character-trances, we can use any method that has already been described for releasing an emotional attitude or freeing ourself from a trance, because without the attitude or trance there is no character. In addition, we can utilize the fact that, when we are in one of these trances, we are believing that who we are is some character with an attitude, and so if we can contact the en-tranced part of ourself with a sufficiently deep awareness of Self, it will remember (through the contact) Who it is and break free of its trance. Of course, the more deeply we are identified with a character or unconsciously believe we need it, the deeper our awareness must go to contact our en-tranced Self and set it free.

Our child character-trances, as we have seen, are usually the most difficult to recognize; because we are so identified with them, we do not realize they are characters. But what is most difficult for us to recognize is also the key to our emotional drama. Because the only thing that prevents us from enlightening our experience of being human is our fear, and because our deepest fears of separation and annihilation are locked within the structure of our scared and needy child-characters, they are our door to freedom, to our Original Child Consciousness. Our scared inner child must become a Free Child, and then it will no longer be a child at all; it will simply be Self experiencing Itself as human. Yet to transform our scared inner child we must bring into that trance a very deep awareness of Spirit and Self, for nothing else but this experience of connection and safety will release the illusion of fear and separateness which maintains our scared inner child.

Whenever we release a child-character, whatever differentiated parental-characters it has generated to support its position will let go. If we try to release a differentiated character directly, whatever reason(s) we had for copying it will manifest itself as a resistance to letting go of it, which will show up in one or more of our other characters, one of which will always be a child-character. This child-character will usually have to be addressed first. (When a parental-character resists the letting go of a child-character, it is really the child-character using the parental-character to maintain its position.)

However, we can release a differentiated parental-character direct-ly in situations where, because of new circumstances, the parental-character is now generating more insecurity than security for the child-character that is maintaining it. An example of this is a woman who came to see me because she had been having anxiety attacks for a number of years, ever since her father died. I was able to show her that it was actually an aspect of her mother's consciousness that she had copied as a child that was having those reactions to her father's death, that they weren't really her own emotions. All she had to do was stop pretending to be that aspect of her mother, and she did, clearing up her anxiety attacks.

With an *un*differentiated parental-character, we can either try to get the child within it to be willing to separate—to differentiate—from its parent, or we can deal directly with that child-character and simply assume that it has the same attitude as the undifferentiated parental-character.

Because of the way our characters function in our personal drama and the way they interact with each other, it usually helps to understand a character's role in our drama and its dynamics with other characters. We can ask questions such as: What is the character holding, resisting, or doing? What is the purpose of this character; what is it used for? Is there another character holding it, in some other way locked into it, or using it for its own purposes? How would I experience myself without this character? (This will sometimes reveal hidden resistances and purposes.) If there is a dynamic between two or more characters, we can use our understanding of it to work on the characters involved. For instance, if we have a dependent child-character that is holding onto a parental-character for security, we can try to nurture that child-character so it will have the courage to stand on its own two feet. That would "evolve" our child-character into a freer character and also weaken our entrancement with the parental-character it had been attached to.

Many therapists today use this process of evolving our child-characters. It is often referred to as "nurturing the inner child," which is really a way of opening up to our Self by nurturing and counseling the child-characters that our Self has become lost (en-tranced) within. When we do this, we are actually using our own nurturing, spiritual consciousness as a parent, re-parenting our stuck inner child so it can become free of its character structures and so our Free Child can emerge. Yet when we nurture our inner child, we must remember that (1) our true goal is not to create a nurtured inner child (who is still a character), but to free the consciousness within that child from its character structures, (2) although we are the nurturers of that stuck inner child, its consciousness and feelings are our own, and (3) nurturance alone is not usually sufficient to free the consciousness within the inner child from its character-trance.

When a character-trance persists in spite of our awareness of the trance and our attempts to let it go, it is either because the reflex habit of becoming that character is still strong (a problem that was described in Chapter 19, in relation to our attitudes), or because we have not gotten down to the place within ourself that is identified with it, or attached to it and holding it. And when we have more than one reason for being attached to a character, then often each one needs to be dealt with for the trance to let go.

Because of how deeply we identify with our character-trances, sometimes our awareness must go very deep to fully release them. Often, this depth of awareness takes time to develop. And we usually have to move back and forth between two different phases of deepening our awareness: (1) ignoring the drama entirely and connecting deeper to our Self, to Love, or to our free awareness (as in Awareness Exercise 10, "Disidentifying with the Weather"), and (2) using the depth of awareness and safety gained in the first phase to release (or partially release) our character-trances. Because releasing a trance requires that we bring a deeper awareness into it than that which is maintaining it, if we struggle with our trances without deepening our awareness, we will usually just get lost in our drama. Sometimes, though, one needs to develop some understanding of the drama first just to quiet the mind so the awareness can go deeper.

Because all of our characters develop out of fear and resistance to life, at every level of getting free of their trances the lesson we must learn is the same: whatever we are afraid of is really safe for us to experience, because we are not characters—we are Free Spirit, unfolding our Self through human form.

AWARENESS EXERCISE 21:
THE BODY

Sit comfortably and close your eyes. Receive a few deep breaths ... and let yourself relax.

PART I

Become aware of your breathing. Experience how your body feels as you relax and breathe. For a couple of minutes, just feel your body.

Then ask yourself: if you were writing a novel, what purpose would you have in mind if you were to give one of your fictional characters the body you have? What kind of fictional character(s) could you easily create with such a body? What kind of spiritual lessons would such a body be a good vehicle for?

If there are any problems with your body, go into the area of the problem—inhabit it—and breathe into it. (If there are no problem areas, skip to Part 2.) Bring your awareness to the inside of that area and receive your breath there. Allow yourself to experience whatever is there as you relax and open to it with your breath. (If you have trouble doing this, it is probably because you are avoiding/resisting experiencing what is there. Acknowledge this resistance to yourself—name it if you can—and then allow yourself to go past it.) You may find that as you open to this area, your body will want to twist in certain ways; if it does, then allow it to, even if this puts you in some strange, convoluted position (which will be the emotional posture of the problem). Then ask yourself:

(1) What is the problem area holding? What kind of emotional attitudes or characters are locked inside of it? What is the emotional posture of the problem area or of the area around it?

(2) What kinds of emotional attitudes have arisen in your life around this problem?

(3) In addition to being useful for exploring the emotional attitudes of (1) and (2), what other kind of learning could this problem be good for?

(4) If you had never had this problem before and one night you dreamed you had this problem, how would you interpret the dream? What would the problem in the dream signify?

(5) How did your body feel before this problem developed (if you weren't born with it)? As you allow yourself to remember—with

both your mind and body—you may become more aware of what the source of the problem is.

(6) What would you need to learn or let go of to heal this problem (if it is not a "permanent" condition)?

(7) Is the part of you that is generating this problem willing to release the condition? (Be careful here, for our *willingness* to release something is not at all related to our *wanting* to release it.)

PART 2

Consider whatever complaints you have ever had about how the government is run and about taxes. Then imagine that you are a king or queen, and that the kingdom you rule is your body. What kind of ruler are you? Do you heavily tax your kingdom? Do you treat it as a slave? Work it to its limit? Ignore it, even when your kingdom is in pain? Or, are you a responsible and benevolent ruler? Do you take the time to enjoy your kingdom?

PART 3

Recognize that your body has a genetic lineage. Be aware of it as the manifestation of the combined genetic pool of your parents' bodies, which were manifestations of their own parents' bodies, and so on. Keep tracing your lineage back, and as you do, feel within your body the presence of all these ancestors—not simply in spirit but in the physical roots of your body, as part of your body's structure. Follow your lineage back through prehistoric man, through reptilian forms, through fish, through more primitive life forms, through single-celled organisms, through basic proteins, through atoms, through subatomic particles, until you come to your very first physical ancestor: the Conscious Energy that is God. Recognize the presence of your first ancestor in every molecule and cell of your body.

AWARENESS EXERCISE 22:
OUR INNER CHARACTERS

Sit comfortably and close your eyes. Receive a few deep breaths ... and let yourself relax.

Think of an attitude other than fear that you often get stuck in. Then:

(1) Experience how you hold this attitude in your body. Notice where you tighten and twist yourself and where the emotional charge seems to be the greatest. Does the attitude seem to originate primarily from one side of your body?

(2) Be aware of the expression on your face when you are experiencing this attitude.

(3) Align yourself with this holding pattern and expression. What kind of character are you being? As this character, who do you think you are? Does the character remind you of one of your parents' characters or of a place you were stuck in as a child?

(4) What kind of beliefs does this character hold?

(5) Align yourself with this character and feel its emotional energy in your body. Do other areas of your consciousness get activated or become uncomfortable when this character is being manifested? Are there places within yourself where you can feel you have attitudes *about* this character? Are there other areas that would react if you were to suddenly let go of this character? If you discover other areas that in some way are interacting with this character, see if these other areas are really other characters, and if they are, ask yourself: What kind of characters are these? How do they relate to the first character?

(6) What is the purpose of this (first) character? What do you or your other characters use it for? What could you do to fulfill this purpose if you didn't have this character?

(7) Remember a time when you were a child and your mother was yelling at you or criticizing you. Remember how your body felt. What kind of character did you become? Can you think of times as an adult that you become this character? Repeat this with your father.

(8) Remember a time when you were a child and your parents were having a loud argument or fight. What is their basic posture toward each other? What is your posture toward the two of them as you experience them fighting? Can you find these postures in your body today?

(9) Think of a wild animal. Stop at the first one that comes into your mind. What is the posture of this animal when it is being aggressive? When it is being defensive? Can you find either of these postures as a chronic holding pattern in your body? What do you experience if you imagine yourself as being this animal?

(10) Pick one of the child-characters you have discovered in this exercise and become aware of the fact that whenever you are identified with being this character you are suffering, because you are lost in an illusion that limits your experience of your Self and separates you from the rest of life.

(11) With the character you picked for (10), find and make contact with the part of your Self that is trapped within it. If you can do this, at the moment of contact the en-tranced part of yourself should become free of its trance.

(12) Repeat steps (10) and (11) with a needy or scared child-character, if you didn't use this character in (10).

(13) Choose a differentiated parental-character. Imagine that this character is a puppet that only seems to be alive when you put your hand inside it and activate it with your energy. Imagine, too, that this is a special kind of puppet in that it is your own consciousness that maintains its form, its outer shell. Then align yourself with this character and imagine yourself withdrawing your life-energy from it. Actually *feel* yourself pulling your own energy back into yourself from inside this character, and notice how the character begins to crumble—a puppet with no hand inside of it. Receive all your life-energy back into yourself, leaving nothing within the character. Notice if you feel any inner resistance to doing this. Notice where the resistance is coming from. (This tool works best with our differentiated parental-characters.)

(14) If you were able to withdraw all your energy from *inside* the character, then withdraw your energy from its *structure,* from the shell and form of the character, and notice how its form begins to dissolve without your energy to maintain it. Again, notice any inner resistance.

(15) Look for the hidden child-characters within the differentiated parental-characters you know you are holding.

(16) If you found within yourself an undifferentiated parental-character, align yourself with the child within that character and attempt to separate—to differentiate—the child from its parent. If you can't, what prevents you?

(17) Choose any inner character and think of some situation that strongly triggered it and still does when you think about what happened. Then enter into this character—become one with it—and as this character, open to the situation with both your body and feelings, remembering that you are *safe*. Allow yourself to receive what is happening without resisting it, experiencing it as okay, just as it is. If this brings up a deeper character, then repeat this with the new character.

(18) Choose one of your characters and align yourself with it. Then get the character to look you in the eye and, as you make eye contact, just be with this character. Even if strong emotions come up, continue to maintain eye contact with the character until either the character dissolves or its emotional charge lets go.

Awareness Exercise 10, "Disidentifying with the Weather," is very useful when you become aware of an inner drama involving several characters. Awareness Exercise 18, "Releasing Attitude-Trances" and Awareness Exercise 19, "Releasing Fear-Trances" are complements to this exercise when working on individual characters.

23

The Reflections of Desire

We have seen that when we can stop projecting our fear of annihilation onto a situation, our sense of survival-need disappears and we experience *desire* instead. Therefore, desire is more fundamental than fear, for it can still exist after fear has evaporated. Although they both grow out of our trance-experience of separateness, desire comes into existence before fear, because the experience of separateness automatically creates a sense of lack and a desire to fill that lack, while fear is an attitude that we add to this situation.

A desire is simply a longing. Although we usually attach all kinds of emotional postures of need and fear to our desires, when freed of these postures our desires are not attitudes. Although a desire defines a specific relationship between ourself and the object of our desire, if there is no need attached to the desire, then there is no grabbing or holding pattern. And while all of our attitudes come into being to support our position of fear in resisting our experience of life, *our desires urge us toward fulfillment.*

Yet, as we have all experienced, the fulfillment we receive from satisfying our desires is always temporary, and then a new desire crops up. Getting what we think we want hardly ever gives us the deep or enduring satisfaction we expect. Yet as we experience this over and over, if we are not completely lost in our desire-drama, we begin to recognize that our desires are outer expressions of deeper, inner urges for fulfillment. Eventually we learn that *all desire has a single inner root: our spiritual yearning for Wholeness which is love longing to return to Itself.* All our desires finally purify down to this one fundamental desire, which arises automatically with our trance-experience of separateness.

Our other—"secondary"—desires come into being when this fundamental desire is experienced through the filter of our various trance-identities. What we desire will be shaped by who we think we are. And, therefore, our desires are also mirrors that we can use as learning tools to become aware of our characters and trance-identities. All we have to do is ask ourself who we think we are when we are experiencing a particular desire.

As we recognize that all of our desires are expressions of spiritual longing, we also realize that to satisfy this root desire we must give up our attachment to satisfying our other desires. This is because our involvement with these secondary desires scatters our attention and weakens our focus on our root desire. And this root desire can be satisfied only when our total being is focused on its fulfillment. H.W.L. Poonja, in *Papaji—Interviews,* states that, "The main obstacle [to freedom] is that the total, absolute desire for freedom is missing."[21] That is why so many spiritual traditions consider these secondary desires to be such a major hindrance on the spiritual path. Yet even so, the problem is really our *identification* with these desires. It is the moment that we *identify* with a desire that we drop from Oneness into separateness. Instead of Oneness there is now a desirer and a thing that is desired. Oneness has broken down into the duality of subject and object. We have moved from infinite Self into some particular self, some identity trance defined by the object that is desired. Instead of being Self, we have become "someone with a desire"; and we enter into a trance-drama that has as its plot our struggle around that desire.

But if desire arises and there is no identification with it, then no identity-trance is created. Although there is the awareness of desire, there is no one having the desire. There is no one being "someone with a desire." There is no one in any drama. There is only the desire by itself, experienced as a part of our landscape, like the sky and the trees. It is just there.

Our lessons around the issue of desire can take many forms. Yet at some point in time, our lesson must take the form of letting go our identification with our secondary desires and bringing the full focus of our being to our basic desire to return to Source. Then, instead of our desire taking us out into the drama of the world, it will take us

---

[21]David Godman (editor), *Papaji-Interviews*, (Boulder, CO; Avadhuta Foundation, 1993), p. 76.

back to our Heart. And finally, even the desire for Oneness and freedom will disappear in the actual experience of That. In Oneness, there is no separate person left to desire anything.

24

*Personal Relationships:
The Double Mirror*

All of our experiences are mirrors that help us to see ourself and vehicles through which we explore ourself and grow. Yet our experiences of personal, human-to-human relationships are unique in that they are double mirrors, for we are being a mirror for the other person while the other person is mirroring us. In general, these personal relationships will usually form the most powerful mirrors in our lives—showing us where we are stuck, where we are free, and where we have learned to allow more love.

Because we will tend to re-create our own inner drama in the outer drama of these relationships, the deeper, more involved a relationship is, the more fully it will reflect the key issues that we are exploring in this human trance. Hence, intimate and sexual relationships tend to form especially intense mirrors, for situations involving love, intimacy, and sexuality tend to bring up and mirror back to us our most deeply seated needs, fears, desires, power struggles, and so on, as well as give us the opportunity to experience our loving, caring heart. Yet even a minor relationship can be an important mirror, especially if we experience a lot of emotional charge in it; even very peripheral people in our lives can be powerful vehicles for our growth.

Every personal relationship, therefore, is an opportunity for us to encounter ourself—to encounter where we are lost in fear and where we are remembering Love. Every relationship is a gift whose sole purpose is to help us grow deeper in Love.

FOUR QUESTIONS

Four questions to ask in all personal relationships, in both intimate and non-intimate ones, are:

(1) *How honest am I being, both with myself and the other person?* Without honesty, our entire life, not just our relationship, will move toward disaster and suffering. Dishonesty always creates walls and becomes issues—visibly or invisibly—in relationships.

(2) *Where am I choosing love in the relationship and where am I choosing fear?* Wherever we choose love over fear, we move toward intimacy, openness, freedom, acceptance, forgiveness, personal growth, awareness, and trust; and as we surrender more deeply into love, our attitudes and holding patterns begin to relax and disappear. Love takes us toward Oneness. Wherever we choose fear over love in a relationship, our intention is to create safety, which usually involves either putting up emotional walls for protection, or turning the other person into a source of Life for ourself (which we believe will give us what we need and save us from our fear). This leads to experiences of neediness (not the same as desire), compulsiveness, emotional addiction, jealousy, control, anger, grief, self-pity, lack, isolation, disappointment, loss, and so on, and we become very manipulative, greedy, blaming, and tense. When we choose fear, we try to use the other person to support our position of fear, which eventually means getting them to withdraw their love. Of course, we will be angry and resentful when he or she does this, but if we choose fear, then we are choosing to create an absence of love. Fear can take us only toward separateness and aloneness; fear always creates walls. In addition, when we operate from fear in a relationship, we believe that our survival is at stake, and this tends to turn the relationship into a battleground on which we struggle for our own survival. (This is why the "negative" emotions in an intimate relationship can get so intense.) When we choose love, we give up the struggle. Choosing love in a relationship is asking the other person to help us move deeper into love. This does not involve trying to "get" love from the other person, for this is fear, rather, it means learning to *receive* more deeply the love that always exists within us, and learning to *share* that love.

Choosing fear will lead us to cling to a relationship or run from it; choosing love will lead us to either be in the relationship or leave it, with love.

(3) *Am I being here-now with the relationship?* Being here-now in a relationship is critical for keeping a relationship alive. If we are not being here-now in a relationship, then we have to keep twisting and distorting the present so that it seems to match how we think the relationship should be, which is often a belief we have about how it was in the past. This stranglehold can only suffocate and kill the relationship, because there is little freedom within such a holding pattern for the kind of spontaneity required for real intimacy. In place of intimacy, a shared holding pattern, with agreed upon roles, is created.

There are several ways that we can keep a relationship locked into the past: we can expect a person to behave, believe, or feel as they did yesterday, last year, or ten years ago; we can hold an attitude toward a person for something that happened in the past; or we can try to create the kind of relationship we had in the past. Living in the past expresses the position that the present is too scary to experience without fixed scripts. This, obviously, is choosing fear. As we have seen, fear cannot exist in the Now. When we choose to be here-now in a relationship, we are choosing spontaneity, openness, creative freedom, and love.

Of course, the issue of being here-now raises the issue of commitment. In committed relationships, the real question is: is the commitment to the other person and/or to living within a fixed pattern of existence, or is it to the ongoing process of choosing love over fear? If we are committed to choosing love, then we must go where love—not necessarily desire—honestly leads us. Anything else would be choosing fear. And when we truly choose love, everyone else in our situation also benefits, whether they recognize this or not.

(4) *Am I acknowledging responsibility for my experience in the relationship?* If we don't acknowledge responsibility for our experience, we will blame the other person for whatever attitudes or unhappiness his or her behavior activates within us—and for a host of other things. We will also perceive any problem in the relationship as something wrong with the other person. (Of course, holding the other person responsible for his or her behavior is completely different from blaming the person for our own experience.) When we acknowledge responsibility for our own experience, we will recognize that we are the cause of our own feelings and that whatever we resist in the other person is a mirror of something that we are resisting within ourself. This doesn't mean that we won't *desire* for a

person to act differently, but we won't need the person's behavior to change. In addition, we can accept—and even love—a person as he or she is, and not desire to continue in an intimate relationship with that person. However, making the other person responsible for our experience leads to arguments and separateness, and it prevents growth; it is a position of fear. Acknowledging responsibility for our experience in a relationship is choosing love, for it leads to openness, trust, communication, and transformation.

PERSONAL RELATIONSHIP ODDS & ENDS

Some other important awarenesses for personal relationships (both intimate and non-intimate ones) are:

(1) Choosing love (rather than fear) will bring to the surface all the places inside ourself where we are afraid to choose love. This can make love seem very scary, but it is never love that is scaring us; it is always our fear.

(2) As with all situations in our life, what we resist in other people is a mirror of some place we are stuck within ourself; and what we avoid dealing with or disown in our relationships will come around again, often more intensely.

(3) The way we enter a relationship—the consciousness we form it with—will shape the relationship we end up experiencing. Whatever we enter with that is not love will usually, in some way, be an issue in the relationship.

(4) The way we leave a relationship—the consciousness we separate with—will shape our experience after the relationship and will usually affect the way we enter our next one. Whatever we leave with that is not love and appreciation will be an issue later in our life and, unless we transform it, it will usually be an issue in our next relationship.

(5) It is easy to confuse intimacy, connection, and involvement with neediness and attachment. The connection (and intimacy) that people feel with each other grows out of the very real connection that they have always had, for we are all connected and are an individuation within the same Source—we are all leaves of the Tree of Life. And our experience of connectedness allows experiences of involvement and intimacy, yet these experiences have nothing to do with neediness and attachment, which occur when, out of fear, we cling to those with whom we experience our connectedness.

(6) Because we are connected to each other through (and only through) the Source, it is the Source that we are experiencing when we feel connected to other people in relationships. Yet when we don't recognize what we are experiencing, we make other people (instead of our Self) the source of our feeling of connectedness, and we become dependent on them and attached to them for our experience of Love and God. Then, whenever we "lose" someone close to us, we feel a loss of fundamental connectedness, as if we have lost part of our Self, as if we have lost part of our connection to God. And because this reminds us of our inner abyss, of the fear and loss arising from our more basic sense of separateness, it will intensify our sense of loss in the present situation and reinforce our fear-belief that we need this person to feel connected to Life and our Self. (For people caught in this trance, the fear of death is often really a fear of losing all their human connections, which they believe they need to stay connected to life and Self.) So, whenever we feel attachment toward someone, it will help to recognize the attachment for what it really is; and whenever we feel a sense of loss toward someone, it will help to perceive the loss in this context, and to remember that we can never lose our connection to our Source or to any individualized being—all we can ever lose is our sense of separateness, and that is just an illusion anyway.

(7) If we feel dependent toward someone and try to disown that feeling, whether because it feels bad or because we know that we are stuck, we reinforce the dependency and the fear that generates it. Instead, we can be responsible for our feeling; we can go into it and bring as much consciousness as possible into our experience of it. Then, what was once a rigidly stuck area becomes an area of new awakening, of emerging love.

(8) Because we are One, the love we receive from others is really an aspect of God's love.

(9) Whenever we do not "feed" ourself (at Home), we will try to satisfy our inner hunger from our outer relationships (in the world), and then we will need these relationships to feed us in particular ways, leading us to manipulate them, so we can get what we think we need from them.

(10) When we resist another person's behavior (or criticism) the first question we should always ask ourself is: why isn't this person's behavior okay for me to experience? How do I believe it threatens

me? We should ask this even when we know the other person's behavior is coming from a stuck place.

(11) Whenever we criticize our partner or the relationship, we should always examine where the criticism is coming from within ourself, even if we believe that the criticism is true.

(12) In our relationships we always know on some level what the other person is doing, thinking, and feeling, and we respond to this whether we are conscious of what we know or not. (Hence "cheating" in intimate relationships is really impossible.)

(13) In every relationship we adopt a basic "position" or "stance"—or several of them—toward the other person, and the other person adopts one or more toward us. These positions express subtle, yet often complex attitudes, that communicate non-verbally where we are in relation to the other person; and by doing so, they also communicate what kind of complementary position we want the other person to take in relation to us. Some examples of simple positions are: "I'll take care of you"; "I need you"; "I'll make you happy"; "Don't expect anything from me"; "Don't get me angry"; and even "I'm great, and you're okay if you agree with me."

Usually we are quite attached to our positions, because we think those are the positions in which we are safest and because some aspect of our identity is tied to them. Many conflicts in relationships are over these positions, because we will want the other person to support our position, but often the other person's position will resist it. It is useful, therefore, to become conscious of these positions—both our own and the other person's—for they can tell us much about the inner dynamics of the relationship. In addition, they point to where we are not in unconditional love, which relates to the world without positions.

(14) Whenever we camouflage an attitude within a relationship, the attitude will use the camouflage to wage a clandestine, guerrilla war against the experience of love in the relationship.

(15) Each of our inner characters will try to use what happens in our relationships to support its own position and attitude.

(16) Whenever we don't trust another person, we will try to use what happens in the relationship to support our position, and we will try to get the other person to validate our distrust (to support our position).

(17) Because we create our own reality (in mutual agreement with other beings), whether we like the other person's behavior or not, we

can always trust that the person will behave exactly as we intend, so we can have exactly the experience we need (for our growth). The issue of trust in a relationship, therefore, really boils down to the question of whether we trust that the life we are creating is safe to experience and, in particular, whether we trust that the relationship we have created is safe to experience, *regardless of what happens.* (Whether we desire the relationship is a different question.) When we trust that life is safe to experience, the idea of trusting another person in a relationship takes on a completely new meaning.

(18) Expectations of the other person always become demands.

(19) Although we may experience it as painful not to have our love received by the other person in our relationship, it is much more painful to block our experience of love.

(20) Although another person may reject us, no one can cause us to feel rejected but ourself. Feelings of rejection are one of the trance-attitudes that we often take toward our trance-experience of separateness; it is, at its core, an illusion. Ironically, when we are afraid of rejection, we withdraw, closing down our willingness to love, essentially rejecting the other person, even as we insist that he or she not reject us.

(21) Often, when we feel hurt or rejected in a relationship, acknowledging responsibility for our attitudes is not sufficient to return to an experience of love. Often we must also forgive the other person, whether the person has actually acted in a hurtful manner or not, because the act of forgiveness will expose any secret blame or anger we still hold, and let it go.

(22) Forgiveness is probably the most powerful healer of conflicts in a relationship.

(23) Feelings of hurt and rejection in a relationship may be considered as a natural consequence of idolatry, of transgressing spiritual law (and the First Commandment: "Thou shalt have no other gods before me"), by making someone outside your Self the Source of your well-being.

(24) When we blame another person for something, or avoid acknowledging responsibility for being stuck, or don't accept the other person as he or she is, we create an argument in the relationship which will find and create many other things to argue about, none of which will be resolvable.

(25) A problem in a relationship is hardly ever what it seems.

(26) A fear of change and of the unknown will create an attachment to what is familiar. This will tend to keep us in a relationship even when it is no longer working, even when it has become a continual source of pain and suffering.

(27) Our fear of dealing with those areas within ourself where we are suffering can cause us either to run from a relationship when there is still much life left in it, or to hold onto a relationship long after the life in it is gone.

(28) Only by completely being ourself in a relationship can we be certain that the other person likes us or loves us as we are.

(29) Relationships tend to bring out the areas where we are the least conscious (stuck in our abyss of fear) as well as those areas where we are the most conscious (Being Love). We're lucky to have such powerful gifts in our life.

(30) Because close and intimate relationships deeply mirror ourself, expect that the person you are (or will be) in relationship with is as crazy, messed up, angry, sad, loving, joyful, sincere, creative, human, and divine as you are.

(31) The perfect relationship is the one you're in now, for it has been perfectly created to help you to grow in whatever way you need to grow now. And this says nothing about whether you should stay in the relationship; it simply directs your awareness to appreciate what IS, and to appreciate the other person for helping you to have exactly the kind of relationship you intended for your growth.

(32) Marriage is qualitatively different than all other intimate relationships, including the situation of an unmarried couple living together. Although bad relationships are not made better by marriage, the act of marriage empowers a relationship and gives it more energy to work with. This energy enters into the relationship as a *blessing,* a unique quality of spiritual energy or consciousness that is called forth out of the universe by the willingness of both people to receive it as a binding force between them. Although it is marriage that calls forth this blessing, it is the power of this blessing that transmutes a relationship into the state of marriage. And this blessing, this infusion of spiritual consciousness has its own purpose: to help each of the individuals grow, with each other, deeper into the unity of spiritual consciousness and unconditional love.

FALLING IN LOVE

For many people, the experience of falling in love is the closest they come to experiencing their true Beingness, their true Self. A man meets the "right" woman and, as if by magic, his heart opens, he feels whole and connected to Life, and he remembers Love, the nature of his Beingness. All of his friends can see how different he is, how happy he is, how much inner light he radiates.

He is like a fictional character from a fairy tale who has been "saved" from ordinary life and is about to live "happily ever after." And this parallel to a fairy tale (as well as to the idea of being saved and going to Heaven) is no coincidence, for the theme of being saved and living happily ever after is really the core of our human drama. It symbolizes what we are all yearning for and where we are all headed as we journey through our incarnations, struggling with the suffering and limitations of our normal human existence, learning the awareness that will ultimately open our hearts and bring us into the transcendence of eternal light and bliss. The possibility of living happily ever after is the birthright that we will all eventually claim, and because we know this and yearn to have it now, we fantasize about falling in love, for that experience gives us a taste of Heaven, and it is an experience that could happen to us now.

Yet falling in love is only the taste of Heaven, not the final enlightenment. Although fairy tales, movies, and romantic novels, being symbolic, can end with falling in love, in real life this is not the end of the story but the beginning of a new chapter that is sitting in the middle of a very long plot. Although the man's experience of falling in love is truly an opening into Self, his experience does not happen in a vacuum, for he brings his previous state of being and emotional point of view into the situation, and they have a lot to do with what unfolds in his future.

To the extent that the man did not already feel whole within himself when he met this woman, he was experiencing lack, and so he will perceive his new experience through the point of view of this lack. Since he is now experiencing a depth of love and wholeness that he wasn't experiencing before he met this woman, he will tend to believe that she is the cause of his new feelings and the source of his experience of love and connectedness; he will tend to believe that he needs her in order to feel this way. These beliefs, which are part of his emotional point of view, immediately begin to limit and distort his experience. At some point, their influence will become clearly visible. Because he will not want to lose this wonderful love he feels, this sense of connectedness to Self he has secretly longed for, his belief that he needs to *get* this love *from* her will lead to various kinds of subtle manipulations, appeasements, addictions, and ego games as he tries to hold on to his experience of love and Self by controlling what he perceives to be the source of it.

In this situation, if the man is not working consciously on his spiritual growth, the best he can hope for is a relationship of mutual dependence (currently referred to as "co-dependence") in which each person takes care of and loves the other person, partly out of genuine love, yet partly out of fear and lack. Although many people consider this an ideal relationship (and it is certainly more nurturing than most), it is limiting, for it supports each person's position of lack and makes the emotional dynamics of lack a fundamental element in the relationship. This automatically blocks some of the love that could have been shared, for *wherever there is clinging and holding on, instead of intimacy and love, there is clinging and holding on.* Although a relationship built on love and lack may evolve into a more whole relationship, until it does it cannot be as full as one created solely from love.

If the relationship ends (as most relationships do that begin with falling in love), then other aspects of the inner drama will emerge. Even if it is he who decides to leave, the break-up will seem to create a hole inside of him. As we saw in the last section, when we unconsciously rely on our connections with other people to feel connected to life and Self, the "loss" of someone close will feel as if we have lost part of our connection to God; it will seem to create a hole inside of us. And since the man's relationship with this woman was a primary vehicle for his experience of connection—even if they have not been getting along for years—the hole he will feel from "losing" her will be a rather large one. Of course, this man's hole was always there, skulking in whatever corner of his consciousness he had hidden it, for his hole is really his own abyss, created by his own fear and sense of lack, which grew out of his experience of separateness. The ending of the relationship simply brings his hole to the surface, making him aware of it. Yet if he blames the woman for it, then just as he originally made her the source of his experience of love, he will now blame her for the hole he is experiencing.

Metaphorically, when we hold onto someone in a relationship, trying to "get" love or connectedness to fill the hole of our own abyss, we are trying to use the person as a "plug" for that hole; when the relationship ends the hole becomes obvious, and we usually blame the other person for creating the hole when all he or she did was take back the plug that was camouflaging it. Hence there are thousands of popular songs about how "she created a hole in my life," yet none about how "she made me aware of the hole I always had, and how grateful I am for the awareness."

To create a different kind of experience requires assuming responsibility for being the source of our experience of love. Then, even if we feel much more connected to love and to our Self through this one relationship, we can recognize that our partner is the *vehicle* for our experience, not the cause of it. For whatever reason, the unique qualities of this person help us to open much more deeply into Life. Yet we will know that we are responsible for the love we are able to experience with this person (as well as for creating this situation in our life). And because we have acknowledged this responsibility, instead of trying to hold onto and "get" love from our partner, we can receive our situation as a gift (which will open us even more deeply to love) and as an opportunity: for learning how to find within *ourself* the love that we feel with this person, and for learning to *share* that love from an experience of inner wholeness. Then the relationship becomes a mutual vehicle for creating inner connection, for finding our inner path; and it is much easier to find the path inside when our outer experience is helping us to remember where we are headed.

The fact that people usually distort their experience of love does not, in any way, negate the significance of their experience. Every time we truly experience love, regardless of how we perceive it or what we end up doing with it, we remember Who we are and some part of us that was asleep, awakens. This stokes our desire for more love, for deeper fulfillment, for deeper connection; and eventually, to satisfy this desire, we will be led into the very core of our beingness, for nothing else will make us whole. Then, we will no longer need to fall in love to remind us of Who we are or to feel connected, for we will be Love Itself, and we will Be Love with everyone and everything in creation. So the next time you fall in love, do not blind yourself with it; surrender to it with your eyes open, reaching for the true Source of your experience of love. Falling in love is ultimately an opportunity—for remembering the Love that We Are.

One other thing about falling in love: since as human beings we are strange and weird creatures, usually with all kinds of fears, needs, dislikes, biases, and other sorts of illusions, and since our life is a mirror, know from the start that the magical, perfect, godlike being you have fallen in love with is also a human being who is as strange and as weird as you.

SEX

Sex is the wild card in the deck of human relationships. Because it is tied into our instincts for life-preservation, we often experience sex as a physical "need." This sense of need is reinforced by the experience of intimacy and connectedness we have in our sexual encounters, for as we saw in the last section, our need to connect with our Source is often projected onto the connections of our human relationships. In addition, the belief system of our cultural-trance, cemented by the beliefs of traditional psychology, can be used to validate the position that we "need" sex. Yet sex is not a need; if it were truly a physical need then we would die without it. Although we can project our sense of need onto sex, sex is simply a *desire* and, as we saw earlier, desires are impulses toward fulfillment that are rooted in spiritual longing, and are thus generated by love. The fact that sex is an instinct also points to its basis in love, for as we saw in Chapter 8, our instincts are not based on need (which grows out of fear) but on love. Love, which is our life-force, acts through our instincts to preserve and re-create life. So sexual desire originates as an expression of love.

Most of the "problems" we develop around sex occur when we project our sense of lack and need onto our sexual desires. First of all, to the extent that we experience sex as a need, the actual experience of sex becomes a relief of tension—with little pleasure in it. Pleasure requires an ability to receive, yet when we think we need something we can't receive it, for we are too caught up in holding onto it; we have to relax our grip and open ourself up to receive. Second, if sex is a need, then we become locked into the position of "needing to get" sex from someone instead of "desiring to share" it in a context of individual wholeness. Since sex is an expression of love, it is not surprising that when we experience sex as a need, we end up in the same position, with the same need-driven attachments and other problems, that we create when we distort our experience of love. Third, when we experience sex as a need, then all of our experience with sex (and our experience of "trying to get" sex from others) becomes a character-drama about need and lack; and this drama both reinforces and validates our position of needing and lacking—which is our basic position of fear—of not being whole within ourself. And, fourth, when we experience sex as a need, we tend to become more unconscious and more irresponsible in our sexual encounters with people. And this always leads to suffering. Sex should be experienced with joy and pleasure.

The other problems that occur around sex are unwanted pregnancies (which from the soul's point of view are never accidental) and all the problems that occur when we allow our inner characters to use sex as a means of supporting their own positions. When we allow our characters to use sex in this way, our sexual experiences become extensions of their dramas as well as dig us deeper into those dramas.

Our experience of sexuality is capable of great variation, and it will tend to shift according to who we (and the other person) think we are at the time. Although some people, when they experience their sexuality, always fix themselves within the same particular identity-trance, others shift among several or more different trances, with each identity-trance having its own unique mix of physical, emotional, and spiritual characteristics, as well as its own mix of attitudes, emotional positions, and a capacity to experience love. So our experience of sexuality, according to who we think we are, can run along a vast continuum, from separate, emotionally isolated people whose bodies are fucking, to two individualized aspects of Love sharing an exquisite, intimate dance of ecstasy. And this is perfect, because according to where we are in our growth, that is what we will explore through our sexuality. If we are torn between two conflicting trance-identities, this conflict will show up in our sexual experiences, and these experiences will be an exploration of our conflict.

In general, the key factor will be the degree to which our trance-identities allow love and intimacy to be present in the situation—at all levels of our beingness. Love creates the experience of connectedness and fulfillment. And because it allows us to be more open, it creates more space for our life-force to flow through us (physically, emotionally, and spiritually), allowing the receiving of more pleasure, on all levels. In fact, love intensifies every aspect of our experience of sexuality because the essence of our spiritual, emotional, and physical beingness, including the essence of our sexual energy, is love.

Perhaps the most intriguing aspect of our sexuality is that, as much as it has been studied, in many ways it remains mysterious. For instance, people often find themselves sexually attracted to people they don't like and don't want to be attracted to, and they often experience a great deal of love and intimacy with people to whom they feel no sexual attraction at all. Webster defines sex as: "the sum of the structural, functional, and behavioral characteristics of living beings that subserve reproduction by two interacting parents and distinguish males and females." You can bet your biology that Mother Nature had a few other ideas, and in Her infinite wisdom put sex in a realm as far from the intellect as possible.

Our sexuality is so mysterious (and powerful) because it is more than a vehicle for the creation of physical life, more than a means of experiencing pleasure, and mote than a convenient arena for projecting and acting out our emotional dramas; our sexual energy embodies the Creative Conscious Energy out of which all dimensions of existence are born, and so it is as mysterious as the Infinite Source of All Creation. And because of this, our sexuality is a door through which we can experience our Source. Yet this door becomes visible only when we experience our sexuality as an expression and receiving of love, for only love connects us to the very essence of our sexual energy, and only in that essence do we experience our Source. (The ancient yogis, recognizing this, developed Tantra Yoga, a form of love-meditation that uses the sharing of sexual energy to enter into the unity behind the male-female polarity and experience God.)

There is a lot of cultural programming about sex—which consists of copied parental-attitudes—that can, at times, make the issues involved seem confusing. Yet there is really only one basic issue that we have to deal with here, and it is the same basic issue we encounter over and over again, in every avenue of our life, at every level of our trance-identity: do we choose need and lack and fear, or do we choose wholeness, safety, and love?

AWARENESS EXERCISE 23:
LEAVES OF LIGHT

PART 1

Sit comfortably, with your spine fairly straight, and close your eyes. Receive a few deep breaths ... and let yourself relax. Then:

(1) Visualize a diamond, one or two inches in size, sitting right on the center of the top of your head, with one point on your head and the other point vertically above it.

(2) Keeping the diamond at that spot, look at the light glistening in it (without tilting your head back). Allow the light in the diamond to get as bright as it can. Play with expanding and shrinking the size of the diamond, until you find the size that radiates the brightest light.

(3) Allow yourself to feel the light that is glistening in the diamond, penetrating into your head and body. Sit with this experience for fifteen minutes.

PART 2

Continue sitting as before.

(I) Visualize the Tree of Life as an infinite Tree composed of threads of Light.

(2) See that the glistening diamond on the center of your head is connected to the Tree by a thread of light.

(3) For a few minutes, experience your connection to the essence of the Tree through the diamond on your head.

(4) Experience yourself as a Leaf of Light that is hanging from the Tree of Life hanging from one of the threads of its infinite branches.

(5) Since, as a Leaf of Light, you are not separate from the Tree Itself, go deeper into the essence of yourself as a Leaf of Light and experience yourself as the Tree Itself that has given birth to this particular leaf.

Take as much time as you like; allow yourself to enjoy this experience.

PART 3

Have someone sit in front of you with his or her eyes closed. Keep your own eyes open.

(1) Visualize the diamond glistening on the center top of your head, feel its light, and then, without losing your connection to your own diamond's light, visualize a similar diamond on the top of your partner's head.

(2) See your partner being filled with the light radiating from his or her diamond.

(3) See that the diamond on your partner's head is glistening with the same light that is shining in yours; see (and, if you can, *feel*) that the light that is filling your partner is the same light that is filling you.

(4) Become aware of the thread of Light that connects you to the Tree of Life through the diamond at the top of your head, and become aware of the thread of Light that connects your partner in a similar manner.

(5) Experience yourself as a Leaf of Light, and as that Leaf, experience your partner as another Leaf on the Tree of Life.

(6) Experience your Oneness with the essence of the Tree of Life, and experience your partner as being the same essence. Then experience, within that essence, that you and your partner are One.

Take as much time as you like.

AWARENESS EXERCISE 24:
CLEARING INTIMATE RELATIONSHIPS

What follows are the requirements for being clear with present and past relationships. As you read them, apply them, yet only to one relationship at a time.

PRESENT RELATIONSHIPS

To be clear in a present relationship you must:

(1) Assume responsibility for your experience of the relationship and for being the source of your experience of love. This includes assuming responsibility for any emotional attitudes you have toward the other person and letting go of any blame you hold toward this person for these attitudes. It also includes giving up any illusions about needing this person (which is different from desiring), even if at the present time you feel a deeper sense of connectedness to your Self with this person than when you are alone.

(2) Allow the other person the responsibility for his or her experience of the relationship and for being the source of his or her experience of love. This also means not supporting any positions of neediness or dependence this person may have toward you, which is different from resisting this person's positions.

(3) Choose to accept the other person just as he or she is. (Wherever you cannot do this, you have a struggle within the relationship, which is, of course, a reflection of a struggle you have within yourself.) This requires giving up and letting go of any secret intentions to change the person (which also gives up the struggle this creates), although it does not mean giving up the desire for this person to grow into a more whole, more conscious, more loving being. If you cannot do this and do not think that you will be able to in the future, then it may be time to consider ending the relationship.

(4) Appreciate, with thankfulness, the role this person is playing in your life, whether you fully understand this role or not.

(5) Forgive the other person for anything that was hurtful (at the same time acknowledging your responsibility for your experience of hurt).

(6) Acknowledge to the other person any lies that you have told, (because as old as they may be, the walls they created still exist).

(7) Be willing to let go of the past and to be here-now with the relationship, just as it is. This means letting go of any expectations of the other person and the relationship.

(8) Be clear about your purpose for being in the relationship (which is not the same as your expectations). This includes rooting out any hidden purposes.

(9) Commit yourself to choosing love in any area of the relationship where you have been choosing fear. This requires honestly asking yourself what you have been doing in the relationship to keep yourself safe and asking yourself what kind of change you need to make in these areas in order to choose love over fear.

PAST RELATIONSHIPS

To be clear with past relationships requires the above nine conditions (put into the past tense) with certain modifications:

(1) Number 3 also requires letting go of any desires for the other person or for the situation to have been different.

(2) Number 6 is necessary only if you are still in some kind of relationship (friendship or acquaintance) with the person.

(3) Let go of any remaining subtle attachments—of any kind—to this person. With sexual relationships especially, subtle sexual, emotional, and security attachments tend to linger, usually unconsciously, sometimes even long after the breakup of the relationship. (And therefore, with past sexual relationships, especially recently ended ones, it is also recommended that you do Awareness Exercise 25, "Releasing Sexual Energy-Cords," to release these subtle holdings-on.)

AWARENESS EXERCISE 25:
RELEASING SEXUAL ENERGY-CORDS

Whenever you end a sexual relationship, doing this exercise will greatly aid and speed up the work of recentering and becoming complete. In addition, if you still feel any kind of subtle attachments to a person you were involved with sexually in the past, it is recommended that you do this exercise with respect to that person, too. Often, this exercise will bring up old, unresolved emotional feelings.

To understand the nature of sexual energy-cords, imagine that (1) when two people become involved in a sexual relationship, they create an energy-connection between their personal energy-fields (they almost always do), (2) this connection takes the form of a thin cord of energy that is constructed from the energy within the personal energy-fields (or auras) of the two people involved, (3) this energy-cord extends from (and connects to) each person at the area above, or above and to one side, of the pubic bone, (4) this cord is created as a way of intensifying each person's sense of connectedness, and (5) whatever attachment each person feels toward the other becomes part of the consciousness with which the cord is created.

You may believe that these energy-cords are only a metaphorical way of representing and making contact with our subtle attachments and holding patterns; yet, whether or not they actually exist, you can experience them as if they do exist, and doing so facilitates releasing these attachments and holding patterns. (My experience is that they do exist and that most people, when directed, can feel these energy cords.)

So, sit comfortably, receive a few deep breaths ... and let yourself relax. Then, to release your sexual energy-cords:

(1) Bring to mind your ex-lover.

(2) Allow yourself to experience how the essence of this person feels to your body, and notice where in the general area above your pubic bone, or above and to one side of it, you feel the person most strongly.

(3) Imagine that an energy-cord was created between you and your ex-lover, that it extends from and connects to your body, as well as your ex-lover's body, in the area you felt most strongly in the last step. (If you didn't feel any area most strongly, imagine that it connects to you about an inch above your pubic bone and a little to the left.)

(4) Imagine that this cord is really two cords: one extending from yourself to your ex-lover, and one extending from your ex-lover to you.

(5) Visualize yourself release, with love, your ex-lover's cord from where it connects to you. If you can, also *feel* this release happen. Then send it back to this person, to the energy-field it came from. It is important to be clear about your intention and willingness to release the cord.

(6) Visualize yourself releasing, with love, your own cord from where you connected it to your ex-lover and feel yourself receive this energy—which is your own energy—back into yourself. Simply draw it back into yourself. Again be mindful of your intention and willingness to release your cord.

25

Living Examples

The following examples are taken from actual situations. Each one illustrates a different facet of the workings or usage of our life-mirror.

(1) A woman who always had a lot of deep anxiety became involved in a relationship with a man soon after he had broken up with his former lover. They moved to a new place together which turned out to be just a few blocks from where the old girlfriend lived. The woman became very anxious about her boyfriend becoming reattracted to the old girlfriend. She worried about this constantly.

The woman didn't realize that the proximity of the old girlfriend was just a mirror of the problem; the problem was her own anxiety, which always found situations to camouflage itself in, situations it could blame for the anxiety. Yet since the woman believed that the old girlfriend was the cause of her anxiety, she felt powerless to change her feelings.

The woman avoided dealing with the real issue of her own anxiety, yet future events showed that her soul-intention was to transform it, because the more she avoided dealing with herself, the more intense and painful the situations that reflected her anxiety became. Eventually, she realized that to change what was happening she needed to deal with her Self as the source of her experience of life and to use the situations in her life as a mirror to help her become conscious of where she was stuck.

Wherever there is a lot of emotional charge in our life, we are intending lessons for ourself and need to pay close attention to our mirror and recognize where the real problem lies.

(2) A man was living with a woman who was "afraid of every-thing." He insisted that it was she who was the anxious one, that he didn't have the fears she had. Yet the woman had to be his mirror. In fact, his body posture and sweaty palms stated quite clearly that he had a lot of fear he was not acknowledging. And occasionally, when the woman got up the courage to do something by herself that she usually would be afraid to do, it was he who objected, revealing his fear, even as he insisted that he was only trying to protect her.

So, this woman both mirrored the man's fears and was a vehicle through which he was exploring them—in spite of his own denial. Yet to transform his fears he must eventually assume responsibility for them. If he continues with his denial, at some point he will have to create situations that will make his fears visible and force him to acknowledge them.

This man may actually believe that he is relatively free of fear, yet if he looked at his life as a mirror and considered what issues he was re-presenting to himself with it, he would be forced to ask himself why he had been drawn to create an intimate relationship with some-one who held so much fear.

(3) A woman who used a controlling parental-character to camou-flage her insecurity and who believed that men were undependable, married a man who was afraid to be an adult, who was stuck in the character-trance of being a rebellious child. Unconsciously, she knew that in this kind of relationship true intimacy would be next to impossible, but there were at least three payoffs: the relationship would enable her to maintain her position as a controlling parent, for with a child-of-a-husband she would feel justified in this role; it would enable her to validate her attitude that men are undependable; and by having a husband she could blame for the poor relationship, she would be able to camouflage her own fear of intimacy. Although these may seem like poor reasons to marry someone, wherever there is fear, safety becomes a critical issue; and since she believes that these attitude-positions have kept her safe (or she wouldn't have adopted them), she believes she will be safe in this situation, for it supports these positions. All of this, of course, goes on in her mind unconsciously.

If this woman wants to become aware of how she is behaving but can't see herself directly because of her trance, she can see her reflection in her husband's behavior, for the character of a rebellious child needs a controlling-parent character to play against and resist. In fact, for as often as she will tell him to grow up, he will tell her to stop telling him what to do (to stop acting like a controlling parent).

In addition, if she were willing to look at her life as a mirror, she would see that the scared, rebellious child she is reacting to in her husband is a mirror of the scared child in herself that uses the character of a controlling parent to protect itself. She would also see that the undependableness she is reacting to in him mirrors her own belief that life is not safe, that her world is out of control.

So, as much as she resists her husband, what she is resisting is what she doesn't feel safe experiencing within herself. Her outer situation with her husband is the creative vehicle through which she re-presents her inner situation, explores it, and creates the experience necessary to ultimately transform it.

(4) A man thought he was very independent, but he always had a strong reaction to people whom he perceived as clinging.

This man's independence was not true independence, but a camouflage for his own sense of dependence. Since he reacted to other people's dependence, pushing it away, their dependence had to be a mirror of his own.

Whatever we push away within ourself, we will push away in other people; whatever we react to in other people is something we are reacting to within ourself. Our reactions are like blinking neon signs, letting us know that we are stuck.

If this man assumed responsibility for his reactions or looked at his life as a mirror, he would know that his reactions and the people he reacts to reflect his own sense of dependence.

(5) A woman left her native country to study at a university in the United States. After being in the U.S. for a year, she decided to end a relationship with a man who still lived in her native country. Soon after that, her car was broken into, her house was robbed, and a man (unarmed) came through her window while she was sleeping, but she managed to fight him off and chase him from her house. During the struggle, a neighbor who was a friend heard her screaming and came running to help.

It turned out that the woman had been experiencing a conflict within her emotional point of view. One set of beliefs maintained that she needed to stay in her native country to feel secure, nurtured, and thus safe; and another set held that she was safe living in the

U.S. and that she would be better off there because more opportunities existed in her field. When she broke off her relationship, cutting some of her remaining ties with her native country, the conflict came to a head and burst on to the outer stage of her life.

The three events were a mirror of this inner conflict and the process through which she was working them out. (And there were probably many other issues being worked on as well—we can never be aware of all of them.) At first glance, the events seemed to mirror, as well as validate, only her fear-beliefs, which held that she needed to return home to feel safe. Yet the intruder who had come into her room had not been armed, enabling her to fight him off, and her friend had come to help her. This mirrored beliefs which maintained that she had the capacity to deal with threatening situations and that she did have support in the U.S. from people she could depend on. And because the events forced her inner conflict and fear to the surface, they provided an opportunity for her to deal with her self-limiting fear-beliefs that were restricting her growth; the events were the process through which she was both exploring and transforming herself.

The woman ended up staying in the U.S. and moving into a wonderful house with a girlfriend. This action deepened her commitment to staying in the U.S., as well as her feelings of connectedness and safety here. Although it might seem that she moved into a house with a girlfriend simply out of fear, this was not the case. Her position about needing to go home to feel safe was weakened and her act of moving into a wonderful house with a friend was an expression of her growth, an external symbol of her willingness to feel safe and connected in a foreign country.

(6) A man was trying to make a decision about something important in his life. Some people he knew thought he should do one thing, while others thought he should make the opposite choice. This confused him. He wished he could separate what he himself thought from what he had heard and been influenced by.

This man didn't realize that he was only influenced by those ideas with which he already agreed. Since he seemed to be influenced by both sides, this showed only that he had thoughts that leaned in both directions. His friends did not create his confusion, they mirrored it.

(7) A man who had felt very lonely and isolated as a child believed that it was very difficult for him to make real friends. As an

adult, none of his friends ever had much time to spend with him, and his girlfriends always left him. He didn't realize that he was unconsciously choosing friends who wouldn't have much time for him and choosing girlfriends who would eventually reject him. These unconscious choices supported his conscious position that the reason he felt lonely was because other people were unfeeling; and they helped him to avoid assuming responsibility for his feelings and life-situations. Yet he was being presented a very clear mirror if he was willing to look at it, because the way these other people treated him reflected his own unconscious beliefs perfectly (and supported his unconscious position) that he was unworthy of love and that it wasn't safe to open up to other people because they would reject him.

(8) A woman was having trouble with her son, who was very violent. Although he had not acted violently toward her, she was afraid of his violence.

To know how to deal with her son, she first needed to know why she had created the situation of having a violent son in her life. What was the significance of this situation for her? It turned out that she had a great fear of violence since childhood because of her father who was violent. Because the woman had not been able to finish her lessons about violence and fear of violence with her father, she had re-created the situation with her son. The woman acknowledged her fear of violence, yet the violence she reacted to was also a mirror of herself—underneath her fear was a dark rage of unexpressed violence. For her to be able to deal effectively with her son's violence, she needed to deal with both her fears of violence and her own violence.

Those areas in our life that give us the most trouble, or that we react to, are always mirrors of places within ourself that are very stuck. Also, those areas in our life that we are most involved in will usually reflect large areas within ourself that we are exploring and learning about. The people we live with, therefore, will tend to mirror large lesson-areas within ourself. And children play a special role: they will usually manifest exactly those parts of ourself we couldn't deal with and suppressed. This is part of the gift of children: they give us the opportunity to encounter ourself and grow.

(9) A man developed a chronic disease which kept him in an exhausted state, unable to work. He moved in with his father (his mother was dead) and became totally dependent upon him. The man

couldn't stand being in this state of dependency, yet he was unable to break out of it because of his exhaustion.

The man was struggling against the dependency of his situation as if it were some external condition that had been imposed upon him. The fact that he had a chronic disease reinforced this belief, since he believed that the disease was some external thing that had taken him over. Yet if he perceived his situation as a mirror of himself, he would have seen a very different picture—that his external dependency was a very accurate reflection of his state of inner dependency and neediness. These feelings had been projected mostly upon his mother, but since his mother was no longer alive, his father was the next best person to explore these issues with. The disease he had was a vehicle for exploring his dependency, an outer mirror of the inner self-limitations created by his beliefs in dependency, a way for him to support his position that he was incapable of living on his own, and a camouflage for the fact that he was afraid of being on his own. (It should be pointed out though, that someone else with the same disease might be exploring completely different issues.)

It turned out, as would be expected, that these issues had been prominent throughout his life, especially during childhood. In addition to having very controlling and overbearing parents, he had been adopted, a situation which is often used by the soul-consciousness to explore deep issues of abandonment and dependency. In fact, his present situation was very much a re-creation of his infancy situation: as an infant, he felt that his true mother had abandoned him and put him in a situation where he was totally dependent upon someone else for his survival; as an adult, he felt that the woman he had turned into his mother had abandoned him by dying, thereby putting him in a situation where he was totally dependent upon someone else for his survival.

Although his adult situation closely re-created his infancy, it would be a mistake to assume that his childhood situation caused his later one; since the earlier situation was itself created to explore the relevant issues, his need to transform certain beliefs and attitudes is the real cause of both situations. (Yet his childhood could still be used *as a tool* in the present for exploring these issues. This will be explored further in Part IV.) It would also be a mistake to assume that he hadn't progressed since childhood, that he was simply repeating himself. Even when we don't transform our issues and the events reflecting them are re-created in our lives more intensely, there is a process at work through which we will eventually transform ourself; as much as we may try to, we cannot stay where we are, we are always growing. With the man in this example, it may be that the situation he created with his father was just the experience he needed to complete his learning about this kind of dependency. At the very least, he will grow in some way from the experience, and that will contribute to his eventual transformation of the issue.

(10) A woman was upset because the man she had a crush on was keeping her at a distance. It turned out that it was the exact same distance she had kept from the last man who had had a crush on her.

It didn't matter who seemed to be creating the distance; the distance was always the same. In fact, if the man she had a crush on suddenly tried to get close to her, she would certainly step back to maintain the original distance. That distance in her outer relationship mirrored an inner emotional position in which she needed to maintain that exact distance from something she resisted within herself.

(11) A man who was very cheerful and happy-go-lucky on the outside had a lot of inner unresolved grief. He always fell in love with happy women who, it would turn out, had a lot of pain underneath their happiness. When he would encounter this in a woman, he would be amazed that he had been unable to see it when he met her, and he would push her grief away.

What we avoid in ourself we either have strong and immediate reactions to when we encounter it in other people, or else we don't notice it all—at first. It always catches up, sometimes in a devastating way in relationships. The way we deal with it will then usually mirror the way we deal with it within ourself.

(12) A woman was married to a man who always lied to her. She didn't understand how she could have married such a liar when she always told him the truth. Yet if she had looked a little deeper into the mirror of the situation and had been willing to trust its reflection, she would have eventually noticed that she was always lying—to herself.

(13) A man with chronic bone pain had run the gamut of medical tests, yet none of his doctors could find anything wrong with him. His conscious worldview was strictly western-scientific, and so he never strayed from the western medical model. One day, after having a talk with a chiropractor in a health food store, he decided to take a

chance and later asked the store's owner for the chiropractor's phone number. But the owner didn't think the chiropractor would help him, so he gave the man the number of a local healer without telling him that this wasn't the chiropractor's number. The man didn't realize until after he had entered the healer's home that she wasn't the chiropractor he had spoken with, she wasn't even a chiropractor, and that her healing methods involved utilizing universal, spiritual energy to balance the body's energy system. This was almost too much for him, as even the idea of using chiropractic had required stretching his world-view. Yet because of his pain, he tried a session with the healer, and it created the first easing of the pain he had experienced. In addition, within a couple of days, he began to have experiences that didn't match his old world view and, after several months of working with the healer, his pain was almost gone, his view of reality had completely changed, and he was having mystical experiences.

This example illustrates several things, the first being the role of the *intentions of our Self.* The convoluted path that brought the man to the healer had not been created by "accident"; it had been carefully devised by his own deeper consciousness, by his out-of-trance Self. Yet his soul-consciousness did not manifest this situation in a vacuum. Although the situation did not mirror any of his conscious beliefs (his conscious beliefs were mirrored by his physical problems), the fact that the man had been able to undergo such a dramatic personal transformation so quickly indicated a certain level of awareness that already existed in him, even if unconsciously. So, this example also illustrates that a soul can be in a more advanced stage of enlightening its human experience than is apparent from the outer form of its human life. In these cases, the soul pretends to forget, while in its human trance, what it has learned, enabling it to create the right situation for exploring certain unresolved issues. When these tangential issues are finally resolved, the person's life will usually undergo a dramatic transformation, enabling what has been learned from previous entrancements to come forward.

This man's experience of chronic bone pain was the vehicle for his final stage of getting ready for personal transformation—when his despair over his pain and his frustration with traditional medicine's lack of answers became great enough, there was a conscious letting go of certain limiting beliefs, enabling him to risk stepping out of the conventional medical model and enabling his soul-consciousness to devise events so that his spirituality could surface again in his life.

(14) A woman with issues about trust and insecurity in relationships was in emotional turmoil after she found out, shortly after her boyfriend had discussed the possibility of marriage with her, that he had been—and still was—sleeping with another woman. The woman felt angry, humiliated, hurt, and enraged. Yet because of the inner spiritual work she had done, she also knew that in spite of his betrayal she was still responsible for all these emotions, that although her boyfriend (now ex-boyfriend) had precipitated an emotional crisis within her, he was activating issues and attitudes that had already been there. She also trusted that what had happened had been created for her own growth, that it was designed to serve Love, and that his behavior mirrored areas where she was stuck within herself (otherwise she wouldn't have attracted this man); yet at the same time, part of her was still caught in all her stuck feelings and attitudes and still blamed him for them.

Since this woman recognized her own responsibility for her experience as well as for where she was stuck, she was in a perfect position to create personal transformation, to bring her awareness of Love into the parts of herself that were entranced with fear and victimization. And because the situation had enabled her boyfriend to become a focal point for her inner attitudes, she now had a perfect mirror in which she would be able to see how well she had transformed certain issues and where she was still stuck: all she needed to do was to think of her boyfriend and notice the extent and intensity of the attitudes and blaming that came up. Wherever she didn't experience unconditional love, she was still stuck.

It should be pointed out that assuming responsibility for her experience will not in itself determine whether she will want to give the man another chance if he asks for one. Assuming responsibility will enable her to stop blaming him for her experience and give her the opportunity to encounter and transform the areas within her own consciousness that contributed to the creation of this experience; yet she must still hold the man responsible for his deceitful, hurtful behavior. If he is willing to assume responsibility for his behavior and use what happened to help himself transform where he is stuck, the woman might decide to try the relationship again. Yet she may not. And either choice, depending upon the situation, could be a choosing of fear or a choosing of love. Three things are certain though: (1) if the woman doesn't assume responsibility for co-creating the situation, she will only be able to choose from fear, (2) if she cannot fully forgive the man, then she shouldn't reenter into a relationship with him, and (3) if she cannot fully forgive the man (whether she stays in the relationship or not), then at some point she will create new life-lessons around whatever is stuck within her that resists and prevents forgiveness.

(15) A man was always complaining that his girlfriend was only half in the relationship, that she always had one foot out the door. The man was committed to the relationship, but the woman couldn't honestly give that commitment, and whenever things started to go a little badly she would talk about leaving. It wasn't until she finally left him that he recognized some of the mirrors in the relationship. He saw that although he was committed to the relationship, his own emotional walls allowed only half of him to actually be in the relationship; in spite of his commitment, he always had one foot out of the relationship, too. In addition, he saw that to camouflage his own emotional holding back, his needy child-character took the position of "I'll take care of you if you'll stay with me," which her own needy child-character agreed to, even though his character used his position as a way of controlling her. He saw that conflicts between them were created when he resented the fact that the position he had taken meant that he himself wasn't being taken care of; he wanted her to take care of him, too. One of his parental-characters would then criticize her, one of her own parental-characters would resent being criticized, and her needy child-character would withdraw.

Without an understanding of the inner dynamics between them (and there were many more than the few mentioned here), her leaving him was almost the only possible outcome of the relationship, in spite of the fact that they both actually loved each other very much.

(16) A woman with many emotional walls had grown up with a brother who constantly beat her up.

One day she had an experience in which her heart opened, and this immediately raised the issue—although she wasn't conscious of this—of whether it was really safe for her to keep her heart open in a world where people like her brother could attack her. Just a few days later, she was attacked by a man while she was working in her office. In the context of the opening she had just experienced, it was obvious to her that this was no "accident," that the external attack had to be some kind of mirror of her inner situation as well as some kind of vehicle for helping her to resolve it.

There are no accidents in life. We live in a world of mutual creation, in which nothing can happen except through the intention of our soul's own free will. Everything serves Love.

Awareness Exercise 26:
General Mirrors
Part 1

For this exercise you will need paper and a pen. This part of the exercise is intended to help you become aware of the general mirrors that you have created in your life.

Write down your answers to the following questions:

(1) What, in general, do you react to or resist? (This includes situations as well as behaviors exhibited by other people or yourself.)

(2) What emotional attitudes do you usually react with?

(3) What do you blame other people or situations for?

(4) What else (in addition to #3) do you not assume responsibility for?

(5) What are the basic problem areas or patterns in your life?

(6) What do you get attached to?

(7) What are you afraid of?

(8) What else, in addition to (6) and (7), brings up your sense of need?

(9) What else (in addition to all of the previous questions) blocks your experience of unconditional love?

(10) What else blocks your experience of peace?

(11) What are your unresolved traumas?

(12) In what kind of situations that people usually react to, do you not react?

(13) What, in general, expands your experience of unconditional love and joy?

(14) What else, in general, gives you a lot of pleasure?

(15) What kind of body do you have? Is it healthy, muscular, frail, bony, tense, relaxed ...?

(16) What are your hobbies?

(17) What are your dreams, hopes, and fantasies?

Part 2

Since all of our life experiences are designed according to our learning needs, we can think of life as a school, The School of Enlightening Our Human Experience, with each of our individual lives a curriculum that we are taking. The idea is not to be overwhelmed or identified with our curriculum, but to experience it with awareness and compassion and to acknowledge responsibility for our experience, since we got here by enrolling, and we designed our own curriculum.

This second part of the exercise is designed simply to help you to be aware of your life as a curriculum, so you can have a better sense of what you are learning. The focus is on your current curriculum.

Draw a dotted line under whatever you wrote down for Part 1, and then right below it, write down: your name, age, sex, spouse or lover's name, parents' names (with the ones that are still living underlined), other immediate family members (also underlined), close friends, occupation, boss (if you have one), coworkers, address, the nature of your residence, hobbies, pastimes, channels for creativity, and the most important plans you have for the next month.

Then meditate on what you have just written, along with what you wrote down in Part 1, as your present curriculum in life.

AWARENESS EXERCISE 27:
MIRROR OF EXTREMES

In your daily encounters, look for people whose attitudes and holding patterns are similar to yours but more extreme. Then, as you interact with them, imagine that you are their therapist. What do you see? What would you tell them about the nature of their patterns? What would you suggest to help them release these patterns?

Examining more extreme examples of your own resistance patterns can make it easier to see your patterns clearly. This is the mirror of extremes.

PART IV

Reincarnation & the Incarnational Personality

26

Levels of Trance-Identity

The irony of this journey
is, there is no place
to get to, and you have to walk
through thousands of lives
to arrive.

At some point in no-time, each of our souls, in its infinite creativity, decided to explore a certain area within its own consciousness that had to do with emotional issues (and forms of creativity) that would arise with the experience of feeling separated from the Source of Life and being bound within the finiteness of time. Yet the soul is always aware of its Oneness—it is a Self-conscious individuation within the One out-of-trance Self—and it always exists outside of time; so to explore this area of itself, it needed to create a trance in which this part of its consciousness would experience itself as a very different kind of being.

The soul could have directly en-tranced itself as a physical being, but then each of its lives would be a separate, disconnected experience; to create a sense of continuity and evolution within time required a being that both lived in time and continued to live from life to life. So our souls created (through entrancement) a being that was neither human nor "physical," but rather an incarnational personality: a being that lived in time yet never died, that was aware of its connection to the soul yet felt separate, and whose primary mode of experience was emotion. Such a being could experience (through entrancement) a succession of physical lives (human and otherwise), which would give it a vehicle through which it could explore and evolve itself. An incarnational drama was thus created, spanning thousands of lives, in which the incarnational personality, having been created as a trance-expression of the soul's consciousness, en-trances itself into physical life, evolving its emotional awareness as it explores (and eventually enlightens) the issues that arise from its experience of separateness. Our human emotions, attitudes, and desires (not including our purely physical desires, such as hunger) are really those of our incarnational personality, experienced in our human body.[22]

Within our human trance, we tend to identify with our humanness and believe that this is who we are. Yet our human experience is the result of our Self en-trancing as a soul (to explore the Mystery within Its own Beingness), the soul then en-trancing as an emotionally-oriented and time-bound incarnational personality, the incarnational personality en-trancing as a human being, and finally the human being en-trancing as various kinds of person-identities and "characters" (for example, a man might experience himself as a competent and dependable truck driver, as a lonely, arthritic old man, and so on). Each level of trance is created as an exploration of the level preceding it, so as we enlighten our experience of being human, we enlighten our incarnational personality, our soul, and our Self. (In terms of the Unified Field, each level of trance corresponds to a different level, or rate, of vibratory energy within the Field.)

Although this may seem confusing at first, these levels of trance-identity are just different levels of our own consciousness through which we are exploring our Self. This is similar to what happens with a tree: the trunk grows out of the roots, and leaves grow from the branches. And just as all these individuations of the tree are still Tree, at every level of our being, independent of our particular identity, we are always our Self, and we always have direct access to every other level of our consciousness, for there are no real boundaries within the Self. So, if we are stuck in our human trance, we never really need to be concerned about what level it is coming from, for anything we are exploring as a human being is an exploration of

---

[22]In previous chapters I used the word "soul" and "incarnational personality" interchangeably, for convienience. Only now am I drawing a distinction between the incarnational personality and the soul's experience *through its trance as an incarnational personality.* In other writings as well, when the word "soul" is used, the context will have to be the indicator of whether the soul or incarnational personality is really being discussed.

our Self, of an area of our own Consciousness that needs more enlightenment, and it is always our Self-as-human-being that is responsible for creating that enlightenment.

As we saw earlier, every level of trance-identity expands the Self's experience of Itself, yet paradoxically, within each level, the being's identity beliefs limit a deeper experience of its Self. This paradox is at the heart of the process through which creation expands and Love unfolds throughout it; because even as the Self creates identity-trances in which it can explore Itself, within each separateness-trance the local consciousness is eventually forced to break free of the limitations of its identity and experience its Oneness with its Self.

As human beings, we are not limited to identifying with our humanness. We can identify with our possessions, with our body or particular parts of it, with our minds or our emotions, with our creations, with our country, with other people, and so on. We can also identify with other levels of our trance-identity, believing we are our incarnational self or our soul self. Each identity we form expands the Self's experience of Itself and traps us within a trance-illusion. Yet this is also part of the process through which we enlighten our experience of being human (and thus enlighten all the other levels of our consciousness as well). Becoming human, therefore, is a wonderful opportunity for us, for it gives us a unique vehicle through which we can explore all the levels of our Self and unfold our Love.

Understanding the levels and dynamics of our trance-identities can be very valuable, yet we must always remember that within all these trances, there is only One Self experiencing Itself, One Creator enlightening the infinite dimensions of its own Consciousness.

27

✧

The Incarnational Point of View

At every level of our en-tranced Consciousness, we experience a sense of identity and have a point of view which reflects our current awareness at that level. Hence, our incarnational personality has its own point of view—an *incarnational point of view*—which is primarily an emotional one, made up of emotional attitudes and desires, as well as awarenesses that allow the experience of love, compassion, and joy. This is in keeping with the dual nature of our incarnational self, for it is aware of its connection to the soul—in fact, it consciously receives guidance from the soul—and knows that it is safe; yet at the same time, its sense of separateness is strong enough to create fundamental feelings of loss and lack, and fears of annihilation. And its point of view also contains this critical awareness: that its path is to use physical life as a vehicle for transforming these areas of darkness and separateness into free expressions of Light and Self.

When the incarnational personality enters a new human trance, it brings its emotional point of view into its new human consciousness, so its fears and past-life emotional charges become the fabric of our human fears and attitudes; its areas of inner darkness manifest as the positions we take as human beings to make ourself feel more safe. In previous chapters, therefore, I was referring to the point of view of our incarnational self whenever I pointed to our emotional point of view, our emotional beliefs, our desires, our inner characters, or our attitudes. In fact, because having a human body tends to amplify the personality's experience of separateness, these areas of inner darkness, which grow out of the experience of separateness, are

213

brought into an especially magnified focus. (Of course, this is why human life provides such a wonderful opportunity for the incarnational personality to work on these issues.) But the incarnational personality is made up of more than stuck emotional attitudes. Outside of its human trance, it has a much larger experience of love-consciousness, and this awareness of love becomes part of our human awareness of love and compassion.

The incarnational personality is also involved in the mutual-creation process described in Part II, and plans soon-to-occur events with other personalities. Yet it is consciously guided by the soul, and it is the soul, being outside of time, that guides the main stream of events into our lives and has the power to "intervene," either by manifesting an event or by acting through us so that we do something that we hadn't consciously intended. So, in spite of the role of the incarnational personality with planning events, the soul will still be referred to as the creator of events in our lives (which is the Self acting through the soul); and in expressions such as "we plan future events," the "we" refers mainly to our souls, yet also to our incarnational personalities as guided by our souls.

The incarnational personality does much of its planning with other beings while we sleep, when the intense focus of functioning within a physical body relaxes. The incarnational personality then "leaves" its physical body to go and interact with other beings; yet because it is still identified with its present human form, it will appear very much like its present human body. Planning can also take place while we are awake, for areas of the incarnational personality's consciousness always remain free of the limitations of its human trance; yet to act at this level while awake, even unconsciously, we need to "blink" in and out of our body, which is analogous to the way we have to shift our attention back and forth to drive and carry on a conversation at the same time.

We design our human lives as vehicles for transforming the fears and illusions we hold as an incarnational personality. And eventually, of course, we do enlighten our incarnational self, which really means that within that trance we will recognize our self-limiting beliefs and attitudes for the trance-illusions they are, and we will remember, within the dark corners of our consciousness, that we are Love. When that happens, the incarnational personality's journey is finished. That human life continues to be lived out, but since the incarnational personality is really just a time-bound entrancement for the soul's consciousness, at the end of that life all of its consciousness returns to the soul consciousness, which is outside of time and space and is conscious of itself as Self.

Although we are usually unaware, within our human trance, of our incarnational point of view, it exists within us, and so its beliefs, emotional attitudes, and intentions operate within our human awareness, even if unconsciously. Most of our unconscious beliefs are related to emotional attitudes and are part of the incarnational point of view that we took with us when we entranced into human form. Even our conscious beliefs, when they contain underlying emotional content, are expressions of our incarnational point of view. For instance, if a woman believes that her children need to be sent to bed without dinner to learn right from wrong, her conscious belief expresses an unconscious emotional attitude that originates within her incarnational point of view. Yet there are no emotional roots to the belief that striking a match will create a flame, so it is not derived from our incarnational self. Sometimes, though, what seems to be a rational, intellectual belief is only a mask for an underlying emotional one. For instance, the woman who believed in depriving her children of dinner probably had many reasons and proofs about why this method was the most effective, yet these are simply justifications for her unconscious emotional attitudes.

In Part I, we saw that our point of view determines our personal reality. As human beings, that point of view necessarily includes our incarnational point of view, as well as the point of view of our body (and the Natural Law it embodies), the point of view of our soul, and our awareness of the Love Consciousness of our Self. They are all part of the structure of our human consciousness, and they will all be reflected in the mirror of our lives.

AWARENESS EXERCISE 28:
OUR INCARNATIONAL SELF

PART 1

Sit comfortably and close your eyes. Receive a few deep breaths ... and let yourself relax. You must allow yourself to get very relaxed to receive what is intended from this exercise ...

Now, you are going to "play dead." (And you thought this was only a trick for dogs.) Just imagine what you would experience if your body simply stopped functioning. Imagine all feeling and sensation gone from your body. Imagine your body filled with dead silence, still as a rock. Actually feel your body go dead. What happens?

If you can allow your body to "go dead" you will notice that it sort of drops away, or conversely, that some part of you seems to move out of it—the part of you that isn't dead. Although you will still tend to project your human personality onto this part of yourself, you may be able to sense that it is somewhat different from your usual human self. The sense of this difference will give you a glimpse of your incarnational personality.

PART 2

For the next few days, whenever you interact with people, instead of being completely focused on their human personality, look for their incarnational personality. Look for the personality that is separate from, but is inhabiting, the body in front of you. You can imagine that these people had just done Part 1 of this exercise; who would they experience themselves to be? You can also try to perceive them as they were before they entered their mother's womb and entranced with their body. Who were these beings then?

In addition, imagine how these people would experience themselves if they were totally ecstatic, totally filled with joy and love, experiencing themselves as blessed. This is a door to their soul-consciousness. Perceive who they become then.

Next time you are emotionally reacting to someone, stop and become aware of your own incarnational personality or soul-self, and then perceive the other person's as well; it will change the way you experience the situation.

28

The Emotional Body/
The Astral Body

In other writings, there are many references to the "emotional body" and to the "astral body." In general, these may be considered to be equivalent to the incarnational personality. Yet when these terms are used, only a particular aspect of the incarnational personality is usually being considered, and unfortunately, that aspect is often believed to be the whole of the incarnational personality.

When the term "astral body" is used, the focus is usually upon the fact that the incarnational personality has its home on the astral "plane" (or trance-level) of consciousness, that it has a human-looking form or "body" that is astral in nature, and that it can travel out of the physical body, traveling through the astral plane, which is called "astral travel."

The term "emotional body" refers to the fact that the incarnational personality is the source of our emotional consciousness and can hold emotional charges. Yet when this term is used, the focus is usually upon the incarnational personality's "negative" or stuck areas of emotional consciousness and all the past-life emotional charges the personality has carried with it into its present existence. Some of these areas can be noticed through psychological perception; but because the incarnational personality's unenlightened issues are expressed in its human-looking "body" as corresponding areas of darkness that hold negative emotional charges, they can also be perceived directly by a trained observer. For instance, a fear of choking will express itself as an emotionally-charged area of darkness in the personality's throat area, containing attitudes and unreleased emotional memories—either present or past-life—connected to choking.

Treating the incarnational personality as an emotional body, therefore, has certain benefits. First of all, a therapist who can see or sense the nature of a client's emotional charges will instantly know what issues the client is working with. In addition, if the therapist or client is able to see the memories stored within those charges—often called "pictures"—some of the context and structure of those issues will be known. For instance, the nature of an emotional charge in a man's throat area may reveal that fear of choking is an issue for him; yet if a past-life picture in which he is being choked by a lover is perceived, then his choking issue will be understood more deeply, and this may shed light on other issues—such as a fear of intimate relationships.

Yet when treating the incarnational personality as an emotional body two things should be taken into consideration. First of all, when a context for an issue is clearly visible, it becomes easy to forget that there is usually more to the story—there is more context. For instance, the man with the choking issue may have had a past life in which he cut someone's head off. This, in turn, may have been a response to a deep sense of powerlessness in that life—an issue which would, of course, have had its own long history.

A second consideration is that it becomes easy to forget that a context perceived in an emotional picture is not necessarily what really happened—it is what the person experienced, which has often been highly distorted by some character aspect of the personality that is attempting to support its position.

There are certain esoteric forms of "healing work" that directly release the emotional charges held in the emotional body. This is a valid way of working with emotional issues, yet what happens with this kind of healing work is generally misunderstood. This is because, regardless of what historical context served to create an issue for the incarnational personality, once the issue is created it becomes an identity for the personality, a fixed emotional position with a belief structure. Releasing the original emotional charges does not necessarily release the beliefs that formed around them, and so the character-identity remains as well, and the incarnational personality will still be struck in its position. Over time, the incarnational personality will simply create new emotional charges as new experiences trigger reactions in the emotional character. But releasing those charges did release the supports for the incarnational personality's position, weakening it, and making its position transparent, thus creating an opportunity for the consciousness stuck in that position to see through its trance. So instead of creating an actual healing, freeing the emotional charges creates a healing *situation*, an opportunity for the stuck consciousness, which has suddenly found itself more open and without supports for its trance-position or character, to change.

With this kind of healing technique, even when the stuck position is not *released,* the person treated will feel *relieved*—for a while anyway—of some burden of "negative" charge they have been carrying. This is beneficial—both because of the openness it creates, even if temporarily, and because frequently the supports for a trance-position need to be released first before the position or trance itself will let go. But because the person treated feels emotionally lighter, they will often mistake this relief for release and believe that this healing technique is more effective than it actually is.

In some forms of healing work, though, the healer is able to bring the awareness of Love or Self directly into the stuck area of the incarnational personality's consciousness. In those situations, not only is charge released but also belief structures; the new awareness awakens the incarnational personality in that part of its consciousness to its true nature, and the character-trance is dissolved completely. This is true healing for the incarnational personality.

Perceiving the incarnational personality as an emotional body can be a valuable tool, as long as one remembers that the incarnational personality's emotional consciousness is really very broad, and is infused with much love and awareness.

29

The Role of Previous Entrancements

In spite of the invisibility of our incarnational point of view, it becomes quite noticeable when two siblings, born to the same parents, exhibit radically different personalities. One is peaceful, the other angry, even violent. One likes the company of other people, the other must be alone. They have the same parents, but the commonality of their history ends there. They have each had millions of years of unique experiences, which have shaped their current experience of life.

In general, over our millions of years of experience, we have done, thought, believed and identified with that which has moved us deeper into limitation, stuckness, and trance; and we have also manifested that which has moved us toward love, awareness and inner freedom. The unique cumulation of both sets of experiences is where our consciousness resides today.

If we invested a lot of time identifying with trance experiences of violence, then today, consciously or unconsciously, part of our consciousness will be caught in trances focused on violence, with all the related issues that go along with that. If we spent much of our last life caught in greed-trances, whether that took the form of greed for money or status or manifested as a general attitude of selfishness, then unless we have freed ourself that trance, part of our consciousness will still be caught in it today. The trance that we live in today is the trance that we have been creating and freeing ourself from for millions of years. This cumulative trance is our current incarnational point of view. (It is also often referred to as our "karmic situation.")

Some of our trances can be quite specific. For instance, if in a previous life I drowned, and while drowning I projected onto the experience all my trance survival-fears, then I would have created a new trance out of these older ones, one in which there would be a lot of emotional charge, especially fear, surrounding the experience of breathing or being in water. If I have not yet freed myself from that trance, then today, I would still have some kind of fear that would reflect that earlier experience. It could be a fear of the ocean, or a fear related to breathing, such as asthma, or chronic chest colds, or even a fear of emotional suffocation.

In spiritual literature, there is frequent mention of the Sanskrit word "samskara," which refers to the lasting, fixed impressions made on the consciousness by an experience. The present effects of our past life experiences are seen as an accumulation of these samskaras. But essentially, this is the same idea as involving our consciousness in a trance, for we will create a trance around any experience that we resist, avoid, struggle with, or identity with; and it is this process that solidifies the experience into a "lasting, fixed impression." Experiences that we totally open to, allowing them to be exactly as they are, pass through us, creating neither trances nor samskaras.

The trances created in this life and in our more recent lives will usually be more active than those from more distant lives, just as our emotional experience from our most recent relationship will tend to be more active today than one from our teenage years. But the trances we created in that teenage relationship became part of the structure of the trances we created in our twenties, and so on. Although our survival-fear trances from millions of years ago may no longer be as active as those created in later lives, they became part of the structure of those created in the lives that followed, which entered into the structure of those that followed them, eventually creating a survival-fear trance with thousands of layers of structure made up of millions of years of experiential history. Today, such a long-standing trance will manifest a new survival drama, perhaps with an issue such as poverty, cancer, or abandonment at its center.

The overall, cumulative trance we existed in before taking birth in this life would be called our incarnational point of view (or karmic situation) at that point in time. This determined which family we would be born into, and formed the background consciousness for all our experiences in this life.

But we are not a victim of either our past trances or our present ones. Whatever trance we are caught in today exists only because we keep believing in, maintaining, and identifying with it today. For instance, a woman who is afraid of becoming pregnant may trace her condition to a past life experience in which she died in childbirth. Although this connection might be true, it would be more true to say that she developed the present-life fear because she had not yet freed the part of her consciousness that was still en-tranced with the earlier experience—and with the issue in the center of that experience (which may have existed as an issue even before this particular experience took place). The past trance continued to affect her only because she kept identifying with it in the present, re-creating it and dragging it along with her into each new present moment, making it part of the structure of her present trance. So, although her present fear of pregnancy is tied to an experience from her past, she cannot blame her past life for her present situation; she must assume responsibility in the present for what she still needs to transform.

Historically, as an incarnational personality, we started with one issue, one trance: our trance-experience of separateness. As we generated fears and experiences of lack within this trance, and as we resisted, avoided, and struggled over this experience, we created new issues and new trances, leading eventually to the unique, multi-faceted trance that we call our life, today. Yet this whole trance still depends upon its original root—our trance experience of separateness. In fact, one can view all the trances that followed as nothing more than supports for the positions of fear and lack that we began with and are still en-tranced with today. When we free ourself from our trance of separateness, all the trances that depend upon our experience of separateness dissolve; our fear, our anger, our neediness, our unworthiness—all cease to exist.

As stated earlier, our present-life trance has also been called our "karmic situation." The Sanskrit word *karma* is generally understood to refer to the universal law of "cause and effect." In the west, this law has been stated in terms of "as you sow, so shall ye reap." The idea of karma, therefore, simply refers to the fact that we are responsible for our actions (and thoughts, beliefs and identifications) and will experience the consequences of them, in this life or another one.

Many people mistakenly interpret karma to be a law of crime and punishment: as you sow, so shall you be punished. But being responsible for experiencing the consequences of our actions is a different concept than being punished for them. It is through experiencing the consequences of our actions that we learn and become responsible, which is a process involving love, free will, and compassion. And it is these principles, along with grace, that are the foundation of the universe, not crime and punishment. (Grace can release karma, or modify it so that, for example, what would have been a crippling car accident becomes a minor fender-bender.)

In a universe of crime and punishment, a man who murders another human being would have no choice but to be murdered in turn. But that is not how karma works. Karma simply says that the murderer's incarnational personality must experience the consequences of his actions. Although experiencing being killed would be one choice, one possible way to experience the consequences of those actions, other choices are possible. The personality might, for instance, choose to "work off its karma" (experience the consequences of its actions) by being a Red Cross volunteer in a war and administering to the ill and dying. Although this would be more indirect, the personality would still experience the consequences of its actions. Another possibility is that the personality would have an "accident" and become crippled for the rest of his life. And regardless of the choice, the personality would also be forced, as consequences, to experience guilt, as well as being caught more deeply in trance. (Of course, the karma from killing someone in self-defense would be different than from murdering someone in cold blood. And even in the case of self-defense, the karma would be different if the killing were performed from a state of detached necessity than if it were performed from a state of hateful vengeance.)

Another mistake people make about karma is believing that until we have "worked off all our karma" we cannot free ourself from our trance. But our trance is like a dream, and the dream does not have the power to hold us en-tranced in its reality if, within the dream, with full intent, we choose to wake up. In addition, no matter what karmic drama we were experiencing within that dream, the moment we wake up, all that drama with all its karmic consequences simply disappears. Karma is a law that applies to this particular dream; it operates only on incarnational personalities in trance-experiences of separateness. When we wake up—when we move through the basic illusion of separateness that keeps us in trance—there is no dream-character, no separate person-ality, left to be subject to or experience karma. The incarnational personality has become a clear and transparent window for the soul, which exists outside of time. Then, it is like waking up from a dream, but allowing the dream to continue to play out in our mind. We are completely free of the dream, it no longer affects us, but we continue to experience it unfold in our consciousness. Within the dream, though, if we had cancer, we will most likely still have cancer. Since we are no longer affected by the dream, there is no reason to change it. So, whatever karmas were still existing in and affecting the body when we were identified with our trance will tend to continue when we wake up.

While we are still living in the dream, though, it can be useful to remember some of the dream-situations that became part of the structure of our present dream. Remembering past lives can quite useful for clarifying our issues and cleaning up our drama today. Yet this kind of remembrance is not necessary. Even a survival-trance that is millions of years old still has only one issue in its core: survival, based on the experience of separateness. We can deal with that issue without remembering other lives and contexts in which we experienced it. When we have cleared the issue in its core, the whole trance falls apart; all we are left with then are the habits of our human consciousness—although the trance is gone from our incarnational personality, by habit our human mind may continue to structure our experience as if the issue still exists.

People are naturally curious about their past lives. They know that there is more to who they are than what they are used to experiencing. And they intuitively sense that their past experience has something to do with their present lives. Knowing that, a small percentage of those people, when they find out about their past lives, will use the knowledge to help them deal with their present issues. But past-life knowledge has other uses as well: it can help us to be aware of unconscious creative potentials that we developed in the past (for instance, as an artist), help us expand our sense of personal self, and help us to free ourself from the narrow identity-trance of our present human self. Even more importantly, remembering past lives helps us to realize that all of our fear-trances are just illusions. For we become able to clearly see that death is just a door and that no experience in human life can destroy us, or even truly hurt us. We may have been tortured to death in the past, and yet here we are, still in one piece, safe and sound. Unquestionably, this is the most important value of remembering past entrancements: it helps us to realize that life is completely safe for us to experience.

꧁꧂

30

The Role of the Womb

At the moment of conception, a door to the Creative Source opens within the mother's physical body and there is an explosion of Life. This door stays open throughout the pregnancy, causing the physical creation process in the womb to vibrate with a very pure quality of Divine Love, as Creative Consciousness unfolds Itself into form. (This presents an opportunity for the parents to deepen their conscious connection to the Creative Source, because a door is right there, and it is wide open.) When the incarnational personality enters the womb and becomes embedded within this light and love, it experiences a deep sense of oneness and Self; and although this is not the full Oneness of enlightenment, it is deep enough that the incarnational personality is able to surrender into the experience and identify itself with it. Yet since this experience is being derived from the creation process that is unfolding through the new body, when the incarnational personality identifies itself with this experience it also identifies with the new body. So, the love emanating from the body in the womb and the relative oneness that it provides acts to help the incarnational personality enter into a very deep trance, which is the trance of human reality. (The quality of love experienced in the womb is usually more intense in the early stages of pregnancy, because as the fetus grows, the personality becomes more conscious of—and reacts to—its actual physical experience, which includes its mother's emotional states and what is happening in her immediate environment.)

Yet even as we surrender into this love and relative oneness, because the body is so susceptible to emotional imprints in the womb, it automatically begins to become imprinted with the holding patterns of our own incarnational personality. (And the imprint will be intensified, as we will see later, by the birth process.) This begins, in a subtle way, to block in the new body the flow of life and love that our incarnational personality had surrendered into so deeply; yet by providing the environment for this to happen, the womb also ensures the integration of the personality into the new body, which will be necessary for their journey together through the schoolroom of human reality.

The womb, as described in Chapter 21, is also the vehicle for our parental womb-imprints, which provide us with a way to force particular holding patterns and attitudes in our emotional point of view into the forefront of our consciousness, thereby helping us to explore these issues.

The womb has one last role to play: because its environment provides us with a sense of relative oneness, it enables us to reenact our experience of becoming separated from our Source, from God, when we are born. (Some babies begin to feel a strong sense of separation from Source while still in the womb.) Yet this reenactment is now experienced in human terms: the womb and the mother are experienced as the source of Life we are being separated from; and since the feeling-tone of the mother is essentially human, we quickly learn to expand our sense of source from mother to any human's love and nurturing, setting up the drama in which we will try to get love from other people to fill our sense of lack. This transfer of our sense of Source into human terms is reinforced by the fact that, after we have been born, our womb experience is our most recent memory of deep connectedness and oneness, and of the kind of love that feels like Home.

So the womb is not simply the place where the physical body grows until it is mature enough to be born; the womb acts as a bridge for our incarnational personality to enter into the trance of human reality, and it is a vehicle for setting up the external drama that the personality will use to explore and enlighten itself.

AWARENESS EXERCISE 29:
OM, THE SOUND OF THE ETERNAL WOMB

Sound has a profound effect on all living things. In the form of music, it can relax us or affect us emotionally; in other forms it can kill. Sound is so powerful because it is vibration, and all the individualized forms of creation are patterns of energy (within the Unified Field), which are patterns of vibration. Just as white light contains all the different colors of light (and all of them combined create white), there is one sound that contains all other sounds, and which all other sounds become when combined. That sound is OM.

OM is therefore in harmony with all sounds, with all patterns of vibration. *OM is the resonant sound of all creation; it is the fundamental vibration of the entire Unified Field.* And since the Unified Field of Creation is really our Self, the sound of OM begins to bring any individualized aspect of our Self—any pattern of energy in the Field—into a deeper harmony with our Self.

OM can be used, therefore, to awaken our awareness to the eternal womb of creation within us, to the infinite peace and love that resides within our Self. (Light is also used by meditators to awaken their awareness. The inner light, like OM, is a primary vibration that is in harmony with all aspects of our Self. Light and sound are simply different vibratory expressions of Consciousness.)

PART I

Sit comfortably, with your back fairly straight, and close your eyes. Receive a few deep breaths ... and let yourself relax.

Now, begin to say the word OM in your mind, and as you hear the OM, feel the vibration of the sound filling and resonating in your head. *You are simultaneously thinking OM, hearing OM, and feeling OM.* Allow yourself to relax into the sound, so that it fills your mind and your head, and then feel the OM resonating in the rest of your body as well. The rate at which you are thinking OM can vary—let it go as fast or as slow as feels natural at the time. This is also true of the loudness of the sound; it can move along the continuum of very loud to barely audible, although in the beginning of the meditation it usually works better to have it louder to set up the vibration.

Notice that in the sound of OM, there is an almost silent "u" sound between the "O" and the "M". It is important to hear and feel that almost silent "u", for it contains the essence of the OM; in fact, where the "u" actually becomes silent is the doorway to the Inner Silence, to the Formless Ground of Beingness that gives birth to the Tree of Life. As you work with the OM, it acts as a funnel, taking you down into that Silence at the root of its sound, into the Silent Beingness of your Self.

At times you will feel the sound more in your head, at other times more in your body. Do not try to control what is happening; simply allow it to happen. Also do not try to control or resist any of the many different kinds of sensations that may be experienced in this kind of meditation.

When you find that you have gone off in your thoughts, simply bring yourself back. Losing your focus temporarily is a natural part of the meditative process, so you shouldn't berate yourself for it. And, you shouldn't resist your thoughts. They will be there whether you go off in them or not—they are just clouds passing through the open sky of your awareness; do not be bothered by them or try to control them or spend time examining them. If you have a sudden awareness about yourself, note it, but do not go off thinking about it; just continue going deeper; continue thinking/ hearing/feeling OM. Merge and become one with the sound of OM.

Do this for at least forty minutes.

PART 2

This part is used for releasing attitude and character-trances.

Begin as before: thinking, hearing, and feeling OM. As you do this notice any places that are stuck, that resist relaxing into OM. The stuck place could be a tight spot in your body, a stuck emotion, or an inner character. If such a place comes up, go *inside* that place and experience yourself *as that place,* thinking, hearing, and feeling OM. More specifically, if a resistant inner character comes up, align yourself with it, enter into it, and experience yourself *as that character,* thinking, hearing, and feeling OM. If an emotional attitude comes up and you don't sense the specific character that is holding it, then go into that emotion, entering into the part of yourself that is feeling or expressing it and, as that part of yourself, think, hear, and feel OM. If the stuck place is a tight area in your body, then enter into that place—inhabit the core of it—and then from within your oneness with that part of your body think, hear, and feel OM.

31

Issues From Birth & Infancy

ISSUES FROM BIRTH

We bring the totality of our emotional point of view with us into our birth experience. (This is composed of whatever emotional trances we still carry from past lives in our incarnational personality, our womb imprints, and the emotional point of view created by the experience of inhabiting a unique, new human body.) As with all experiences, to the degree that we are en-tranced with self-limiting emotional beliefs, we will try to use whatever happens in birth to support these beliefs and the attitudes they generate (because we believe this is how we stay safe). Yet birth is unique in that the emotional experience of birth is usually imprinted much more deeply in our body than other experiences—more than other intense and traumatic ones—because (1) the birth experience is our body's first intense experience (unless our mother was traumatized during pregnancy), (2) it is our new human consciousness' first intense experience in that body, and (3) the emotional imprint that our body will receive during birth (determined mostly by our emotional point of view), will shape our body's first breath, creating a deep imprint on the breathing process itself.

Thus, through our birth experience, we imprint our emotional point of view deeply into our physical body, and our body acquires a holding pattern that matches our own resistance to life. From the point of view of our soul and our incarnational personality, this makes our birth experience a wonderful opportunity to set up the particular kind of life-drama that will best feed our growth. In fact, very often, we re-create in relationships and in other areas of our life the exact emotional drama we created for ourself with our birth experience.

Although we can project our emotional point of view onto any kind of birth situation, as an incarnational personality we will be drawn to the particular birth situations that match our karmic situation and that we believe will most help us to explore the areas of ourself that are stuck. For instance, if we are exploring dependency issues, we may choose a birth situation in which we will cling to the womb, resisting being born, and the doctor induces the birth. Or we may choose a situation in which we will have to depend on an artificial lung machine for some time to survive. Yet we may also choose a birth situation that is gentle and nurturing, if this would more effectively help us to explore and enlighten where we are stuck. To set up the life-drama that will best feed our growth, we choose our birth experience (and the imprint it will create) very carefully, matching the situation to our emotional point of view and our learning needs. And we are always guided by our soul-consciousness.

In the same manner, groups of incarnational personalities may all use a particular kind of birth situation or technique to set up similar kinds of imprints, facilitating certain kinds of group dramas. For instance, the increase of social violence and the disintegration of the family happened with the generation that was birthed with the "modern" medical technique of taking the newborn away from its mother and putting it in the controlled environment of a hospital nursery. This kind of separation allowed the imprint of a much deeper kind of separation anxiety (reinforced by bottle-feeding and having babies sleep alone, which they do only in "modern" industrialized societies), which prevented a certain kind of bonding with the mother that had always existed with "primitive" birthing techniques. Yet this scenario also helped that generation to develop a much deeper yearning for spiritual connection (to fill the hole created by weak bonding and separation anxiety) and has facilitated the kind of spiritual growth that is happening in this culture today.

The most important factors in our birth experience are our parents, the particular body being born into, the person doing the delivery, the nature of the physical birth itself (including the birthing techniques being utilized and what is done with the baby immediately afterwards), and most importantly, the emotional point of view of our new human consciousness with which we experience our birth.

Our emotional point of view is the most important factor because that will determine what we actually experience. Whereas one person may not be bothered at all by forceps, the attitude of another one might be that the doctor is trying to kill him. Yet the other factors are still important, for when they correspond to a primary attitude within the emotional point of view, the imprint on the new body and new human identity is deeper.

As we have seen, as human beings we are attached to the attitudes we hold (believing they keep us safe), and we attempt to use our life-experience to validate our position in holding them. What follows is a list of issues and attitudes, with explanations as to how we could have perceived our birth experience so as to project these attitudes onto it, imprinting them into our new human body and identity:

(1) *Feelings of irreparable loss, rejection, and abandonment:* imprinted if we perceive, in these terms, the experience of having the relatively peaceful womb-state of physical oneness with our mother destroyed by our forced expulsion from the womb and the severing of our umbilical cord.

(2) *Feelings of separateness and aloneness:* imprinted if we believe that our separation from the womb is separating us from our Source of Life and condemning us to being alone. This imprint may later take the form of fear of all separations, where we cling to everything, afraid to live and afraid to die, or it may take the opposite form—a fear of intimacy and connectedness (because it may later be lost). If we are separated from our mother at birth, this imprint is deeply reinforced, and if we believe that our mother is dead when we are taken away from her, we may imprint the belief that separations mean death.

(3) *Fear of physical death:* imprinted if we perceive the separation from our mother's womb—and hence our birth—as some kind of death or near death. Or, imprinted if our umbilical cord is cut before it stops pulsing and we choose to believe that we are being cut off from our one source of nourishment. These imprints usually take the form of "Life will kill me," or "Growing up will kill me," or separation from _____ will kill me," or "I can't get enough (to nourish me/ satisfy me/ make me feel safe)."

(4) *Guilt:* imprinted if we believe that we must have done something horribly wrong to be expelled from the womb (part of the experiential basis of "original sin"). Or imprinted if we are separated from our mother at birth and believe that she is dead and that we

must have killed her by being born. Or imprinted if our mother has a painful birth and we believe we are responsible for her pain. (Later, this last one may take the form of "For me to live or be happy, someone else must suffer.")

(5) *Feelings of worthlessness or unlovableness:* imprinted if we believe that we were ejected from the womb because we were not "good enough" to stay or are unlovable.

(6) *Dependency and helplessness:* imprinted if we focus on the experience of ourself as a tiny, helpless being who is totally dependent upon parents (or other beings or life-support machines) for physical survival; and this imprint is amplified to the extent that we believe that we also need our parents for emotional and spiritual survival.

(7) *Need for control:* imprinted if we believe that we survived birth by "holding on" long enough to get through the experience, or survived through some expression of our own personal will (and we believe that we will survive Life by acting in this way). Or, imprinted if we believe that we almost died from birth because we were not in control of what was happening, or that with more control we could have prevented ourself from being expelled from the womb.

(8) *Being rescued:* imprinted in Cesarean births if we believe that we survived birth because someone "rescued" us from the womb (and believing that this is how we can survive life).

(9) *Distrust:* imprinted if we believe that our ejection from the womb, and thus our experience of separation, was made possible because while we were in the womb we relaxed and trusted the love we experienced there. This belief may later take the form of "If I trust love I will be separated from it or lose it."

There are many more possible attitudes that can be set up and imprinted at birth; these are simply the most common.[23] And some

---

[23]A study by Dr. Bertil Jacobson at Stockholm's Karolinska Institute found that a correlation exists between the method a person chooses for suicide and the kind of birth trauma experienced. For instance, those who experienced trauma through forcep delivery were more likely to kill themselves using a mechanical instrument, such as a knife; whereas those who were born with their umbilical cord around their neck were more likely to kill themselves by hanging or asphyxiation. This shows that emotional patterns that are imprinted at birth and not dealt with will still exist in the adult's psyche. Yet again, the particular kind of birth was chosen so as to imprint these patterns onto the new life, in order to focus on particular issues.

of these birth attitudes can be additionally reinforced by what a parent tells a child about his birth later on. For instance, a parent can reinforce guilt attitudes by telling a child how difficult and painful her birth was.

Most of us did use birth to validate at least one of these attitudes and imprint it into our human body, and those we imprinted most strongly most likely became our most fundamental emotional issues. Yet depending upon the intensity of our attitudes, the degree of health of our new body, and whether we had considerate, creative, and loving parents who managed to meet most of our desires, we could have stayed in a vibration of love, receiving joy and pleasure from our body, and been very happy for quite some time. Or, we could have blocked our experience of aliveness, made our body a source of suffering, and been miserable from the moment of our birth.

It is also important to realize that, in spite of the significance of our birth situation, because our relevant issues were not caused by birth but by our emotional point of view, we don't need to remember our birth to deal with them; whatever is still stuck is here-now in our emotional point of view today. Yet in the same way that we can use past lives as a tool for our growth today, the memory of our birth can be a valuable tool, because our experience of birth embodied—with great emotional intensity and clarity—many of the most important issues that we are working on today.[24]

ISSUES FROM CHILDHOOD

A valuable way to think of our childhood is as our most recent past life, and the one we most vividly remember. Most people believe that our childhood experiences, especially with our parents, are to blame for whatever we don't like about our emotional self. Unfortunately, this belief keeps them stuck, for if they assume no responsibility for their emotional point of view, they have no way to transform it.

As we move from birth to infancy, we take with us all the attitudes and awarenesses—including those that allow love—within our

---

[24]A healing technique such as "Rebirthing," which works with freeing the breath and clearing the emotional patterns that hold it, can help to bring up birth-memories, as well as to release the emotional imprint imposed on our breathing pattern at the time of our first breath. For information on this technique, read *Rebirthing, The Science of Enjoying All of Your Life* by Jim Leonard and Phil Laut.

incarnational point of view. Our parents (and any other family members) are a vehicle and an opportunity for us; they enable us both to test our love and explore our stuck attitude-positions through particular dramas (as we help them to do the same).

To make use of this opportunity, all we have to do is become fully involved in our outer drama and shape our attitudes to match our new family. This happens automatically though, because our identification with our new body sets us up, after we are separated from the womb, to experience ourself as a human child that is physically and emotionally dependent on our parents for survival. And the emotional intensity of this experience is deeply reinforced by the fact that this situation is a living metaphor, a physicalized re-presentation, of our more basic incarnational situation—our experience of separation from, yet total dependence on, our Source of Life. In our experience of neediness and lack, it becomes very easy for us to project our fundamental incarnational situation onto our parents, seeing them as our Source of Life, and seeing the loss of them (especially our mother) as leading to our total annihilation. Hence, rejection by our parents becomes the equivalent of being cut off from Life Itself; abandonment by them becomes an abandonment by God. (Even the best and most loving of parents, who have also used the most gentle birthing techniques, cannot prevent this kind of drama from unfolding in some fashion.)

En-tranced with these projections, we solidify our scared and needy child-characters (sometimes developing an "autistic" child-character); and identified with these characters, we are pulled into our new drama as we look for ways to make ourself safe. Yet as we interact, we begin to shape our fears and other attitudes to fit our new situation. For instance, what was a fear of violence in a life with violent and abusive parents could become a fear of poverty in another kind of family situation, or a fear of rejection.

Perhaps our most important tool for reshaping our attitudes is our ability to adopt parental-characters, because then we experience our attitudes in terms of our parents' characters and in relation to the emotional dynamics of our new family. When we adopt parental-characters, though, not only do we reshape our attitudes and become more deeply identified with our outer drama, but we set up an inner drama between our child and parental-characters that reflects our new human situation; and this will be the drama that we will work with and continually reenact in some fashion with all the people we meet—until we transform it.

To the extent that our drama is driven by fear, our scared child-character will be active and will activate all the other characters that were created to support its position. In addition, because these characters believe that we are not safe, when we are identified with them our drama will focus on getting love (or some approximation of it), on getting some vehicle for obtaining this, on staying in control, or on avoiding or denying certain experiences, for this is how we think we stay safe. As children, we will usually be most focused on the dynamics of "getting love," because love reminds us that we are safe, and it dissolves our sense of need and lack. Yet if we happen to have chosen a situation in which getting almost any approximation of love is next to impossible, our drama may evolve into one about denying the reality or importance of love, or may even become a drama about destroying other people's experience of love (issues of hatred and revenge). In a world in which we think we need to get love to be safe but can't get it, we may think we will be safer by denying love in some way. In fact, if this was our parents' attitude, then our closest approximation to getting love may be through "sharing" this attitude with them, even though this causes us so much suffering.

One important factor in all the dramas we develop, is that we tend not to notice that all our attempts to get love (or get safety) involve adopting certain positions, and because all positions are resistance patterns, they block our ability to receive what we get, leaving us feeling even less safe than before and feeling that we need to get (or deny) even more to feel safe. This feeds our dramas and resistance patterns, reinforces the self-pity trance which maintains that our parents don't love us enough, and helps us to sink deeper into our suffering; yet this also eventually leads us to transform the illusions that are creating our suffering.

Although some children do receive more love than others, and some receive a lot of abuse, the bottom line, regardless of our particular experience, is that if we didn't receive *enough* love, we wouldn't be alive today. The belief that we didn't get enough love is just an attitude, and we are responsible for our own attitudes. Of course, this doesn't relieve our parents of their responsibility for how they treat us (which is different from blaming them).

In spite of the importance of our childhood for setting up our inner drama, to transform ourself we don't really need to delve into what happened to us then. Yet doing so can be an extremely valuable tool for enlightening our present issues, because our childhood intensely embodied most of our core issues for this life. Our relationship with our mother, for instance, always embodies and re-presents certain key issues that we are exploring. So to the degree that we can release the issues and illusions that we were involved in during our childhood, especially those concerning our relationship with our parents (although sometimes siblings or other adults will play a more important role), we will release many of the issues that we are working on, in other dramas, today. For example, a man who has difficulty opening up to women discovers that, at a very early age, he shut down emotionally toward his mother after she left him for a month with his grandmother. If we recognize that his mother's trip was not really the cause of his shutdown but what he used to support a pre-existing victim/abandonment position (as well as other positions), then it is clear that her trip is also not the cause of his resistance toward women today. Yet because he is still projecting his attitude onto that experience, he can use that experience to work on his attitude. And if by doing this he transforms his attitude, then he will no longer have it to project onto the women in his adult life. So his childhood memory is a useful tool; yet it is not a necessary one, for he could have also dealt with his attitude by focusing on the present—by working on opening up to the women who are in his life today, or simply by confronting within himself the illusion that he is a victim and that he has been abandoned by life.

In spite of the depth to which our attitudes became embedded in our relationships with family members and seemed to originate there, we were totally responsible for en-trancing ourself with any attitudes that we held or manifested. Our childhood was our own creation which we used as a tool for exploring and enlightening our Self. *Regardless of what happened, it was ultimately an expression and unfoldment of Love.* Of course, most of our characters will resist this idea, for it is exactly this love which they must deny to maintain their attitudes and positions. Yet we can choose not to identify with our characters; we can acknowledge responsibility for our childhood experience and appreciate what we created. Our only alternative is to spend the rest of our lives having had a miserable childhood, resisting what no longer even exists, digging ourself deeper into our web of trance-illusion.

AWARENESS EXERCISE 30:
WOMB REGRESSION

For this exercise you will need some paper, a clipboard or some other lightweight yet stiff surface to write on, and a regular, non-mechanical pencil that is not too sharp. (You can use a pen if you have to, but pencils seem to work better.) Have a warm blanket within arm's reach; you may want it later in the exercise. It is also important to be able to complete this exercise without outside interruption. (Take your phone off the hook.) The exercise will take about an hour, yet it may take longer, you may want to savor your trip. If you find that you can't get all the way back to the womb, relax; you will probably be able to another time.

Once you begin, you will not want to stop in the middle to read the instructions; it will completely take you out of your inner process and you may have to start over. Therefore, I suggest you either have a friend guide you through the exercise, use a tape recorder in the manner I suggested in the section, "A Note on Using this Book," or memorize the instructions well enough that you will remember what to do.

If you had a very traumatic childhood, be aware that this exercise may powerfully bring up some of those memories. This in itself is not a problem, for remembering is part of the process of healing; yet if you think you still have deep unresolved trauma I would suggest that you have a friend read this exercise to you, so that if you feel overwhelmed by this old stuff you will have some emotional support.

To begin the exercise, sit on a bed with your back supported by a few pillows that are leaning against a headboard or a wall; or sit on a well-carpeted floor, with your back supported by pillows against a wall or other firm surface. This exercise may not work as well if you are sitting on a chair, but if chairs are more comfortable for you, use a soft one that you can relax in.

Once you are comfortable, take your pencil in hand and sign your name anywhere on the sheet of paper as you write it today. Then close your eyes, receive a few breaths, and let yourself relax. You are going to travel back in time.

Now, allow your hand to remember how you wrote your name when you were in the third grade. You are not going to remember this with your conscious intellect; rather, you are going to *let your hand remember* how it felt writing your name. Your hand remembers how it held the pencil, how it moved the pencil, the speed at which it moved the pencil, and how it wrote your name. And as you do this, you will remember how it felt to be in your body at that age, how it felt to sit and to breathe in your body then. Notice these sensations; allow yourself to re-experience them as you write your name.

(Writing your name is simply your focusing device; it keeps you focused in being a particular age and it prevents you from drifting off too far into free-associations and day-dreams. The purpose here is not really to write your name but to get you back into your past; yet you need to keep focused by writing your name to accomplish this.)

If you were able to write your whole name in the third grade, then do so. Otherwise, just write what you can. Repeat this several times, or more often if you like. (It is important to do this with your eyes closed; do not open them until the exercise is finished. It does not matter if you write over something you have already written.)

Then allow your hand to remember how it wrote your name in the second grade. Again, allow your conscious, curious intellect to relax, and let your hand remember how it felt writing your name. Notice all the body and emotional sensations that go along with this age. You might remember how, at that age, in that body, you related to other people or your family. Write your name at this age several or more times, and then allow yourself to remember how it felt to write your name in the first grade.

Keep going back like this; you can travel as slowly as you like. Yet don't get too caught up in any one age for now; you can always return later. At this point you can regress in yearly or six month intervals. Keep allowing your body to do the remembering—don't try to remember with your mind—keep focusing on how you held and used a pencil at those ages and the memory will be there.

At some point, of course, you will reach an age at which you weren't able to write your name. But you were still able to scribble then. So when you reach these ages, just scribble. Remember how much fun it was to scribble. (And don't worry about scribbling over the names you have written.)

When you get to the age at which you could no longer scribble, then just remember how it felt to hold a pencil in your hand.

As you get back to these young ages, let the memories of how you experienced grown-ups come in. Remember how you perceived your parents and how it felt to be held and carried, to be breast or bottle fed, and so on. For some, there will be trauma associated with some ages. If this comes up, for now just let it be there; you don't have to do anything with it. Just notice your experience. At some point you can return to it to deal with it more specifically. And if you are having trouble, you can always regress yourself a little quicker to get back to a time before the trauma.

As you become very young, you can begin to remember both your experience of birth and how it felt to be in the womb. (At these ages you may want to lie down and cover yourself with the blanket; but don't let go of the pencil—it is still your time machine, and it is still a good focusing device.) Allow those memories to keep getting stronger as you keep getting younger, and then use the momentum that you have created, aging backwards, to keep yourself moving through your birth and back into the womb. Allow your body to remember.

Once you have made it back to the womb, notice how peaceful you feel. Notice your experience of love. Allow your body to remember. (If you don't feel peaceful in the womb, then you will have to go back even further—go as far back as you need to go— until you do.) If you surrender to this memory of peace and love, you will probably also sense in your memory those beings of light who were with you in the womb, who escorted you to the door of birth, and who are still with you today, even if your experience of human-ness has hidden them from your awareness. If you can even vaguely sense these beings with you in the womb, your sense of peace, love, and connectedness will go even deeper.

Now, notice any attitudes that you already have, here in the womb, before you have been born. This last awareness can give you a sense of your incarnational point of view (amplified in certain areas by womb-imprints).

Then look at the life you are going to enter. You have the benefit of knowing what is going happen. But look at it from your viewpoint in the womb. Look at your life as a river that you will jump into, get wet in, and step out of at some time in the future. It is inherently safe, you are just going for a swim, through some years of experiences, in a different body than you've ever swum in before. Look at where the most intense experiences (some of which you have viewed as traumas) will be and at the kind of attitudes that you will project onto those situations. Look, in particular, at your birth experience; exam-ine the experience and the attitudes you generated the first time through. Look at how you moved deeper into your identification with separateness, and how this veiled you from your connection with the light-beings who were with you. What awareness would you have needed in order to go through birth (or your other traumas) without resistance or developing the kind of attitudes and holding patterns you did? Find the transformative awareness you will need, for when you age forward, you will take that awareness with you and change the way you experienced these situations.

When you are ready, you are going to start aging forward again. And you will take your sense of peace and love and your transformative awareness with you as you age; you will allow your body and emotional awareness to remember.

Starting with birth, allow yourself to begin coming down the canal (or however you were born) and take with you your sense of peace and love and your transformative awareness. If you sensed light-beings with you in the womb, feel their presence still with you as you move through birth. And remember: you're just going for a short swim through the river of physical life. Everybody gets dry again on the other side of the river, no one ever drowns, so you have perfect freedom to enjoy your swim, to enjoy all of your experience.

Just as you incrementally aged backwards, now incrementally age forward, taking your new awareness with you into each age. Go very slowly at the beginning, examining different aspects of your birth, your first breath, the cutting of your umbilical cord—taking your new awareness and sense of peace with you—and get a sense of how these experiences feel different with your new awareness. If you felt light-beings with you in the womb, maintain contact with them at each age, as you grow older.

When you can, take hold of your pencil again—at this age just hold it, but use it again as a focusing device. Age slowly through the first few months, noticing your experience as a baby with your new awareness and sense of peace, and keep aging forward, with bigger increments, doodling again when you're old enough to, and writing your name when you can, up to the third grade. Notice (with your eyes still closed) that you hold the pencil differently with your new awareness, with your remembrance of love and sense of peace, and that it feels different writing your name.

Now, although you jumped to the third grade when you were regressing, you are going to age forward more slowly, so you can integrate your new awareness into your personal history. Use whatever increments that you need to maintain continuity—remember you can always go back and fill in gaps—and age yourself, with your new awareness, writing your name as you go, all the way to the age you were when you started this regression. Then write your name one last time, as you would write it now with your new awareness, with your new experience, with your new sense of peace and connectedness, and when you are ready, you may open your eyes.

There are many other kinds of awarenesses and explorations that can be experienced from the womb. Yet on this first trip back, I just wanted you to focus on the state of peace and the experience of love you felt in your body in the womb. On your second trip, I strongly suggest that you keep going back to before you entered the womb, to get a clear experience of your incarnational self and of the incredible light that you emerged from to enter this human life. By going that far back you can also explore the shift that happened as you entranced with your body. On another trip, you could explore past lives, for the womb is an easy place to remember them. It is also a good place for examining what you wanted to achieve in this life, what is getting in your way, and what you can do to change that. In addition, you can use this technique to go back to and explore any particular time in childhood. Be creative and explore some of the possibilities that occur to you.

32

The Garden of Eden

The story of the Garden of Eden is a delicately woven metaphor of all the issues surrounding our separation from Oneness as well as separation from the womb. Adam and Eve, being individuations of God (created in God's image), follow their divine-creative urges (represented by the serpent[25]) to expand their awareness when they freely choose to eat the apple. Eve tells us that she eats the apple because she desires wisdom (which would expand both her consciousness and the individuated aspect of God she represents). God never says that eating the apple would be "wrong" (which would be meaningless, since they won't know right from wrong until after they eat the apple); he simply tells them not to eat it because of the consequences—they will die. Dying here represents what becoming separate and being expelled from Eden (being born) will feel like (including the fear of annihilation they will experience as separate beings), and dying also represents the experience of physical death they will "surely" have after they are expelled (born) from Eden. They take this threat pretty lightly though, because before they become separate the idea of separateness or physical death is meaningless.

---

[25]In most cultures, serpents represent the divine creative will acting in Life. We see this in the caduceus, a symbol used by doctors and ancient healers (pictured with two serpents rising intertwined on a staff) to represent the divine healing power as well as the kundalini energy—an intertwining energy in our spine that the yogis awaken to expand their consciousness and reconnect to God. Traditionally, the kundalini energy has been called the "sleeping serpent." So the snake, as the divine creative will within Adam and Eve, also represents their kundalini energy, which has the power, if awakened, to create enlightenment. In fact, the snake's actions here represent the beginning of that awakening.

Before they eat the apple they are in Oneness, represented by being in Eden without the awareness that they are naked. Eden is Oneness. Eating the apple and obtaining the Knowledge of Good and Evil is a manifestation of their free choice to expand their awareness (in their quest for wisdom), which will involve separating out of the Oneness by becoming an individual (incarnational) personality, entering into a womb, and identifying with a body.[26] This shift in their consciousness is represented by being in Eden but identified with their bodies, experiencing separateness, and by their experience of emotional attitudes. Eden now represents the womb they are about to be ejected from, and paralleling this change, God is perceived as an angry, jealous, rejecting parent, which also reinforces the idea that they have shifted from a spiritual to an emotional level of consciousness. When God asks Adam why he is hiding (why he is separating himself, why he is acting as if he is separate), Adam says that he is *afraid because he is naked.* Being naked represents his state of vulnerability to the world "outside" himself and to the threat of annihilation that has arisen with his experience of being separate. Even God, now separate and part of his outer world, is a threat. So he hides when he hears God's voice because he is scared of this vulnerability, and paralleling this, what he has covered with fig leaves is the place where, as a separate human being, he is most vulnerable. (Covering is also a symbolic act of separation.) It is interesting that although Adam now knows good and evil, he doesn't say that he is hiding because he has done something wrong; he won't feel that he did something wrong (and again, God never said that eating the apple would be wrong) until after he is punished and expelled from Eden (until after birth).[27]

---

[26]The symbolism of eating forbidden fruit, as well as the aspect of the snake as a sexual symbol (which is the snake as divine creative will becoming sexual energy to give life) points to the sexuality necessary for them to manifest their choice to become separate human beings.

[27]The experience of being expelled from the womb is part of the source of the experience of "original sin." The feeling is not created out of the action of doing something wrong, but out of retrospectively believing that we must have done something wrong to have been so harshly punished and rejected.

The rest of our sense of original sin comes out of an attitude of guilt and a sense of failure for not manifesting what we inwardly know is our true Self: perfect unconditional love. (These attitudes, in turn, reinforce the belief that our expulsion from the womb was a punishment.)

When God throws them out of Eden, He is described as an angry parent, which is how we often perceive our mother when she expels us from the womb. (According to this interpretation, the Old Testament isn't saying that God is an angry, jealous God, but rather that human beings, caught in their trance of separateness, experience God in this way.) They are sent out from the east side of Eden (they are born), with God telling them about the sorrow they will experience from the expulsion, and a flaming sword (the knife that cuts the umbilical cord) is put there to make the exit permanent.[28] They cannot get back into Eden the way they left (through the womb). If they are to return and eat of the Tree of Life, they must find a different path (a *spiritual* path, which returns to Eden from directions other than east, other than the womb). They can return to Oneness only by their own evolution through physical life as human beings. And the fact that they are leaving Eden through the east bodes well, for they are walking toward the rising sun, which means they are starting a new day, embarking on a new beginning (a new birth or incarnation) for exploring and expanding their consciousness; and walking toward the rising sun says that on this new journey they are *moving toward the Light.*

By now, of course, they have long forgotten why they ate the apple; they may even regret it. Yet they have ventured onto a path through which they will eventually achieve the wisdom they desired (the Light they are moving toward), and the Oneness they will reenter will be expanded by their quest.

---

[28]God's curse of the serpent—that it will crawl and its head will be stepped on by humans—simply reflects the change in consciousness that has transpired. The serpent, as kundalini energy and divine will, must have been previously erect, which in kundalini terms means connected to Divine Consciousness through the energy center (the "chakra") at the top of the head. When the serpent is required to crawl on its belly, this reflects the fact that the focus of the kundalini energy has been pushed down to the energy center closest to the ground, the one that deals with physicality, survival, and survival fears. Reinforcing this symbol is the image of the snake's head, our conscious connection to Divine Consciousness, being pushed directly to ground when it is stepped on by humans—when our human experience of separateness completely suppresses our awareness of Divine Consciousness.

In addition to being a powerful metaphor for our experience of separation and our journey-quest for wisdom, we can use the image of the Garden of Eden as a tool to help us on our path. We simply imagine that our path through Life is taking us back toward the Garden. We know that everything in Life is really One, that it is all God; yet since we experience ourself as a separate being, we can imagine that all that exists is God and ourself. Since we cannot reenter the Garden in our present state of fear and negativity—we must be "purified" first—God keeps assuming the form of people and situations that will help us to purify. Because of our inner blindness, though, we project our experience of separateness onto these people and situations and imagine they are threatening us; we don't see that it is all just God guiding our way. In every situation God is reminding us of love and re-presenting to us where we are stuck in illusion, so we can purify ourself and return Home. For instance, if we need to purify anger, God takes the form of a human being or a situation that triggers our anger. We get angry at this person or situation, not realizing that we are really getting angry at God, whose only motivation is love, and whose only purpose is to help us find the wisdom we left the Garden to seek, so we can come Home again.

Yet as we walk down our path, we can begin to notice that all that we encounter in life is God. And when we fully recognize this and experience our Oneness with life, we will have reentered the Garden, for it was always here-now, wherever we went, with only the illusion of our separateness preventing us from seeing it and Being Home.

33

Being Love (Here) Now

Each of us carries within us, not only the memories of this life, stretching back to birth and infancy, but memories stretching back through millennia of past lives, and even into worlds we don't consciously know exist. Sometimes these memories can be useful tools for illuminating the issues we are working on today. Yet focusing on them is frequently a trap, for more often than not, we use them as excuses for whatever we are holding onto or resisting today—we use them to support our position of fear—or we get caught up in the old drama, reliving it and reanalyzing it, creating new understandings that end up generating new attitudes, that don't set us free. What we really need to practice is opening our Hearts to receiving this moment, to Being Love here in this moment, as it Is Now.

This open-hearted fullness of being/receiving Now is what we are really searching for. So ultimately, we will have no choice. To fulfill our quest, we will have to stop looking backwards and forwards; we will have to open our Hearts to experiencing Life as it Is Now.

We simply begin here, in this present moment in time. All of our history has unfolded into this present moment. And we have died a thousand times, evolving ourself so that we could be exactly where we are, so that we could experience being *alive in this moment*. This is the moment we have been striving for. By choosing to open our Hearts and Be Love here in this moment, we give ourself the gift of fully experiencing it; and in doing so, we move beyond this moment, for Love is the very essence of our Self, of Conscious Beingness, forever Being Now.

AWARENESS EXERCISE 31:
QUIETING & LETTING GO OF THE MIND

This exercise is actually an ancient Zen meditation. It will help you to let go of your identification with your mind as well as quiet your mind, which will help you to release (to exhale) holding patterns and be here Now. Our identification with our mind is one of our deepest trance-identities, and when this trance predominates over our identification with our body and emotions—when we get caught up in our mind—we become "ungrounded," which roughly means that we are living so much in our head that we have lost our experience of our body (not the same as losing our identification with it), with its two feet connected to the "ground." So this exercise, by helping us to let go of our mind-identification and by bringing us into our belly, is also very "grounding."

The basic tactic of this meditation is to give your consciousness something that exists here and now to focus on, and to have this thing both (1) be very boring to your mind, so that your mind will have difficulty creating distracting mind-realities about it, and (2) require enough of your mind's attention so that it cannot wander off and think about other things. Under these circumstances, after a while you start to let go of your attachment to and identification with your mind, because it is no longer very interesting. Of course, your attachment to your mind will try to get you to escape from the drudgery that will be assigned to it. Some common escape routes are going off into daydreams, or even having such thoughts as: "I'm bored," or "I don't like this," or "my neck hurts," and so on. When these daydreams and thoughts come up, just let them go by.

To do this exercise, sit comfortably, yet with your back fairly straight. You can sit cross-legged on the floor on a pillow (with your back against a wall if you like), on a firm chair, or on the edge of a chair. Then close your eyes, bring your attention to your breathing, and count your exhalations: with your first exhalation you think-breathe "one," with your next exhalation you think-breathe "two," and so on, up to "ten," and then you begin with "one" again. Just be here Now, with your breath and with the counting of your exhalations. To get the full effect of this exercise, it should be done for forty minutes or more.

While doing this, you will, of course, go off into other thoughts. That is to be expected, so don't berate yourself for losing your focus;

when you become aware that you have gone off, simply bring your attention back to counting your exhalations. The idea is not to push your thoughts away or to try to control them, for that only gets you caught up in a struggle with your mind and your thoughts. (People who "blank out their mind" are neither quieting it nor letting go of their identification with it; they are simply hiding their mind in a mental sound-proof closet.) Do not be bothered by your thoughts; allow them to be there, just as they are, and keep bringing your focus back to your breath and to counting your exhalations. As you go deeper into this exercise, you may even have bizarre thoughts or images—the mind is full of all sorts of oddities, as you probably know from dreams. Rather than get caught up in considering these to be either frightening or interesting, just allow them to be there, and focus on your breathing and exhalations.

In addition to trying not to control your thoughts, you are not trying to control your breathing; you are simply being aware of it, as it is Now, and counting the exhalations; let your breathing breathe by itself. (At times your rate of breathing will naturally speed up— especially at the beginning—and at times it will get very quiet.) In this exercise, you are not trying to control anything; you are allowing everything to be just as it Is Now, and while everything is being that way, when you are remembering to, you are being aware of your current breath and counting your exhalations.

You may have an experience in which it seems that thousands of thoughts are all going on at once in your mind. Do not be disturbed by this, for this is what the mind actually sounds like all the time; we never notice though because we are usually focusing on only one of those thoughts at a time. You had to have let go of some of your identification with your mind to have this experience, so you may consider it a sign of progress; but don't think about your progress, just count your exhalations. In this exercise, any thought you have is to be considered as just "mind stuff," and thus unimportant. Even the thought, "nothing is happening" is just another thought; return to your breathing and counting your exhalations.

As you go deeper, your sense of breath—which is manifest spirit—and your sense of mindfulness or awareness will become more subtle. Eventually, your mind will quiet down by itself, you will move from being caught in time to experiencing what Is Now, and then, in Silence, with no thought to limit your experience of yourself or Reality, you will be amazed.

AWARENESS EXERCISE 32:
I AM

Sit comfortably on a chair with your back fairly straight and with your feet on the floor. Then close your eyes, receive a few breaths ... and let yourself relax. Take twenty minutes or longer to do each part of this exercise.

PART I

Become aware of your breathing. Then as you inhale, think the word "I" and as you exhale think the word "AM." You are thinking these words with your breath, so that you think-breathe-in "I" and think-breathe-out "AM." Allow your breathing to do whatever it wants to do; do not control it in any way. It will change as the exercise proceeds.

Now, as you are doing this, have the sense of affirming your beingness with your words "I AM." Have the sense of affirming your life-force. In particular, have the sense of affirming whatever "I" you experience yourself to be in that moment. If a sad "I" comes up, do not say, "That is not me" and try to push it away. Rather, affirm the beingness of the "I" that is feeling sad. This is not the same thing as affirming the sadness, for you are not saying that you are sad, you are simply saying "I AM." And the "I" which in that moment experiences Itself as sad is Real; it is your own true Self that has en-tranced Itself within a character who holds the attitude of sadness. So affirm the "I" that exists, hiding within this trance. As you affirm Its being-ness, you will increase Its sense of life within that trance, helping it to remember Who It IS, and It will let go of Its sadness and Its constructed self.

While you are doing this exercise, you will become aware of places within yourself that are stuck in emotional attitudes or places that don't feel alive—places which have forgotten that their very essence is "I AM." When you come across such a place, align your-self with it and affirm the "I AM" within it; simply think-breathe "I AM," being the "I" within that trance.

PART 2

Keep saying I AM with your breath as before. But now think of the "I" as the universal "I", the One "I" that IS in all things, the essence of Life Itself. Imagine that all of Life, in all of its dimensions is saying "I AM" through you, is expressing its total aliveness through you, in rhythm with your breath, and experience yourself as that I AM. Notice any place where you are holding Life back from expressing its aliveness through you, and simply let go of holding it back; allow the aliveness of Life to be and flow through you.

PART 3

Repeat Part 2 with your eyes open while walking outside. Sense the universal "I" within everything you see, and experience all of Life around you and within you saying "I AM" through you, as you think/breathe I AM.

PART V

Going Home

34

34

Walking the Path

If you cannot love each other you cannot achieve your goal.
— Neem Karoli Baba, in *Miracle of Love*

As we walk down our path, on this trance-created journey of exploring and unfolding our Self, it is important to keep remembering Who we are and where we are going, for it is easy to get lost in the labyrinth of our human drama.

We get lost for several reasons:

(1) We don't recognize when we are lost. We believe that our trance-illusions are Reality, and that our trance-identity is our Self.

(2) Our fear and neediness, created out of our sense of separateness, leads us to struggle with our drama as well as become attached to it, deepening our entrancement with it.

(3) Our human drama is fascinating. It attracts our attention and involvement, deepening our en-trancement with it.

(4) Even after profound experiences that open our Heart and help us remember our Self, we quickly become lost again—often just minutes later—because of the areas of our consciousness that are still stuck.

Therefore, it is useful to have some method of keeping our consciousness aligned with where we are going, some way of staying free of our drama and keeping the Light continually present within our Heart. Then, instead of always getting lost within our maze of illusions, we can connect to the Beingness of our Free Self, and we can bring this awareness into our human experience, to enlighten the dark corners and trances of our life.

Every deep meditation technique, including prayer and conscious service, is designed for this purpose. A few of these methods have been presented as ideas or as exercises in this book and can be used on a regular basis. In addition, the idea of using our life as a mirror is a basic tool that can supplement any path, because our life-as-mirror always lets us know when we have wandered from our Heart and become caught in illusion—either we see that we are suffering, or in situations involving other people we see that we are not relating with unconditional acceptance and love.

Yet no form of meditation can fully serve its purpose unless we are committed to bringing the awareness we gain from the meditation into our daily life. Our life itself must become a conscious process of opening and unfolding, a continual meditation of surrendering to our own deepest love and awareness. Then, as we walk our path, enlightening our experience of being human, we will not even be concerned with when we will finally arrive Home, for our commitment will align us with the knowing that we are always Home, and that we are Free Spirit, exploring our Self through this incredible journey of Living Now.

35

The Choice

We live within a magical universe that manifests according to our own creation. And so we have a choice, which is always before us: do we choose to remain unconscious within our human drama, reacting to life out of our trance-illusions of fear and separateness, or do we choose to remember Who we are, to awaken?

Our human trance is familiar and cozy. We have gotten comfortable in it. Even our sense of suffering and our habitual reactions of blame and other attitudes have acquired a cozy, familiar feeling that we cling to. And so the process of awakening, if we truly choose it, will turn our lives topsy-turvy, confront us with our deepest fears, force us to be responsible for all of our experience of life, and catapult us, in all our vulnerability, directly into the heart of the unknown.

Yet there is an inconceivable beauty and joy that surrounds us and is within us, an ecstasy and freedom that pulses within the very unfolding of Life. And this experience is the gift of our awakening.

The choice—the *free* choice—is always before us, and we must choose over and over and over again. For no matter how many times we have chosen one way or the other, in the next moment, the choice is always there again: familiar unconsciousness, or stretching ourself to continue awakening within this moment, *now*.